D0913291

Hummingbirds of North America

Dedicated to the memory of Luis F. Baptista
for whom hummingbirds were one of so many inspirations
and who likewise inspired so many

Hummingbirds of North America

The Photographic Guide

Steve N. G. Howell

Princeton University Press
Princeton and Oxford

Published in 2003 by Princeton University Press, 41 William Street,
Princeton, New Jersey 08540
In the United Kingdom: Princeton University Press, 3 Market Place,
Woodstock, Oxfordshire OX20 1SY

First published by Academic Press

Copyright Text © 2002 by Steve N. G. Howell
Copyright Photographs © Photographers

ISBN 0-691-11603-2

Library of Congress Control Number 2002115443

British Library Cataloging-in-Publication Data is available

This book has been composed in Stone Serif

Printed on acid-free paper. ∞

www.birds.princeton.edu

Printed and bound in Spain by
Grafos S.A. Arte Sobre Papel, Barcelona

1 3 5 7 9 10 8 6 4 2

Contents

List of Species Covered

Preface

Hummingbirds, true avian jewels, have long held a special place in the human psyche. They have fascinated mankind from the earliest native tribes, through waves of European explorers, to modern-day birders and scientists. In the U.S. and Canada, though, we're only sitting at the tip of the iceberg. Of the 320 or so hummingbird species recognized today, only 14 breed regularly in North America, north of Mexico, with the greatest diversity being far off in the Andes of Colombia and Ecuador. A further eight species have turned up in North America as post-breeding visitors or vagrants from Mexico and the Caribbean and, on rare occasion, some of these visitors breed or have bred in the southwestern U.S. This photographic identification guide treats these 22 species, plus two others: Cuban Emerald (sight records from Florida) and Bumblebee Hummingbird (two 1896 specimens from Arizona). Two other species have been reported from North America but the records were not considered valid by the American Ornithologists' Union[2] and the natural occurrence of these species here seems unlikely. These are Antillean Crested Hummingbird (*Orthorhynchus cristatus*) and Rufous-tailed Hummingbird (*Amazilia tzacatl*).

While hummingbirds include some of the most striking and unmistakable birds, they also include some of the most challenging in terms of identification. Indeed, some species (albeit mainly female and immature birds) can be identified to species in the field only by assumption, based on their geographic range, perhaps in conjunction with habitat or season of occurrence. Hummingbirds have been the subject of many books, yet none of these specialist works has been aimed specifically and critically at field identification. Regional field guides treat their relevant species in varying degrees of detail, and in-hand identification criteria were summarized by Peter Pyle in part one of his *Identification Guide to North American Birds*[13]. The most useful field-oriented identification texts for North American hummingbirds are undoubtedly Gary Stiles' seminal work on California hummingbirds[18], Kenn Kaufman's excellent summary in *A Field Guide to Advanced Birding*[9], and David Sibley's new guide to North American birds[16].

This guide aims to provide identification criteria that, given good views of a bird, should allow you to identify the majority of individuals. Remember, though, that responsible field identification always includes the ability to 'let birds get away' as unidentified, and also that some individuals (perhaps hybrids, or just oddballs) may defy specific identification, even in the hand.

References are on page 37.

Acknowledgments

The vast resource of museum specimens is often overlooked by birders, yet has been largely responsible for the text and illustrations of most field guides that we all use and take for granted. This book could not have been written without reference to museum specimens, and in particular I thank personnel at the California Academy of Sciences (CAS; the late Luis Baptista, Douglas J. Long), the Museum of Vertebrate Zoology, University of California, Berkeley (MVZ; Carla Cicero, Ned Johnson), the American Museum of Natural History, New York (AMNH; R. Terry Chesser, Jacqueline Weicker), the National Museum of Natural History (Smithsonian Institution), Washington, D. C. (USNM; James Dean, Gary R. Graves), and the Academy of Natural Sciences, Philadelphia (ANSP; Nathan Rice, Robert S. Ridgely) for their assistance and permission to examine specimens in their care.

During the preparation of this guide I traveled widely in search of hummingbirds and constantly encountered hospitality and a willingness to share information from others who harbor a passion and wonder for these avian jewels. In particular I thank Kimberly Baldwin of Puerto Vallarta, Jalisco, Mexico; Tom and Edith Beatty of Miller Canyon, Arizona; Woody and Betsy Bracey of Abaco, Bahamas; Alan Contreras; Paul Dean of New Providence, Bahamas; Jon Dunn; Richard Erickson; David Fix; Kimball L. Garrett; Geoff Geupel and many field biologists of Point Reyes Bird Observatory; Jennifer Green; Robb Hamilton; Sacha Heath and the 'East Side' crew of Point Reyes Bird Observatory; Tom and Jo Heindel; Jesse Hendrix of Nogales, Arizona; Rich Hoyer; Matt Hunter; Donna Knox of Rockport, Texas; Denise LaBerteaux; Daniel Lane; Gene and Leta Mallon of Tom's Place, California; Michael O'Brien; Brainard Palmer-Ball; Wally and Marion Paton of Patagonia, Arizona; Jon Plissner; Peter Pyle; Fred Ramsey; Will Russell; David Sibley; Sophie Webb; and Tony and Trina White of New Providence, Bahamas.

Logistical support was provided by Jonathan Alderfer, Robert A. Behrstock, Anthony Collerton, Gretchen Mueller, Point Reyes Bird Observatory (in particular Grant Ballard, Tom Gardali, Geoff Geupel, and Mike Lynes), Pete and Nancy Spruance, and Oriane and Michael Taft. Will Russell, Greer Warren, and Parker Backstrom of WINGS all helped directly and indirectly in numerous ways.

Information on status and distribution was gleaned from a number of published sources, in particular *North American Birds* and its predecessors *Field Notes* and *American Birds*; much seasonal data were summarized from the *Regional Reports* and I thank all who have contributed their observations to these invaluable publications. More specific queries were addressed by correspondence with numerous colleagues whose time and responsiveness are appreciated greatly. Paul Lehman reviewed status and distribution drafts of all species, and regional help was provided by Giff Beaton (Georgia and South Carolina), Kelly Bryan (Texas), Jim and Marian Cressman (Nevada), Bob Curry (Ontario), Daniel Gibson (Alaska), Kim Eckert (Minnesota), Kimball Garrett (California), Greg Lasley (Texas), Bruce Mactavish (Newfoundland), Ron Martin (North Dakota), Ian McLaren (New Brunswick and Nova Scotia), Karl Overman (Michigan), John Parmeter (New Mexico), Jack Reinoehl (Michigan), J. Van Remsen, Jr., (Louisiana), Gary Rosenberg (Arizona), Scott Seltman (Kansas), Thede

Tobish (Alaska), Philip Unitt (California), Sartor Williams (New Mexico), and Alan Wormington (Ontario). In addition, Jon Dunn and Will Russell reviewed the entire text; Robert A. Behrstock, Gayle Brown, Matt Heindel, Rich Hoyer, Don Mitchell, Stephen M. Russell, and Robert R. Sargent read and commented on specific accounts to improve their accuracy; and Octavia Cathcart, Keith Hansen, David Lukas, Peter Pyle, and Sophie Webb helped brainstorm with series of photos to determine and articulate field marks. Any mistakes remaining are mine.

And lastly, but obviously not least, a photographic guide would be nothing without photographs. I am indebted to numerous photographers who provided photos for review and, in some cases, took it upon themselves to target certain 'missing' images: Robert A. Behrstock/Naturewide Images, Steve Bentsen, William Bernard, Rick and Nora Bowers, Kelly B. Bryan, Jim and Deva Burns/Natural Impacts, Mike Danzenbaker, Larry Ditto, John Dunning/VIREO, Kimball L. Garrett, William E. Grenfell, Bruce Hallett, Jo Heindel, Matt Heindel, John H. Hoffman, Kevin T. Karlson, Greg W. Lasley, Peter La Tourrette, David S. Lee, James Lomax, Charles W. Melton, Narca Moore-Craig, Alan Murphy, Ralph Paonessa, Sid and Shirley Rucker, Larry Sansone, Peter E. Scott, Brian E. Small, John Sorensen, Mark M. Stevenson, Ian C. Tait, Dan True/VIREO, and Kristof Zyskowski. In addition, Sophie Webb painted a few plumages that appeared to be inadequately represented by available photos.

This is contribution number 944 of the Point Reyes Bird Observatory.

Introduction

What are Hummingbirds?

Hummingbirds (often called simply 'hummers') include the smallest of living birds and are endemic to the New World, with at least one species found almost everywhere between Alaska and Tierra del Fuego. They comprise the avian family Trochilidae (meaning 'small birds') which is considered most closely related to the swifts (family Apodidae; meaning 'unfooted' birds!). Traditionally, as done for example by the American Ornithologists' Union[2] and as followed here, these two families are united as the order Apodiformes, while the DNA-based classification of Sibley and Monroe[17] considers swifts and hummingbirds to comprise the super-order Apodimorphae, and treats them as separate orders: Apodiformes and Trochiliformes. Two subfamilies of hummers are widely recognized: the relatively dull-colored Phaethornithinae (hermits and allies) in which the sexes look mostly alike; and the Trochilinae (so-called typical hummingbirds), in which the sexes are often strongly dimorphic.

Characteristics shared by swifts and hummingbirds, in addition to their tiny feet, are proportionately long wings with a short, thick upper arm bone (or humerus) and long 'hand' (or manus, to which the primaries are attached), which contribute to remarkable flight powers. Apodiform birds also have short secondaries, 10 tail feathers (most passerines, by contrast, have 12), usually only a single molt and plumage per year, unmarked white eggs, and are further united by a number of internal anatomical features.

Hummingbirds as a group are perhaps best known for their small size, remarkable flight powers, and brilliant colors. They have slender, pointed, and proportionately long bills that vary from straight to curved and which are used primarily to probe flowers for nectar; their extensile, tubular tongues have brush-like tips to aid in nectar gathering. Hummingbirds are unique in being able to reverse their primaries while hovering (in effect rotating their wings through $180°$), which enables them to fly backwards, and their wings beat so quickly that they usually appear as a blur. Often the wings make a humming sound in flight, hence the name, and adult males of some species have modified outer primary feathers to enhance their wing buzz, or wing hum.

Most hummers have *iridescent* (metallic-looking) plumage, at least dorsally and, on many North American species, the throat of males often appears as a solid patch of iridescence, known as a *gorget*. These brilliant colors are largely structural and are caused by the interference of light reflected via tiny melanin granules on the feather barbules; the microscopic structure of the melanin granules determines the iridescent color and, to some degree, its intensity. The most intense colors, such as manifest by gorgets, come from feather barbules that act as flat mirrors, so that reflected light is concentrated in one direction. Hence the color is only visible at certain angles. Less intense iridescence, such as the glittering-green upperparts of many species, results from barbules that resemble concave mirrors, so that light is reflected in all directions. Thus some color is always visible although it is less intense than the concentrated reflection from a flat surface. The complicated physics of this process were described by pioneer hummingbird photographer Crawford H. Greenwalt[5]. Because of the nature of these colors, the apparent color, and especially its intensity, can vary with the angle of viewing – unlike the constant colors caused by pigments, such as on a male Northern Cardinal (*Cardinalis cardinalis*).

Sexual dimorphism in plumage is marked in typical hummingbirds, the males adorned with patches of brilliant color, especially on the throat and crown, the females often colored in much more sombre hues. In South America, the iridescent colors and plumage ornamentations attained by males of some species approach sensory overload for birders accustomed to the relatively conservative garb of North American hummingbirds. In terms of size, though, it is often females that are larger in mass and bill length, as with the small gorgeted hummers of North America.

Hummingbird molt (that is, the cyclic renewal of feathers) is a poorly studied subject but, in general, it appears that North American species have only a single, protracted molt once a year, after breeding[8], when all of their feathers are replaced. Often this molt occurs on the winter grounds, e.g., in Mexico, and in general the molts start with the flight feathers and end with the head and gorget. Immature hummingbirds insert a complete or near-complete molt (often termed their complete first prebasic molt) into their first plumage cycle, and immature males of some species may also have an additional molt of some gorget feathers in their first fall and winter[8]; thus immature male Black-chinned and Ruby-throated hummingbirds migrate south in fall looking much like females and return in spring in their stunning adult plumage, yet they are less than a year old.

Although in North America it has been said that Anna's Hummingbird is different, unique even, in having an obvious, relatively complex song, most hummingbird species have songs (some startlingly loud), and instead it is the more familiar North American species, with their spectacular aerial displays, that are in a minority. In addition to vocalizations that proclaim territories and attract mates, hummingbirds make a variety of calls, mainly chipping notes while perched or feeding, and squeaky to buzzy, fast-paced twittering chatters in interactions, such as while fighting at favored feeding sites.

Hummingbirds feed mostly on nectar, insects, and spiders, and many plants are pollinated by hummingbirds – the frosty-crowned birds often seen, and which may at first cause confusion, are simply laden with pollen. Insects are taken while hummers are on the wing, mainly gleaned from foliage, picked from spider webs, or chased and caught in a darting, dancing flight – the sight of an adult female engaged in such flights in summer is often a sign that she is feeding young in a nearby nest.

Because hummers have a fast metabolism and do not feed at night, they have evolved the ability to lower their metabolic rate and temperature and become torpid. If birds have accumulated adequate food during the day, are not experiencing an energy drain (such as molting), and the night temperature is not that cold, they simply sleep without becoming torpid. Torpidity, then, usually reflects a level of reduced energy, and torpid hummers can appear dead, nailed to a perch. As they warm up, however, they seem to come back to life, and some early American tribes believed that hummingbirds were resurrected birds.

Hummingbird nests are small cups of lichen, plant down, spider silk, hair, and other fine material. Nests in most North American species are usually saddled on a branch or similar structure, or nestled in a fork, although some (notably the Blue-throated Hummingbird) construct their nests on near-vertical surfaces such as rock faces. All North American species lay two unmarked white eggs and the male plays no part in nesting – males simply sing and display and copulate with as many females as they can. Hummingbirds hatch virtually naked, helpless, and blind, and remain in the nest until they are fully feathered, usually within about three weeks in North American species (**Pics I.1–I.3**).

The hummingbird breeding system helps explain the high ratio of females to males in some species, especially the small gorgeted hummers most familiar in North America. And this ratio is apparently increased in fall when all the immatures also look much like females. So, while identifying male hummingbirds to species is often relatively easy, more often than not you may be seeing females and immatures, which are much more challenging.

I.1 Black-chinned Hummingbird nest with egg and hatchling. Sid & Shirley Rucker. Kickapoo State Park, Texas. June 1997.

I.2 Black-chinned Hummingbird and young nestlings. Although some references note that this species' nest has 'lichen absent from exterior' (Ehrlich *et al.* 1988:328), nest material probably reflects local availability, and Black-chinned Hummingbirds frequently have lichen on their nests (and see Pic I.3). Diagnostic features of the adult (compared with Anna's and Costa's hummingbirds) are the relatively narrow inner primaries and broad outer primaries, relatively long bill, buff flank spot, and plain whitish undertail-coverts. Charles W. Melton. Miller Canyon, Arizona. August 1999.

I.3 Black-chinned Hummingbird and old nestlings. See comments on nest material and diagnostic characters of adult under Intro Pic. I.2. William E. Grenfell, Placer Co., California. 18 June 1995.

Taxonomy and an Identification Framework

An important first step in identifying many birds is being able to place them in context, and to this end a simple understanding of taxonomy (the science of classification) is useful. Most of us make subconscious taxonomic distinctions daily, such as between a dog and a cat, or a duck and a sparrow. What to look (or listen) for when identifying hummingbirds depends on the group of species involved and, at a finer level, on the age and sex of the bird.

Birds, like all living organisms, are classified by a hierarchical system, the category most familar to birders being that of a species. An important category just above the species level is the genus: each known bird on Earth has a scientific name, which is italicized and comprises its genus name (capitalized) and species name (lower case). For example, the Rufous Hummingbird *Selasphorus rufus* can be classified as:

Class: Aves
Order: Apodiformes
Family: Trochilidae
Subfamily: Trochilinae
Genus: *Selasphorus*
Species: *rufus*

Each genus (the plural is genera, not genuses) has certain characteristics and, while taxonomists often argue over whether or not genera are really 'valid,' birders can still benefit from an appreciation of generic characteristics. For example, the genus *Selasphorus* in North America comprises three species of small hummingbird (Rufous, Allen's, and Broad-tailed), males of which have flame-colored to rose-pink gorgets, green crowns colored like the back, and make a strong wing buzz in flight; female *Selasphorus* have a rufous wash on their sides and at least some rufous on their tails. By contrast, in the genus *Calypte* (Anna's and Costa's hummingbirds), males have the gorget *and* crown rose-pink to violet and in flight the wings make an 'average' hum; female *Calypte* have dingy, grayish or whitish underparts and lack rufous in their tails. Knowledge of such characters can really help in narrowing your choices when making an identification.

Hummingbird taxonomy is in need of a critical revision at both the specific and generic level. For the time being, though, the hummingbird species recorded in North America, north of Mexico, can be considered in the following genera.

Genus *Colibri* (Violet-ears)

Four to five large species that inhabit temperate, primarily montane habitats from central Mexico to Brazil and northern Argentina. Violet-ears have straightish, medium-short to medium, black bills and fairly long, broad, and squared to slightly notched tails that have a dark subterminal band. As the name suggests, all species have erectile violet auricular tufts. One species, the Green Violet-ear, occurs as a rare vagrant north of Mexico and should be unmistakable if you're lucky enough to see it in North America.

Genus *Anthracothorax* (Mangos)

A complex of from six to eight species whose taxonomy is vexed. Mangos range mainly in tropical lowlands from eastern Mexico and the Caribbean to Brazil and northern Argentina, with greatest diversity in Central America and the Caribbean. They are large hummingbirds with fairly thick, medium-length, arched black bills and large, broad tails that are squared to slightly cleft. Males of most species are predominantly deep green, often with a dark patch or stripe on the underparts. Females of most are pale gray to whitish below, often with a dark median stripe. Several mangos look very similar and species identification may not always be possible, although the Green-breasted Mango is the most likely species to occur in North America and is the only species so far recorded – as a casual vagrant to Texas.

Genus *Chlorostilbon* (Emeralds)

A genus of about 18 species (taxonomy remains unresolved) ranging from Mexico and the Caribbean to Brazil, these emeralds are named for the overall glittering-green plumage of the males. They are small hummers with medium-short to medium, straightish bills, and tails that typically are cleft to deeply forked, most strongly so in males. Bills often have some reddish or pink, at least on the mandible. Hypothetical in North America: one species (Cuban Emerald) has been reported from Florida.

Genus *Cynanthus* (Broad-billed Hummingbirds)

A small genus of from two to four species (again, species limits are vexed) largely endemic to Mexico, with one species (Broad-billed Hummingbird) occurring north into the southwestern U.S. These are lightly built, medium-sized to medium-small hummers with medium-long, straightish bills that are broad across the base. Their broad tails are cleft to forked and are often wagged by hovering birds. The bills of males are bright red with a black tip, while females and immatures have reddish mostly restricted to the mandible. The male Broad-billed is bright green overall, the female is pale grayish below with a broad dark mask; by virtue of structure, plumage, and habits this species is distinctive in North America.

Genus *Basilinna* ('*Hylocharis*') (White-eared Hummingbirds)

Typical *Hylocharis* comprise a fairly distinct group of about six species known as sapphires, and which occur mainly in tropical lowlands from southern Mexico to northern Argentina. Two other species (White-eared and Xantus' hummingbirds), typical of temperate habitats in northern Middle America, are also sometimes placed in *Hylocharis*[2]. These two are distinct in several ways, however, and consequently have been separated in the genus *Basilinna*[7,14,15]. *Basilinna*, then, are two species of fairly stocky, medium-sized to medium-small hummers with medium-length, straightish bills that are broad across the base. Their broad tails are squared to slightly notched, and are held mostly rigid by feeding birds. The bills of males are bright red with a black tip, while females and immatures have restricted reddish at the bill base. All age/sex classes have a boldly contrasting white post-ocular stripe and blackish auricular mask, and both are striking species that are unlikely to be mistaken if seen well.

Genus *Amazilia* (Amazilia Hummingbirds)

These comprise what have been termed 'typical' hummingbirds in Middle America, where about half of the 30 or so species occur. They are medium-sized to medium-large hummers with medium to medium-long, straightish bills and 'average' to fairly large and broad tails that are cleft to squared at the tip. The bills show at least some reddish at the base and some species have bright red bills, tipped black. Underparts range from all-white to cinnamon to green. Four species (Berylline, Buff-bellied, Cinnamon, and Violet-crowned hummingbirds) are known from North America, north of Mexico.

Genus *Lampornis* (Mountain-gems)

About 6–10 species (taxonomy, again, is controversial) endemic to temperate and subtropical habitats in Middle America. Most *Lampornis*, but not the Blue-throated Hummingbird found in North America, are aptly called mountain-gems. Think how a change in this species' common name would spice up birding in Arizona – 'Have you seen any Blue-throated Mountain-gems?' sounds a lot more exotic than 'just another hummingbird.' *Lampornis* are large to fairly large hummers with straightish, medium-short to medium, black bills and fairly long and broad tails that are slightly double-rounded to cleft. They favor shady and often moist areas, and commonly feed 'inside' flower banks, rather than in the open.

Genus *Eugenes* (Magnificent Hummingbird)

This genus comprises a single species, the Magnificent Hummingbird, endemic to the mountains of Middle America and the southwestern U.S. As its name might suggest, the 'Mag' is a large hummingbird, and it has a long, straight, black bill, and a fairly long, broad, and cleft to slightly double-rounded tail. It often favors relatively open situations within woodland and perches prominently, at times making prolonged flycatching sallies. The Magnificent is often considered similar to the Blue-throated Hummingbird but, besides being very large, the two genera differ obviously in structure, behavior, voice, and plumage.

Genus *Heliomaster* (Starthroats)

Four species found in tropical lowlands from Mexico to Brazil and northern Argentina. Starthroats are large hummers with long to very long, straight bills, and squared to forked tails. At least the two Middle American species spend much time flycatching conspicuously, especially over streams. Only one (Plain-capped Starthroat) occurs as a casual vagrant north of the Mexican border, and is unlikely to be confused except perhaps with the female Magnificent Hummingbird.

Genus *Calothorax* (Sheartails)

I include in *Calothorax* the Bahama Woodstar, recently placed in the genus *Calliphlox*[2] but for many years included in *Doricha* and before that in *Calothorax* (see Ridgway[14]), plus the two species of *Doricha* (as done by Howell and Webb[7]). These species share striking similarities in displays, flight behavior, vocalizations, plumage pattern, and structure. As with Blue-throated 'Mountain-gem,' the North American species of *Calothorax* could stand to be re-named 'Lucifer Sheartail' and 'Bahama Sheartail' to set them apart from the mass of generic 'hummingbirds' and to avoid misleading association between the latter and the quite different Middle American woodstars. *Calothorax* are small hummers with medium-long to long, arched black bills and, as the name suggests, tails that are forked, especially deeply in males. Sheartails are typical of open and semi-open areas, and the two species known from North America should not be confused with other hummingbirds in the region: Lucifer Hummingbird occurs in arid canyons of the SW U.S., while Bahama Woodstar is a casual vagrant to S Florida.

Small Gorgeted Hummers

The genera *Archilochus*, *Calypte*, *Stellula*, and *Selasphorus* comprise North America's 'small gorgeted hummers,' a highly migratory group among which the commonest identification challenges lie. At the generic level, *Calypte* and *Stellula* may not be different enough to be separated from *Archilochus*[7], and the same may be true of *Selasphorus*, in which case all would become *Selasphorus*, because that genus was the first to be named. Regardless of taxonomic pedantry, there are some differences that separate these groups and which can be useful for field identification. In many cases, determining the age and sex of a bird will be critical to specific identification (see **Field Identification of Hummingbirds**, following).

Genus *Archilochus* (Black-chinned Hummingbirds)

Two widespread species (Ruby-throated and Black-chinned hummingbirds) comprise this genus. These are small hummers with medium-length to fairly long, straightish, black bills, and tails that are forked in males, slightly double-rounded in females. The inner six primaries are proportionately narrower than the outer four, and this is an excellent character to eliminate other species. Adult male gorgets are shield shaped, ruby-red to bluish-violet, and chins of both species are black. Females have mostly plain underparts with an indistinct to distinct buffy wash on the flanks. Both sexes have a white post-ocular spot set off by dusky auriculars, and at rest the wingtips fall short of the tail tip.

Genus *Calypte* (Helmeted Hummingbirds)

Two western North American species (Anna's and Costa's hummingbirds) comprise this genus. Small hummers with medium-length, straightish black bills, and tails that are cleft in males, slightly double-rounded in females. The inner primaries are evenly broad, like the outers. Adult males have the gorget *and* crown rose-pink to violet, and the gorgets are elongated into 'tails' at the corners. Females typically have dark to dusky lores, a short whitish supraloral stripe, a whitish post-ocular spot or line, and grayish to whitish underparts that typically lack buff on the flanks.

Genus *Stellula* (Calliope Hummingbird)

The Calliope Hummingbird of western North American mountains is the single representative of this genus. It is a small, relatively short-billed and short-tailed hummingbird (at rest, the wing tips of females and most immatures project slightly beyond the tail tip); the primaries are broad throughout. Adult males have a cleft tail and a uniquely 'streaked' rose-magenta gorget elongated at the corners, females have a slightly rounded tail and a distinct buffy wash on the flanks.

Genus *Selasphorus* (Rufous Hummingbirds)

This genus comprises eight species (including *Atthis*, merged by Howell and Webb[7]) of small to very small hummers that breed in temperate habitats from western North America to timberline in southern Central America. Three species breed in North America: Rufous, Allen's, and Broad-tailed hummingbirds, and a fourth (Bumblebee Hummingbird) may have occurred as a vagrant. Bills are black, straightish, and medium length (to medium-short in Bumblebee). Males have solid gorgets slightly elongated at the corners, graduated to rounded tails, and make a strong wing buzz in flight. Females have graduated to rounded tails, a rufous wash on their sides, and rufous in their tails. At rest, the wingtips fall short of the tail tip and P9 and P10 are about equal in length, with P10 sometimes covered by P9.

Field Identification of Hummingbirds

Field identification of hummingbirds usually requires at least a reasonable view of the bird in question, and many of the finer points of distinction may be apparent only after a lot of critical and comparative experience with several species. However, many encounters with hummingbirds 'in the wild' (i.e., away from feeders) can be frustratingly brief, with birds simply buzzing by or feeding in view for only a few seconds – and even birds at feeders often do not stay long enough to identify. This is a problem for experts and beginners alike, and one should recognize that many hummers 'get away' as unidentified. Having accepted this, consideration of the following points should increase your ability to identify hummingbirds in the field.

Appreciating Variation

If you look hard enough, all species of birds exhibit variation of one kind or another. Fortunately, geographic variation is not a concern for identifying hummingbirds in North America. The trick is to gain an understanding of individual variation within each species, and within each age and sex class, and to learn when differences are great enough to indicate a different species. There is no short cut to this: it takes time and observation. While field marks can be found to separate many species and age/sex classes, a synthesis of several features, not simply one or two, is usually needed to be certain of an identification.

As with any identification challenge, the key to distinguishing hummingbirds lies with time spent watching and studying the common species around your home and at regular birding haunts. Don't take them (or it, in the case of Ruby-throated in eastern North America) for granted, pay critical attention to plumage variations, bill size and shape, molts, behavior, calls, and so on. Also, don't rely on your memory, write things down or make sketches in a notebook. For example, look at the throat patterns of female hummers visiting a feeder and soon you'll be able to distinguish different types of pattern or even different individuals. In this way, you will be much better prepared to recognize unusual species.

At least in western North America, be prepared to see birds you can't identify. At first it may be best to ignore these. Perhaps start with only adult males, get to learn their structure, behavior, and calls, and so on. Then work into females and immatures. After a while you'll come to recognize the normal range of variation in some commoner species, such as Ruby-throated Hummingbird in the east, or Anna's and Black-chinned hummingbirds in the west.

Assuming they stay still long enough, most hummingbirds can be identified to species fairly readily, some even border on unmistakable. The worst problems lie among the small gorgeted species, i.e., the genera *Archilochus*, *Calypte*, *Stellula*, and *Selasphorus*.

Hybrids

Hybrid hummingbirds – derived from mixed-species pairings – can cause serious identification problems. By virtue of hummingbird mating systems, hybrids occur more frequently than among many other groups of birds – but they are still relatively rare. The 'commonest' combination may be that of Anna's x Costa's hummingbird, but all manner of hybrids have been reported. Most described hybrids are males, but this probably reflects an ease of identification – think how easily a hybrid female Black-chinned x Anna's hummingbird could be passed over. In some cases, a hybrid may resemble some rare species, while in others it may appear truly different enough to cause a double-take. In the early years of ornithology, some hybrid hummingbirds were described as new species but, with time, the true identity of most of these oddballs has been ascertained.

It should also be noted that, because hummingbird colors are structural, hybrids could show a color different from either parent – a change in the angle of light interference does not necessarily produce an 'intermediate' color. For example, a presumed hybrid Azure-crowned Hummingbird *Amazilia cyanocephala* (white throat) x Green-breasted Mountain-gem *Lampornis sybillae* (green gorget) in Honduras showed a gorget that was orange-red, similar to an Anna's Hummingbird[10].

In twenty years of watching hummingbirds I have seen a few striking hybrids and been shown photos of several others. Thus, while rare, the possibility of a hybrid should be considered when confronted with an odd bird that defies ready identification[4,8] (**Pics I.4–I.7**).

I.4 Presumed Magnificent Hummingbird x Berylline Hummingbird hybrid. Charles W. Melton. Miller Canyon, Arizona, 22 August 2000.

I.5 Presumed Magnificent Hummingbird x Berylline Hummingbird hybrid. Jim & Deva Burns (Natural Impacts). Miller Canyon, Arizona, August 2000.

I.4 and I.5 This bird's structure, large size, and voice (pers. obs.) suggested Magnificent Hummingbird, while the pinkish mandible, solidly iridescent throat and chest 'shield,' pale buffy-gray belly, and small area of pale cinnamon at the bases of the remiges suggested Berylline. The crown, throat and chest often looked intense, iridescent beryl-turquoise, a color not normally shown by any North American (or Mexican) hummingbird. The uppertail-coverts and tail often appeared coppery golden, again a color not shown by any North American hummingbird, but other times looked coppery rufous, similar to a Berylline. Without knowledge of these facts, or prior experience with Berylline Hummingbird, however, this bird could be (and was, at times) misidentified as a pure Berylline (see Heindel and Howell 2000).

I.6 and I.7 Hybrid male hummingbird. This bird shows features of both a *Selasphorus* (perhaps a Rufous) Hummingbird (rufous sides, wing shape including outer primaries) and Calliope Hummingbird (face pattern, elongated gorget, tail pattern) but without in-hand examination its parentage is little more than guesswork. Kelly B. Bryan. Davis Mountains Resort, Texas. 31 July 1998.

Environmental Factors

As if inherent variation and hybrids were not enough, observers contend with a variety of environmental conditions when watching and identifying hummingbirds. Environmental factors may operate directly on the bird, or may be indirect but affect an observer's perception.

Distance and lighting are two environmental factors that affect the observer. As in all groups of birds, distance is an important factor. If a bird is simply too far away to distinguish features clearly, there is not a lot to be gained by watching it – more can be learned from studying closer birds. Assuming a bird is close enough to study, an appreciation of the effects of lighting on your perception of features is important.

The most striking feature of much hummingbird plumage is its iridescence. As noted

I.8 and I.9 Adult male Anna's Hummingbird. Often, the intense iridescence of gorgets simply looks black or shows only a hint of color. Turned slightly, the gorget flashes intense rose-pink, and can even reflect on the bill to give the appearance of a pinkish mandible. William E. Grenfell, Sacramento, California, December 1986.

I.9

earlier, these brilliant colors are caused by the interference of reflected light, so that a gorget can look glowing one second, simply black the next (**Pics I.8–I.9**). If the iridescent pink crown of a male Anna's Hummingbird doesn't catch the light (e.g., **Pic. I.10**) the bird might be mistaken for a male Broad-tailed or Ruby-throated hummingbird. For such reasons, use of multiple characters should be used in any identification. In addition, worn iridescent feathers can look different from fresh feathers. The bluish-green or emerald-green cast of fresh back feathers can change with wear to dark green or to a dull, grayish green. Gorgets also may change slightly in color, the intense rose-pinks and ruby-reds of fresh gorgets becoming duller and more orangey when feathers are worn, while violets may become bluer when feathers are worn. Photographs can be particularly misleading when attempting to evaluate iridescent colors, as variation in the intensity of lighting and angle of light can be compounded by different films and developing processes.

Lighting can affect more than iridescence. Strongly backlit wings on hovering birds can appear reddish, especially if the remiges are worn and relatively brown rather than fresh and more blackish. The same can be true of spread tails that appear to show rufous but, in fact, lack it.

Another aspect of lighting is the potential for reflection of red tones from hummingbird feeders: in bright light, reflected red light can cause the underparts of some species to appear pinkish when they are not. In some cases, red from a feeder or a lit gorget can reflect on to the mandible and suggest a pinkish base to the underside of the bill (e.g., **Pic I.9**).

I.10 Male Anna's Hummingbird. In some lights the gorget can be illuminated but the crown remains dull or even looks green. To tell this bird from a male Broad-tailed Hummingbird (and cf. Pic. I.11) or Ruby-throated Hummingbird note the post-ocular droplet of iridescence, solidly reddish chin, and dusky-mottled chest. Molt timing would be another clue to check. Matt Heindel. Ramsey Canyon, Arizona, July 1997.

1.11 Adult male Broad-tailed Hummingbird. Note the heavily abraded outer primaries which, in this condition, would not be expected to make the wing-trill normally diagnostic of a male Broad-tailed in flight. The whitish chin, pale face, broad inner primaries, and long green central rectrices eliminate a male Ruby-throated Hummingbird. Robert A. Behrstock. Houston, Texas, 20 January 1998.

In terms of direct factors, plumage wear probably has the most important potential effect on field identification of hummingbirds. Beside affecting subtleties of iridescent color, as noted above, plumage wear can alter wing-tip shape or tail-tip patterns. The shape of the outermost primary tip can be critical in the separation of some species (e.g., Ruby-throated and Black-chinned hummingbirds) and, given a good view, this feature can be seen in the field. However, in mid to late winter, when the wings are at their most worn, the primary tips can be heavily abraded so that the diagnostic shapes cannot be discerned. Similarly, the heavily worn wing tip of an adult male *Selasphorus* hummingbird may cause the bird's normally distinctive wing buzz to be modified or even lost completely (e.g., **Pic. 1.11**).

Female hummingbirds often use their tails as props when feeding young at the nest (**Pic. 1.17**). Over time, this can cause the white tips of the longest rectrices to wear off, and also cause the tail to become slightly shorter overall. This should always be considered when evaluating relative wing/tail projections. It can also be an ageing clue in fall – birds with heavily worn tail tips are most likely adult females rather than immatures.

Because hummingbirds pollinate plants their crowns, throats, or bills can become laden with pollen such that these areas appear to be whitish, pale yellowish, or even milky greenish (**Pic. 1.12**), and this could cause momentary confusion. Partly or fully albino or leucistic hummingbirds are sometimes seen (**Pics 1.13–1.15**) and can be difficult to identify except by structural features and call notes. Partial albinism may be symmetrical – perhaps the outer one or two rectrices on each side – or non-symmetrical – perhaps the inner primaries on one side only, or an irregular spattering of white feathers in the green upperparts.

One other factor to consider relates to the increasing interest in, and study of, hummingbirds. Sometimes researchers color-mark hummingbirds to keep track of their movements and you may see a bird with odd-looking colored patches or spots on its head or throat (**Pic. 1.16**). Although these painted markings are unlikely to resemble normal plumage variation they could cause momentary surprise and possibly confusion.

I.12 Adult male Rufous Hummingbird. Pollen can discolor the crown and/or throat and is often most striking as a whitish crown patch. Here the forecrown and chin are frosted with pollen, creating a greenish color. Charles W. Melton. Gila Cliff Dwellings National Monument, New Mexico, 30 July 1999.

I.13 Leucistic female or immature Ruby-throated Hummingbird. On such birds, structural clues and voice are the best means of identification. Other photos of this bird show the narrow inner primaries typical of *Archilochus*, and the slightly falcate P10 with an evenly narrow outer web further indicates Ruby-throated. Robert A. Behrstock. Houston, Texas, 19 September 1994.

I.14 Mostly albino Anna's Hummingbird. Structure and active primary molt at this season identify this bird to species. Larry Sansone. Kern County, California, 26 July 1997.

I.15 Partly albino adult male Ruby-throated Hummingbird. The relatively deeply forked tail and ruby-red throat feathers identify this bird to age, sex, and species. Robert A. Behrstock. Houston, Texas, 14 September 1995.

I.16 Adult female Black-chinned Hummingbird. Sometimes researchers color-mark hummingbirds to keep track of their movements (also note the tiny metal band on this bird's right leg). Markings such as the almost metallic pale blue crown patch on this bird might puzzle an observer and is something to bear in mind should you encounter an odd-looking bird. From this photo the bird's specific identify is problematic. This is a fairly dingy individual late in the season and it shows somewhat vested underparts. The lack of a dark central throat splodge and of distinct green mottling on the sides points away from *Calypte*, and by default to *Archilochus*, and note the hint of a cinnamon spot above the banded leg. The tail is a good clue to identification: the white-tipped outer rectrices are rather broad for Costa's, too tapered for Anna's (more truncate) and Ruby-throated (more evenly rounded), and best fit Black-chinned. Peter LaTourette. Kern River Preserve, California, 6 July 2000.

Hummingbird Topography and Appearance (Pics I.17–I.20)

An understanding of hummingbird topography is crucial to being able to describe accurately what you see. Hummingbird have the same general structure as most birds; it's just that some of the proportions differ (**Photos I.17–I.20**).

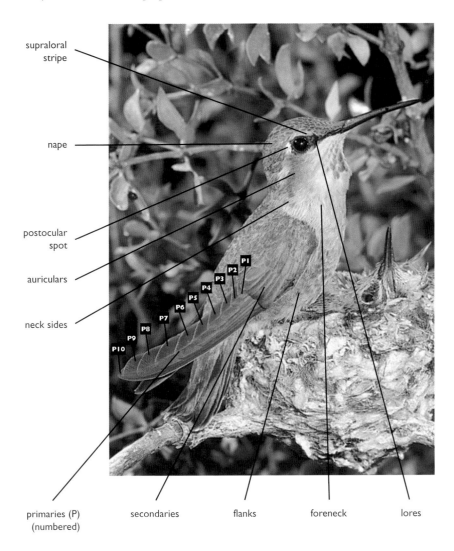

supraloral stripe

nape

postocular spot

auriculars

neck sides

P1 P2 P3 P4 P5 P6 P7 P8 P9 P10

primaries (P) (numbered)

secondaries

flanks

foreneck

lores

I.17 Adult female Costa's Hummingbird. Note how the tail is used as a prop at the nest, such that white rectrix tips can abrade and tails can appear shorter than usual. The broad inner primaries, green-mottled sides, and lack of rufous in plumage point to *Calypte*; the dingy upperparts, short tail, and plain whitish malar region (usually spotted in adult female Anna's) indicate Costa's Hummingbird. Charles W. Melton. Anza-Borrego Desert State Park, California, March 1998.

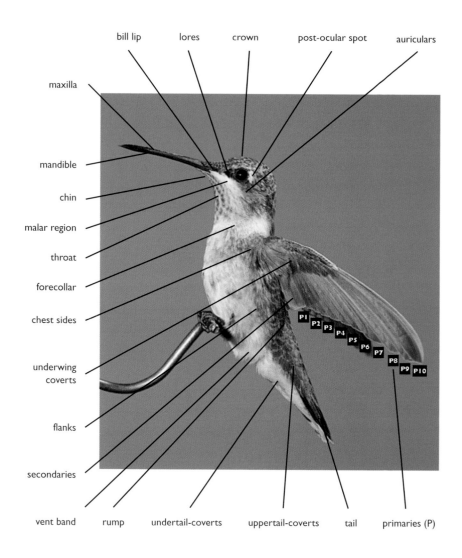

bill lip   lores   crown   post-ocular spot   auriculars

maxilla

mandible

chin

malar region

throat

forecollar

chest sides

underwing
coverts

flanks

secondaries

P1 P2 P3 P4 P5 P6 P7 P8 P9 P10

vent band   rump   undertail-coverts   uppertail-coverts   tail   primaries (P)

I.18 Immature male Black-chinned Hummingbird. The fresh wings and buff-tipped upperparts are typical of juvenile hummingbirds in summer and autumn, in contrast to worn adults at this season. Over the course of the winter this bird undergoes a complete molt and ends up looking like an adult male by spring (cf. Pics I.24–I.25). Note the relatively broad outer primaries, diagnostic of *Archilochus*, and the club-tipped P10 with a slightly swollen outer web, diagnostic of Black-chinned. Charles W. Melton. Madera Canyon, Arizona, September 1998.

scapulars

mantle

upperwing
coverts

rump

secondaries

uppertail-
coverts

cleft tail

primaries(P)

inner web
of P10

outer web
of P10

I.19 Immature male Broad-billed Hummingbird. Note the 10 primaries (numbered from the short, innermost P1 to the long, outermost P10) and six secondaries (the innermost secondary much shorter). The dark mask, whitish post-ocular stripe, pinkish mandible base, and blue-black tail with pale gray tips to R1–R3 and narrow whitish tips to R4–R5 identify this bird to species and age/sex. Mark M. Stevenson. Tucson, Arizona, June 1997.

mantle

inner primary molt

secondaries

rump

uppertail-coverts

slightly rounded tail

R5
R4
R3
R2
R1

rectrices (R)

vent band

undertail coverts

I.20 Fighting Anna's Hummingbirds. Note that the spread tail has 10 rectrices (i.e., five pairs), unlike the 12 typical of many other birds, including most passerines. The rectrices are numbered from the central pair (R1) to the outer pair (R5). The central rectrices lie on top and cover and protect the other rectrices as the tail closes. Thus, from below on a closed tail you can see the pattern of the outer rectrices. The overall tail pattern shown here is typical of many species, with R1 colored green like the upperparts, and white tips and a black subterminal band on the outer rectrices. In this species, the broad and truncate outer rectrices and clean-cut black subterminal band indicate an adult female. Broad rectrices, relatively squared tail tip, and primary molt in June indicate Anna's Hummingbird. William E. Grenfell. Placer Co., California. June 1994.

Overall Size and Structure

All hummingbirds are relatively small, but some are smaller than others. Slight differences in relative size can only be judged with two species together or with a known point of reference. In this regard, hummingbird feeders can be useful as a standard from which to judge relative size. In your own yard you may soon learn the typical appearance of a given species at a known feeder – when a different species appears it may immediately stand out by virtue of slight differences in size. Note, though, that one feeder does not necessarily look like another, and at each site you'll need to re-calibrate for distance, angle, and lighting before subtle clues can be appreciated. Even without other species for comparison, and given some critical field experience, three sizes of hummer can be distinguished fairly easily: small, medium, and large.

Basically, most North American hummers (and all of the widespread ones) can be considered 'small', with the stockier Anna's tending towards medium-sized. The distinctive *Amazilia* species (mainly Violet-crowned in Arizona, and Buff-bellied in Texas) and a few vagrant species are medium-sized. Magnificent and Blue-throated hummingbirds are, relatively, 'huge' and in direct comparison they dwarf most North American hummers (**Pic. I.12**). Gaining an appreciation of relative size takes a little practice but can be useful. For example, some beginners mistake female Broad-billed Hummingbird for Blue-throated Hummingbird based on a superficial similarity of face pattern – yet the former is medium-sized and lightly built, while the latter is very large and heavily built, and the two should be readily distinguished by these features alone.

Unlike relative size, structural features can be discerned on a lone bird, although comparing species side by side can also be very useful for appreciating differences – e.g., in comparison, the large-headed and thick-necked appearance of the stocky Anna's Hummingbird is noticeably different from the smaller-headed appearance of the sleeker Black-chinned Hummingbird. Relevant structural characters are discussed within each species account, as well as under the following sections.

I.21 Female Magnificent Hummingbird (left) with Black-chinned Hummingbird. In overall plumage, female Magnificent is not too different superficially from female/immature Anna's or Black-chinned hummingbirds, but size alone is diagnostic. Features that distinguish this bird from Blue-throated Hummingbird, the only other really large North American hummingbird, include the long and sloping forehead, spotted throat, and green tail. Mark M. Stevenson. Miller Canyon, Arizona, July 1999.

Bill Shape and Color

The bill comprises upper and lower halves: the *maxilla* (often called the upper mandible) and the *mandible* (or lower mandible). On hummers, the base of the maxilla typically flares out slightly to form a black 'lip' or flange that protects the nostrils. Noting bill shape should be an automatic reaction when viewing a hummingbird. Is the bill really straight, or 'straightish' (the default option for many species), or is it arched? The arched bill of Lucifer Hummingbird is distinctive in comparison with the straightish to slightly decurved bills of other small gorgeted hummers. Bill length is also good to check, say in relation to the head. Is the bill about the same length as the head, a little longer, or much longer, than the head? Magnificent Hummingbirds have proportionately long bills that usually set them apart quite readily from Blue-throated Hummingbirds and which are more reminiscent of a Plain-capped Starthroat's bill. Note that female hummingbirds generally have longer bills than do males. This can be quite striking, such as comparing a short-billed male Black-chinned Hummingbird with a long-billed female. Also, immature hummers have shorter bills than adults, although such differences usually become negligible within 1–2 months of fledging[12].

Most North American hummers have all-black bills but some species have red

I.22 Adult male Black-chinned Hummingbird. Note the smooth, glossy-looking maxilla, cf. Pic. I.23. John H. Hoffman. Sonoita, Arizona, September 1997.

I.23 Immature Black-chinned Hummingbird. Note the 'grooved' maxilla characteristic of young hummingbirds, cf. Pic. I.22. John H. Hoffman. Sonoita, Arizona, August 1997.

bills, tipped black, or have a mostly black bill with some red or pinkish on the mandible base. This last type of bill pattern can be hard to see, so it is useful to check bill color carefully when confronted with a problem bird. As noted above, reflection from a feeder or lit gorget can cause the appearance of a pinkish (or even greenish) mandible base on an all-black bill (e.g., **Pic. I.9**). The distribution of coloration on a hummer's bill is best made in reference to the maxilla and mandible, e.g., 'reddish pink was restricted to the basal two-thirds of the mandible.'

One character for ageing hummingbirds (mainly when you have them in the hand) is the nature of the surface of the maxilla. In adult hummers this is smooth, hard, and shiny (**Pic. I.22**), while in immatures (through fall and into winter) the maxilla is marked by parallel rows of oblique scratches, or grooves (**Pic. I.23**). Banders use the presence and extent of this 'bill grooving' to help determine the age of a bird[13,20]. Given the views afforded by hummingbird feeders, together with the increased quality of modern optics, bill grooving occasionally can be seen in the field and contributes information about the age of a bird.

Head Topography and Pattern (see Pics I.17–I.19)
An appreciation of feather tracts is useful for recognizing and describing face and head patterns. The crown and nape featherings are continuous, and distinguishing between them is subjective – the break in angle at the rear of the head is an arbitrary point of separation. Crown feathers are generally smaller and more tightly packed (especially near the bill), while nape feathers average larger and more loosely packed. The dorsal feather covering of the head often narrows in extent on the hindneck, immediately above the mantle. The crown feathers taper to a sheath that covers the base of the maxilla and may spread out laterally to cover the lores. Some species have a paler supraloral/supraorbital line along the sides of the crown, forward from the eyes, and on many species the maxilla extends back as a 'lip' projecting into the lores. The throat feathers spread back from the gape and, on gorgeted males in particular, can be elongated so that they fan up over the lores and also may cover much of the auriculars. The chin refers simply to an arbitrary area of the upper throat. The lores (the area between the eye and the bill) often appear as a narrow 'seam' between the forecrown and throat, and merge below the eyes with a small, fan-shaped region of auricular feathers, or ear-coverts. On many females and immatures of the small gorgeted hummers, the lores appear as a dark wedge. From the eye back along the lower edge of the crown/nape there is a narrow post-ocular tract, often featuring a whitish *post-ocular spot* immediately behind the eye. On some species the post-ocular tract is colored like the crown (e.g., *Amazilia*), on others (e.g., Broad-billed Hummingbird, and many female *Calypte*) it is contrastingly paler and forms a pale *post-ocular line* that may be duller than the white post-ocular spot, or the whitish post-ocular spot may continue back into a post-ocular line. On some species (e.g., most female *Archilochus*) the dusky auriculars fan back and cover/merge with the dusky post-ocular tract, thus isolating a white post-ocular spot.

Below the throat is a band of feathers across the foreneck, and often this tract is colored differently from adjacent areas of the underparts. For example, on male *Archilochus* and *Selasphorus* the foreneck forms a contrastingly white band between the gorget and the underbody. The relative contrast of this forecollar with the throat and underparts can be useful for identification – is it contrastingly whitish, as on typical female/immature Rufous Hummingbirds, or is it washed buff and not strongly contrasting, as on female/immature Broad-tailed Hummingbirds? Because this tract originates from the neck, which can be stretched and contracted, the width and prominence of the forecollar can vary with a bird's posture, i.e., it is wider when the neck is stretched out.

When viewing a hummingbird its face pattern should be noted carefully. Is there a contrasting white post-ocular spot (as on a typical Magnificent or female Black-chinned), or a whitish post-ocular stripe or line (as on a typical Blue-throated or female Costa's)? Is there a really bold white post-ocular stripe contrasting with blackish auriculars (as on White-eared Hummingbird), or a duller whitish post-ocular stripe and dusky auriculars (as on Broad-billed Hummingbird)? These are all questions that may pass almost instantaneously through the minds of experienced birders when confronted with an unfamiliar hummingbird.

Throat pattern is often an important identification character. On males, what shape and color is the gorget? On females and immatures, is the throat unmarked, flecked or spotted with dusky, with or without patches of iridescent feathers? What is the distribution of any iridescent color? Adult female Rufous/Allen's Hummingbirds generally have an overall whitish throat with an obvious central splash of iridescence, while immatures have the dingier throat overall flecked with bronzy green, and at most only scattered iridescent feathers. Immature male Black-chinned Hummingbirds typically have a whiter throat with distinct median lines of dark flecks, while immature females have a dingier throat that typically lacks any dusky flecks. Throat patterns can change with wear: e.g., the heavy dark flecking on the throats of recently fledged Rufous/Allen's Hummingbirds often fades by fall or winter when their throats can look dingy whitish overall with faint dusky flecks.

Most head shape differences relate to the angle of slope of the crown – whether it slopes shallowly up from the bill or whether it is more evenly rounded, or domed. The way in which the feathers are held can affect apparent head shape, but head shape is always worth noting on a perched bird.

Body Color and Pattern (see Pics I.17–I.20)
The **upperparts** comprise the mantle (i.e., the interscapular area), rump, scapulars, and uppertail-coverts. In general, the mantle grades smoothly into the rump at about the point of the tertial tips, while the rump grades into the uppertail-coverts at the point of the uropygial gland; the scapulars of hummingbirds are small and not very noticeable. The upperparts of hummingbirds tend to be glittering green overall. Whether the back is more of a bluish green or golden green is worth noting, although usually this will be only a supporting rather than diagnostic character in an identification. The pattern of the lower rump and uppertail-coverts can be useful, e.g., the presence or extent of rufous edgings can help with age/sex identification of Rufous/Allen's Hummingbirds, or the separation of either from female Broad-tailed Hummingbird. Alternatively, are the lower rump and uppertail-coverts largely concolor with the back (as on Buff-bellied or female Magnificent) or contrastingly darker (as on Berylline or Blue-throated)?

The pattern of the **underparts** can be very useful for field identification, especially the color and pattern of the sides/flanks, and to a lesser extent the undertail-coverts. The vent feathers of many species are white and often show as a contrasting and puffy white band, immediately forward of the sleek undertail coverts. Often the wings cover much of the sides/flanks on a perched hummer, but the flanks show well on hovering birds. Are the flanks washed strongly with rufous as on typical *Selasphorus*, washed with dingy grayish and limited buff as on typical *Archilochus*, or mottled with bronzy green as on female Anna's Hummingbird? Alternatively, do the undertail-coverts have dusky centers and appear dusky overall, like a female Anna's Hummingbird, or do they appear overall whitish, in contrast to the underbody, as on many female Black-chinned Hummingbirds?

Wing Structure and Pattern (see Pics I.17–I.19)

Hummingbirds, as do most birds, have 10 *primaries*, i.e., the main, or primary, flight feathers (**Pics I.17–I.19**). These are numbered from innermost (primary number one, or P1) to outermost (P10). Usually, all 10 primaries of a perched hummer can be seen readily, and the long primary projection is a striking feature of a perched bird. On *Selasphorus*, however, note that P10 is often covered by P9. Looking carefully at the closed wing can be very useful for identification and you should take the time to familiarize yourself with checking closed wings, and counting the individual primaries. Then, for example, detecting wing molt on a hummingbird will be easier, and this can be important in identification, e.g., for *Archilochus* versus *Calypte*, which have different molt timings.

The relative widths and shapes of individual primaries can be very useful for identification but seeing these characters requires a good view. Still, if you have a telescope set up at a feeder or favorite perch, the relatively narrow inner primaries of an *Archilochus* hummingbird are a diagnostic feature to separate it from *Calypte*, which have broad inner primaries.

The shape of individual primary feathers, particularly P10, can be critical to the specific identification of some species (e.g., Ruby-throated versus Black-chinned hummingbirds), although you should note that the shape of primaries varies among age/sex classes of the same species. Such details can be seen on birds perched at feeders or can be determined subsequently from good photos. Note that the exact shape of an outer primary cannot always be determined when the feather tips are worn (e.g., **Pic. I.11**).

The *secondaries* (i.e., secondary flight feathers) of hummers are very short and typically number six in North American species (**Pics I.17–I.19**). The inner three secondaries are also known as tertials (i.e., third-degree flight feathers). In terms of structure, you don't really need to worry about secondaries for identification – when in doubt, look for the shape of primaries. Pale tips to the secondaries can be useful for ageing birds in fall – immatures have pale tips and relatively fresh secondaries, while adults have relatively worn feathers that lack neat pale tips.

The pattern and color of primaries and secondaries (collectively called the remiges) are rarely useful for field identification of North American hummingbirds – most species have all-dark remiges, darker and sometimes with a blackish or purplish sheen when fresh, paler and browner when worn. An exception is Berylline Hummingbird, which has prominent rufous bases to the remiges.

The upperwing-coverts form the 'shoulder' of a hummingbird and comprise a relatively small area that is generally not relevant for field identification. The color of the underwing coverts (seen on hovering birds) tends to be similar to that of the flanks, e.g., buffy or rufous on *Selasphorus* hummingbirds, dingy grayish on *Calypte*.

An important feature for some identifications is the projection of the wing tip relative to the tail tip on a perched hummingbird. This usually reflects tail length. For example, on females of most small gorgeted hummers the wings fall short of the tail tip on perched birds, but on female Calliope and Costa's hummingbirds (which have relatively short tails) the wing tips project slightly *beyond* the short tail. This feature can require practice to evaluate in the field and is best judged on a bird viewed in profile with its wings held against, and slightly under, the sides of the tail. Note, though, that a bird facing away on a feeder can hold the wings drooped such that the tips appear slightly longer than the tail (when in fact they are shorter), or that wings held raised above the tail can appear slightly shorter than the tail tip (when in fact they are longer). Also consider how molt (of either the outermost primary or longest rectrices) might affect the apparent wing/tail projection on a bird (e.g., **Pic. I.24**).

Tail Structure and Pattern (Pics. I.18–I.20)
A hummingbird's tail comprises five pairs of *rectrices* (or tail feathers), the singular of which is *rectrix*. These are numbered from inner (rectrix number one, or R1) to outermost (R5), such that hummers, unlike most passerines, have only 10 rather than 12 rectrices (**Pic. I.20**). In some cases, the shape and width of individual rectrices can be useful for identification (e.g., between Rufous and Allen's hummingbirds), but be aware that shape and width can vary noticeably among age/sex classes of the same species. In some hummers (e.g., *Amazilia*), adults generally have broader and more square-tipped (or truncate) rectrices than immatures, while in others (e.g.,

I.24 Female Blue-throated Hummingbird. Note that P10 is growing and P9 retained, such that wing/tail projection could appear misleading (with tail apparently projecting well beyond wing tips) if worn P9 were assumed to be outermost and longest primary. The face pattern, all-black bill, and, especially, the bold white tail tips are diagnostic of this species, while lack of blue in the throat indicates a female. Primary molt could complete in November, which may indicate a failed breeder or non-breeder, possibly a second calendar-year bird that did not complete primary molt the previous winter (cf. Pic. I.10). Most adult Blue-throated Hummingbirds molt on the non-breeding grounds between November and April. Mark M. Stevenson. Madera Canyon, Arizona, 27 October 1996.

Selasphorus) adults have narrower and often more pointed (or attenuate) rectrices than immatures. In addition, males of small gorgeted species have narrower tail feathers than females. Also note that, in general, males (including immatures) of most North American hummingbirds have proportionately or absolutely longer tails than do females.

The overall impression of tail length and shape should always be checked – is the tail long, short, forked, cleft, notched, squared, graduated, double-rounded? This is best seen on a tail that is not fully closed or widely spread: closed tails can appear squared when really they are cleft or even deeply forked, and squared or notched tails can appear rounded when fully spread. Be aware that birds molting or missing some rectrices can show different tail shapes. For example, adult male Anna's Hummingbirds usually have a moderately long and cleft tail with the longest outer rectrices blackish. However, adult male Anna's in fall often appear to have a relatively short and squared, all-green tail. This is because the longer outer rectrices have been shed and/or are not fully grown (see **Figure 5**, p.148).

An important point to check on perched hummers is if the wing tip projects beyond the tail tip, or *vice versa* (see under *Wing Structure and Pattern*, above).

Tail patterns can be very useful for identification of some problem groups of hummers. In some cases, the tail pattern may allow you to determine the age/sex of a bird which, in turn, can help with identifying the species, such as the notoriously similar Rufous and Allen's hummingbirds. Is there any rufous on the tail feathers? If so, how much and where, and on which feathers? What is the pattern of green, black, and rufous on the tail? How many outer rectrices have white tips? Are these white tips large or small? For example, Blue-throated Hummingbirds have very large and bold white tips to their blue-black outer rectrices, while female Magnificent Hummingbirds have much smaller white tips to their greenish outer rectrices.

Molt and Plumage

Feathers are not permanent – they wear out and need to be replaced. Molt is simply the cyclic replacement of feathers which, for most species of birds, occurs once a year, after breeding. This single complete, or near-complete, molt is termed the prebasic molt, and it produces basic plumage. Some species of birds (but not hummingbirds) fit a second molt into their annual cycle, the prealternate molt producing an alternate plumage. Hummingbirds, then, simply molt from one basic plumage to another basic plumage, each year. Although an 'eclipse' plumage, i.e., a second plumage in the adult cycle, has been reported for some hummingbird species[15], this is unsupported by critical data.

An Overview of Hummingbird Molt

Most North American hummingbirds molt on the non-breeding grounds, which largely lie south of the U.S., mainly in Mexico. The increasing trend towards over-wintering by many hummers in the southern U.S., however, means that molting birds can often be studied at feeders. Because the primaries are long and conspicuous it is often easy to distinguish molt in progress, e.g., the difference between newer and blacker inner primaries and older, faded brownish outer primaries, often with a gap in sequence between the new and old feathers, where a primary has been shed or is just starting to grow. Primary molt can be seen easily on perched birds (**Pics. I.25–I.26**) and often shows up well in photos of flying birds (**Pic. I.27**).

Precise details of molt are poorly known for most hummingbirds, both in terms of timing and the sequence in which feathers are replaced. A few papers have addressed these issues for particular species (e.g., for Anna's Hummingbird[17], Allen's Hummingbird[1], and Ruby-throated and Black-chinned hummingbirds[3], while Pyle[13] provided a summary of molt periods for North American breeding species). Based on these references, personal field observations, and photographs provided by Robert A. Behrstock of wintering *Archilochus* hummingbirds in Texas, molt sequence of the small gorgeted hummingbirds can be summarized as follows, and this overall sequence also appears typical of other North American breeding hummingbirds.

Molt of primaries starts with P1 and progresses outward to P8, then P10 and lastly P9 are replaced, i.e., a variation on the P1 first to P10 last sequence typical of most birds. The short inner primaries are often dropped in quick succession, and it is common to see large gaps in the wing from P1 or P2 through P5 or P6 (**Pic. I.27**). Usually not until P5 is fully grown and P6 growing does P7 drop, and molt of the long outer primaries is quite protracted and may even be suspended at times (e.g., **Pic. I.28**), perhaps over migration or during periods of limited food supply. Molt of the tail usually occurs during the period that P6/7 to P10/9 are growing (**Pic. I.25**), while the secondaries are molted while P7 to P10/9 are growing (**Pic. I.25**).

Head and body molt may start on the lower rump and proceed anteriorly, or may start in various tracts but with an overall anterior progression[3]. The last feathers replaced during a hummingbird's complete prebasic molt are usually head feathers, most obviously the gorgets of males, which are attained during or after the molt of outer primaries and tail (e.g., **Pics I.29–I.30**). Molt of the gorget feathers in immatures males is highly variable. Some individuals have striking patches of adult-like color in fall, usually on the lower throat, while others attain just a few scattered iridescent feathers before the adult male gorget is molted in. To what extent iridescent gorget feathers attained over the winter are re-molted during attainment of the adult gorget remains to be satisfactorily determined, and probably is highly variable. In addition, molt of feathers around the bill base (of all ages and sexes) appears to have a facultative basis and may occur at any season in

I.25 Immature male White-eared Hummingbird. On this bird, P1–P6 are new, P7 is growing (and lies just short of the tip of P6), P8 is growing and short (visible at the base of the wing), and P9–P10 are old and worn. The innermost secondary is new and blackish in contrast to the old and faded, brownish tertials, and most of the tail has been dropped. The thick white post-ocular stripe, blackish mask, red bill base, and green-mottled throat and chest identify this bird to species and age/sex. Charles W. Melton. Miller Canyon, Arizona, September 1998.

I.26 Adult female Costa's Hummingbird. P1–2 are growing, P3–4 have been shed, and P5–10 are old and relatively faded. Evenly broad primaries, summer molt schedule, and lack of any rufous tones point to *Calypte*, although the face pattern of this individual (with a contrasting white post-ocular spot) suggests Black-chinned Hummingbird; the plain throat sides indicate Costa's rather than Anna's. Ralph Paonessa. Mojave Desert, California, June 1998.

I.27 Immature male Black-chinned Hummingbird. The large gap in the middle of the wing is typical of when the inner primaries are growing. P7–10 are old. This bird has a large amount of dark in the throat, and its tail is still that of a juvenile. Late winter molt timing (versus *Calypte*) and whitish underparts (versus Calliope and *Selasphorus* hummingbirds) point to an *Archilochus* hummingbird, and R3 being this much longer than R4–R5 indicates Black-chinned. Robert A. Behrstock. Houston, Texas, 12 February 1993.

response to the wear and nectar-damage these feathers can sustain during feeding[7]. An appreciation of the timing of molt can be useful for identification. For example, most Costa's and Anna's hummingbirds have a summer molt schedule, while Black-chinned Hummingbirds have a winter molt schedule. Thus, a Costa's/Black-chinned Hummingbird showing obvious primary molt in May through July would be a Costa's (which can even start primary molt while still feeding young, **Pic. I.**26), because Black-chinneds typically don't start primary molt until they reach the non-breeding grounds, usually in September or later. Some immature Costa's and Anna's, however, have late molt schedules that overlap with adult Black-chinned's, so a winter-molting bird could be any of the three species.

Molt timings are less well known for some of the larger species, although adults breeding in the southwest USA generally have a complete prebasic molt after breeding, sometimes suspending molt between breeding and non-breeding grounds. Immatures, however, appear more variable in their molt timings and strategies. For example, the postjuvenal wing molt of some White-eared Hummingbirds starts in late summer, relatively shortly after hatching, while in some *Amazilia* and Blue-throated Hummingbirds the postjuvenal wing molt often appears delayed until late winter or spring and occurs during what would be the first breeding season, completing in summer or fall of the bird's second calendar-year.

Age Terminology

The plumage in which a bird fledges is called its *juvenal plumage*, and birds in this plumage are termed *juveniles*. In hummingbirds the juvenal plumage often looks much like that of an adult (especially the adult female), unlike the lax and fluffy juvenal plumage of many passerines. Because the first-year molts of hummingbirds remain poorly documented (e.g., whether or not males replace some throat feathers twice in their first year), I use the term *immature* to refer to a hummingbird in its first year prior to the attainment of adult plumage. By their first spring, when less than a year old, most North American hummingbirds are in a plumage that is adult-like, although *subadults* ('first summer' birds) can be distinguished in some species.

Molt and Changing Appearance

Immature hummingbirds of many species in fresh plumage have distinct, pale buff or cinnamon tipping to the feathers of their upperparts (e.g., **Pics I.18, I.23**), and most such birds can be distinguished readily in fall from worn-plumaged adults. Some early-hatched immature Anna's and Costa's molting in fall can be hard to distinguish from adults but typically show relatively fresh, pale-tipped secondaries and relatively fresh primaries.

Pale tips to the upperparts of juveniles vary greatly in width and prominence among and within species. Many immature Costa's have broad, buffy-white edgings that create a pallid, or 'floury' look to their upperparts, while the pale edgings of immature Calliope and *Selasphorus* hummingbirds tend to be narrow and darker, buffy cinnamon, so that their upperparts look overall bright green. Most immature Black-chinned Hummingbirds have distinct to very distinct pale buff edgings to their head and upperparts, and on some birds these edgings wear off by early fall to reveal bright green upperparts distinct from an adult female Black-chinned and much more like a typical Ruby-throated Hummingbird.

The sequence of hummingbird molt is variable (see above) but tends to finish with the throat of males, late in winter. Thus, some mid-winter immature males may

I.28 Female Black-chinned Hummingbird. Primary molt has reached P7 and appears to have suspended, at least briefly (wing molt of this individual had reached the same stage by 5 January, or earlier), with contrast between new P1–P7 and old P8–P10. On some adults in summer, the outer primaries (P8–P10 or P9–P10) appear contrastingly fresher than the inners, probably resulting from suspended winter molt such as this. Note the relatively narrow inner primaries, diagnostic of *Archilochus*, and the overall broad and blunt primaries typical of Black-chinned. Robert A. Behrstock. Houston, Texas, 18 January 1996.

I.29 Immature male Black-chinned Hummingbird. The outer two primaries are more-or-less fully grown (whitish sheaths are still present on the shaft bases) and the tail is adult-like, but the throat is still that of an immature. The relatively short tail (assuming it is fully grown) is typical of male Black-chinned versus Ruby-throated. Robert A. Behrstock. Houston, Texas, 15 February 1994.

I.30 Immature male Ruby-throated Hummingbird. This bird's first full molt is almost finished, the last feathers to molt being those of the head, especially the gorget, which bursts forth in a very short period after completion of the wing and tail molt. Robert A. Behrstock. Houston, Texas, 3 April 1996.

have adult male-like wings and tail but retain a female-like throat. In addition, because of the P8-P10-P9 sequence of outer primary replacement (see above), one could see a bird with P10 growing and a worn P9 retained, and mistakenly assume that P9 is the longest (i.e., outer) primary. This could affect judgement of relative wing/tail projections on perched birds, and should be borne in mind (e.g., **Pic. I.24**). Also consider how tail molt (usually occurring when the outer primaries molt) could affect perception of wing/tail projections.

Another potential effect of molt is that birds in active wing molt may sound different in flight from fully winged birds. For example, an Anna's Hummingbird in active wing molt, with one or more missing and/or growing primaries, makes a relatively loud and labored wing rattle, unlike the faster-paced and quieter hum of an Anna's not in wing molt.

Voice and Wing Noise

Vocal characters, especially call notes, can be very useful for separating some similar-looking hummingbird species, e.g., Black-chinned and Costa's hummingbirds. They can also allow you to identify birds that simply fly by, when there is not time to look for structural or plumage features. Observers should take time to become familiar with the typical calls of any species that occurs regularly around their home or at favorite birding spots. As well as simply listening to the calls, make a critical effort to describe them in words – high-pitched, ticking, hard, clicking, sharp, smacking, piercing – whatever adjectives work for you are good. With time and critical appreciation, the calls of your local Ruby-throated or Anna's hummers will become etched onto your template of bird vocalizations, and when you hear, say, the chipping of a *Selasphorus* hummer, it may stand out as being different.

Note that context can be important in using voice for identification, because most hummers (e.g., the small gorgeted group) have a number of different calls. Feeding and perched birds can be silent or give a simple chipping call, often single or paired notes that can be repeated steadily from a perch. In apparent inter-specific or intra-specific warning, slightly longer and often buzzier calls may be given, and most species have a rapid-paced twittering or chattering 'chase call' given in aggressive interactions, such as one bird chasing off another. Typical 'feeding calls' are very useful in many species-level identifications. Chase calls are more complex and variable but still can be useful for identification. The songs (and flight displays when relevant, see **Habitat and Behavior**) of adult males can also be useful for identification.

The humming sounds made by different species in flight may also be useful for identification. The best known example is the unique, relatively shrill wing trill of an adult male Broad-tailed Hummingbird, which is quite distinct from the lower wing buzz of an adult male Rufous/Allen's Hummingbird, or the low wing hum of an adult male Black-chinned Hummingbird. Note, though, that wing molt, or heavily abraded outer primaries, may cause birds to sound different, and that male *Selasphorus* with worn or molting outer primaries can lack a wing trill (e.g., **Pics I.11**).

Habitat and Behavior

Hummingbirds can occur just about anywhere there are suitable flowers, or feeders, but some broad habitat characteristics can still be useful. For example, Blue-throated and Magnificent hummingbirds occur mainly in temperate, forested mountains, while Broad-billed Hummingbirds occur mainly in desert washes and tropical and subtropical woodlands. Finding a Blue-throated Hummingbird in a low elevation desert wash would be highly unusual. Still, a dozen or more species (including these three) can occur contemporaneously at feeders in the canyons of Arizona in late summer and fall.

Hummingbird behavior can provide useful clues in an identification but should only be considered a supporting rather than primary character in any problem identification, except perhaps for flight displays of territorial adult males. The best way to start is by watching adult males or any individuals of known (or reasonably presumed) identity (e.g., by default in eastern Canada and the eastern U.S. in summer, virtually all hummers can be assumed Ruby-throated). By contrast, going in late summer to feeders in Arizona, where there are lots of immatures of several confusing species, is not a good way to start but can be valuable after you have gained experience with a few species.

Things to note include how the tail is held habitually on perched birds: is it closed or spread (usually the former)? Do birds (which sex?) perch prominently on bare twigs or inconspicuously? On feeding birds in flight, is the tail held cocked above the body plane, in the same plane as the body, or depressed? Is the tail held closed or flashed open? Is it wagged habitually or rarely? A striking example is the frequent tail wagging and fanning of hovering and feeding Broad-billed Hummingbird, quite different from the relatively rigid or quivered tail of feeding White-eared Hummingbird. Some Broad-billeds, however, feed with their tail held fairly rigid, or quivered slightly, although it is often cocked above the body plane, rather than held close to the body plane, as on White-eared. Note that any hummingbird maneuvering among flowers or approaching a feeder often fans or twists its tail.

Some species typically dominate others at feeding aggregations, e.g., Anna's usually chase off Black-chinned Hummingbirds, Rufous/Allen's hummingbirds tend to be very aggressive and dominate Anna's and Black-chinned, most species chase off the diminutive Calliope Hummingbird, and most species yield to Magnificent Hummingbird. Inter-specific aggression is variable, however, and depends on a number of factors so that it is unlikely to be of use in identification. For example, birds resident in an area may dominate migrants, and particularly aggressive individuals of smaller species may chase off larger species.

The small gorgeted hummingbirds all have flight displays that typically comprise two components: dive-displays with a distinct vertical component and a U-shaped or J-shaped trajectory, and shuttle-displays, which mostly involve short-wavelength rocking with a mostly horizontal component. Flight displays are mostly given by territorial adult males in the breeding seasons, although immature males (from a month of age or younger) give dive-displays that can help with species identification (e.g., Rufous versus Allen's hummingbirds). Dive displays are species-specific and conspicuous; they reflect aggression and courtship, and can be directed at other males and other species (including non-hummingbirds, even people at times!), as well as at females. Shuttle displays are more similar among closely related species and seem related mainly to courtship, and 'pinning down' a female, although they can also be used in an aggressive, territorial context; often they occur in or near cover and usually are observed less often than dive displays.

A Summary of Identification Characters

While the foregoing may seem an almost overwhelming amount to digest, there is no rush. Time and the associated experience gained are a key part of watching and identifying hummingbirds. The above discussions simply provide a background that should put your observations into context. Armed with this information you are in a position not only to identify most hummingbirds you see, but to contribute to the field identification process. Many species can be identified readily and quickly, others may defy specific identification even with prolonged views.

In general, when confronted with an unfamiliar hummingbird, place it in the small, medium, or large category right away, then look at relative bill length, tail shape, and, if it's perched, the relative lengths of the closed wing tip and tail tip. Check plumage characters – face pattern, throat pattern, and tail pattern being the most useful features in almost all cases. While doing this, note the bird's behavior (tail wagging or tail flashing, etc.) and any vocalizations it is making. With practice you can assimilate a remarkable amount of information in only a minute or so of viewing time. As you begin to recognize certain problem species pairs or groups you'll learn which features to key into – e.g., looking straight at the shape of the inner primaries (for *Archilochus* versus *Calypte*) or the shape of P10 (for Ruby-throated versus Black-chinned), or the width and pattern of the outer rectrices (for Rufous versus Allen's, taking into account age and sex). Having said all of this, remember that many hummingbirds get away before they can be identified, even by experts – that's just part of the magic and challenge of these remarkable birds.

How To Use The Book

Each genus is introduced by a summary of its characteristics, and then the species accounts are broken down into categories to make information more easily accessible. First, a species' English and scientific names are given, followed by its length in centimeters and inches. These are standardized lengths taken by me from museum specimens laid on their back, and are full length from tip of bill to tip of tail. In addition, bill length is given (in mm). In general, females have longer bills than males but in most species there is a fair amount of overlap between the sexes in bill length.

Each account opens with an identification summary that covers the key points for a species, followed by three introductory sections that provide background information. Then come details on characters that relate more directly to field identification, and last is a list of references cited in each species account.

Identification Summary: The key points that identify each species are summarized here, although in some cases you may need to refer to more detailed information in the *Similar species* section.

Taxonomy: This includes a brief notation about subspecies (if any) and other taxonomic aspects, such as differing generic treatments of some species by the AOU. If no subspecies are described for a species it is termed monotypic.

Status and Distribution: Knowing where you are and what should, or could, occur there at a given time of year can be important in an identification. While it may seem that any migratory species of North American hummingbird could turn up almost anywhere on the continent, vagrant occurrences remain rare and should be documented thoroughly. The geographic range and overall seasonal occurrence of each species are summarized in this section, and maps are included for the more widespread species; this book is not intended as a compendium of all vagrant records of hummingbirds in North America. Rather, records of rare migrants or vagrants are synthesized to indicate broad-scale geographic or seasonal patterns of occurrence, and often the most far-flung records are noted rather than all records. Thus, for example, because Green Violet-ear has been found 'as far afield to the N and E as W Ontario, North Carolina, and Alabama,' records from Wisconsin, Michigan, and Kentucky are not mentioned because they fall inside a net cast over the farthest points noted. Data were derived from the AOU Checklist[2], general regional sources, and review of records published in American Birds (AB), National Audubon Society Field Notes (AFN), and North American Birds (NAB), followed by review by several national and regional authorities (see Acknowledgments). When I summarized and synthesized AB/AFN/NAB data this is cited simply as NAB (including AB and AFN). For exceptional records, specific issues and page numbers may be cited, e.g., AB 47:441, rather than full citations involving author and date. Records are mostly summarized through 1999, sometimes later, depending on the availability of local information.

In general, most hummingbirds are fairly common to common where they breed, becoming less common to rare at the edges of their range. Because of factors such as difficulty of detection and 'feeder bias,' I have avoided using relative abundance terms in some cases. For example, a rare species may seem 'common' if it comes to a feeder regularly, while numerically fairly common species may be detected rarely in the field if they do not visit feeders. Alternatively, a species may be common one year at the edge of its range or as a migrant through an area, and then rare the next. Such fluctuations may result from broad-scale climatic factors (especially rainfall) that influence year-to-year variation in the abundance and distribution of flowering plants, or from more local weather conditions that could cause migration routes to shift slightly.

Hummingbird distributions are dynamic and, furthermore, the distinction between a vagrant (a bird outside its 'normal' range) and a rare migrant (within its 'normal' range) is subjective. My use of terms such as 'casual' (less than annual in occurrence) or 'rare' (annual in occurrence, on average) often refer to what traditionally have been considered vagrants, but which are often listed here (with spans of seasonal occurrence) without a status designation. Much of the apparent changing status of some species may be due to the increasing year-round presence of feeders, particularly in parts of southeastern North America. This, in combination with increased planting of exotic plants and perhaps a greater interest in hummingbirds, is helping re-shape or at least re-write the distribution of many species in North America, particularly in winter. For example, 10–15 years ago winter records of hummers in the eastern U.S. were rare, but in recent years up to eight species have been found wintering regularly in the southeast.

Range: The world range of each species is summarized for reference.

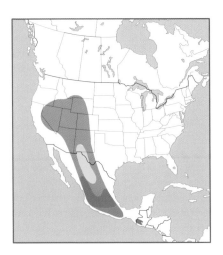

◼ Seasonal breeding ("summer") range

◼ Permanent resident

◼ Non-breeding ("winter") range

☐ Transient migrant

Field Identification

Up to nine of the following sections cover aspects that relate to field identification.

Structure: The overall structural characters of each species are noted, including age/sex differences when relevant.

Similar species: Distinguishing features for each age/sex class of a species are given in comparison to other similar species.

Voice and Sounds: The calls (and songs, if relevant) of each species are described here, if known. Non-vocal sounds, e.g., wing-buzz, are also discussed if relevant to identification. Sounds produced in flight displays often involve modified outer primaries and, apparently, outer rectrices (such as in *Selasphorus*[11]), so full displays tend not to be given by molting birds in the non-breeding season. All voice and sound descriptions are based on my own observations unless stated otherwise.

Habitat: A broad indication of habitat is given.

Behavior: A summary of behavioral characters is noted, including displays when relevant. This information is based upon my own observations unless noted otherwise.

Molt: Approximate dates are given for the periods of start and completion of wing molt. Details are incomplete for several species (mainly vagrants to North America) and should be viewed as provisional. Primary molt is usually the most conspicuous aspect of molt and also appears to span the overall period that molt occurs in most other tracts (and see above). These data are derived from museum data collected by myself and Peter Pyle, my own field observations, and examination of photographs.

Description: Detailed descriptions are given for each age and sex class.

Hybrids: Any known or presumed hybrids involving a species are listed.

References: References (to both published and unpublished data) are noted by use of superscripts throughout the text and are listed by author and date at the end of a chapter or species account. Full citations for published works can be found in the literature cited section near the back of the book.

Photos: A series of photos accompanies each species account, and captions highlight identification criteria for each species and age/sex class. I reviewed over 3000 photos and tried to pick a combination of portraits (showing features in detail) and 'field photos' that show the birds more as one usually sees them. In a few cases, suitable photos were not found and four plumages (of two species) are shown by color paintings.

References

[1]Aldrich 1956, [2]AOU 1998, [3]Baltosser 1995, [4]Graves and Newfield 1996, [5]Greenwalt 1960, [6]S. N. G. Howell, personal observation, [7]Howell and Webb 1995, [8]Jones 1983, [9]Kaufman 1990, [10]B. Mila, unpublished data and photos, [11]Ortiz-Crespo 1980,[12]PRBO unpublished data, [13]Pyle 1997, [14]Ridgway 1911, [15]Schuchmann 1999, [16]Sibley 2000, [17]Sibley and Monroe 1990, [18]Stiles 1971, [19]Williamson 1956, [20]Yanega *et al.* 1997.

Violet-ears Genus *Colibri*

Violet-ears comprise four to five large hummingbird species that inhabit temperate, primarily montane habitats from central Mexico to Brazil and northern Argentina. They have straightish, medium-short to medium-length black bills and fairly long, broad, and squared to slightly notched tails that have a dark subterminal band. As the name suggests, all species have erectile violet auricular tufts. One species, the Green Violet-ear, occurs as a rare vagrant north of Mexico.

I Green Violet-ear

(Colibri thalassinus)

11–11.5 cm (4.2–4.7 in); male > female. Bill 18–22 mm.
Pics 1.1–1.4

Identification summary
Medium-large size. Green overall with violet auriculars, bluish-purple chest patch. Tail bronzy blue-green with broad blue-black subterminal band. Female and immature duller than adult male. Rare vagrant to North America.

Taxonomy
North American records refer to the northern subspecies, nominate *thalassinus*, found from Mexico south to northwestern Nicaragua (the race *minor* described from Honduras is considered a synonym of *thalassinus*[6]). Populations from Costa Rica south lack violet-blue on the chest and lores and have been considered a separate species, *Colibri cyanotus*, Lesser Violet-ear[8], with *thalassinus* called Mexican Violet-ear[8].

Status and Distribution
Casual to rare visitor (mainly May to August, with a few records from mid April and into early November[2,7]) to widely scattered locales in E North America. Most records have been from Texas (29 accepted records, 1961–2000, mid April to mid September[9]), but also found as far afield to the N and E as W Ontario, North Carolina, and Alabama[1]. Two reports from California (August to early September) are considered hypothetical[3].

Range
Montane forests from central Mexico to Andes of Bolivia (and see under Taxonomy). Mexican populations undergo poorly known local migrations[4,10,11] and wandering birds reach North America on occasions.

Field Identification

Structure
Fairly large and well built hummingbird. Bill straightish to very slightly decurved and medium length, often looking proportionately short. Tail fairly long, broad, and notched (adult male) to squared or slightly cleft (female). Primaries fairly broad with P10 narrower and tapered at tip. At rest, wing tips slightly (female/immature) to distinctly (adult male) < tail tip.

Similar species
In North America the Green Violet-ear is largely unmistakable but still should be studied carefully to confirm an identification.

Male Green-breasted Mango (vagrant to Texas) has longer, strongly arched bill and mostly purple tail.

Slightly larger Sparkling Violet-ear (*Colibri coruscans;* 12.5–14 cm, 4.8–5 in; bill 22–25 mm) may be kept in captivity in North American aviaries, and escapes would probably be passed off as Green Violet-ear. Note that Sparkling Violet-ear has violet from auriculars extending forward in a broad band under eyes to chin.

Southern populations of Green Violet-ear might also be kept in captivity, and are told from Mexican populations by lack of bluish violet on lores and chest (but similar to some Mexican females/immatures), broader buffy edges to undertail-coverts (again, similar to Mexican immatures).

Also beware the possibility of hybrids that might resemble violet-ears superficially.

Voice and Sounds
Periodically gives a hard rattled *trrrr* or *trrr* while feeding, also a single hard chip, *tk,* that can be repeated and run into rattles, *tk, tk, tk, trrrr.* Warning call (?) a single, abrupt, low metallic *tchk!* Song (unlikely from vagrants?) a mostly disyllabic, metallic chipping, given with slightly jerky rhythm and often repeated tirelessly from perch on exposed twig: *tíssik-tíssik tíssik-tíssik tíssik-tíssik...* or a more varied *ch-it chi-i-it chi-chi-it ch-it chi-it...,* etc., at times punctuated with *tik* and *tssi* notes. An immature male in Texas gave prolonged series of rough, wheezy buzzes and rattles interspersed with sharp chips[5].

Habitat
In Mexico favors humid to semi-arid pine-oak, oak, and evergreen forest and edge, adjacent clearings with flowers. In North America has occurred in a wide variety of habitats, with most birds found at feeders.

Behavior
Feeds low to high and regularly chases off smaller species such as White-eared Hummingbird. Flight fairly quick and often keeps 'inside' flower banks when feeding, rather than in open situations. Tail usually held in or near body plane and quivered, being flashed open in maneuvers. Singing males perch on prominent bare twigs at mid to upper levels in trees, the wings slightly drooped and tail variably fanned; they turn their head from side to side, so the song changes volume and can be hard to pinpoint, and intermittently flutter their wings.

Molt
In central Mexico, primary molt of adults apparently occurs mainly during January to August.

Description

Adult male: crown, nape, and upperparts deep golden green with glittering purple lores and auriculars, and with violet-blue extending narrowly and diffusely under the chin; distal uppertail-coverts usually bronzier than back. Throat and chest iridescent bluish green with violet to purplish-blue patch on upper chest; rest of underparts bronzy green to bluish green, undertail-coverts with variable cinnamon-buff edgings. Tail bronzy greenish blue, greener on R1, with broad blue-black subterminal band. Bill black, feet blackish.

Adult female: slightly smaller and shorter tailed. Plumage overall duller and less intense green, crown duller and more bronzy, auricular tufts smaller and less expansive, chest patch bluer (less purplish) and less extensive, sometimes reduced to a few bluish and poorly contrasting spots.

Immature (sexes similar): crown, nape, and upperparts bronzy green with fine cinnamon tips most distinct on head; purple reduced to absent in lores and averaging less on auriculars. Throat and chest dull bluish green with scattered iridescent feathers and trace of blue on chest; rest of underbody dusky bronzy green, undertail-coverts dusky pale cinnamon-buff with variable darker centers. Tail like adult but R1 averages bronzier green.

Hybrids

None reported (?).

References

[1]AOU 1998, [2] AFN 50:68 (1996), [3]CBRC unpubl. data, [4]Howell & Webb 1995, [5]G. W. Lasley tape, [6]Monroe 1968, [7]NAB 53:56, 117 (1999), [8]Ridgway 1911, [9] TBRC unpubl. data, [10]Wagner 1945, [11]Wilson & Ceballos 1993.

1.1 Adult Green Violet-ear. The solidly iridescent throat and chest indicate an adult, probably a male based on the extent of purple and blue. Robert A. Behrstock. Volcán de Fuego, Jalisco, Mexico, 18 December 1995.

1.2 Apparent adult Green Violet-ear. Unmistakable. Steve Bentsen. San Benito, Texas, 18 April 1991.

1.3 and 1.4 Immature male Green Violet-ear. The gray ground color to the throat and chest indicates an immature bird, the relatively extensive blue and purple (for an immature) point to a male (confirmed by song). Greg W. Lasley. Sandy Creek, Travis Co., Texas, 18 June 1995.

1.4

Mangos Genus *Anthracothorax*

A complex of from six to eight hummingbird species whose taxonomy is vexed. Mangos range mainly in tropical lowlands from eastern Mexico and the Caribbean to Brazil and northern Argentina, with greatest diversity in Central America and the Caribbean. They are large hummingbirds with fairly thick, medium-length, arched black bills and large, broad tails that are squared to slightly cleft. Males of most species are predominantly deep green, often with a dark patch or stripe on the underparts. Females of most are pale gray to whitish below, often with a dark median stripe. Several mangos look very similar and species identification may not always be possible, although Green-breasted Mango is the most likely species to occur naturally in North America and is the only species so far recorded – as a casual vagrant to Texas.

2 Green-breasted Mango

(*Anthracothorax prevostii*)

11.5–12 cm (4.5–4.8 in). Bill 24–30 mm (female > male).
Pics 2.1–2.4

Identification summary
Large size. Black bill fairly thick and arched. Male deep green overall with purple tail. Female and immature have whitish median underparts split by dark central stripe. Casual vagrant to S Texas.

Taxonomy
Birds in Mexico and N Central America are nominate *prevostii*, the subspecies most likely to occur in North America. Other (more southern) populations average slightly shorter and more slender bills but identification to subspecies requires a bird to be in the hand. Populations from the Pacific slope of western Panama were formerly treated as a subspecies of Green-breasted Mango[1] but are now considered specifically distinct, as Veraguan Mango *A. veraguensis*[2,8] (but see Wetmore[12]). Green-breasted and Veraguan mangos form a superspecies with Black-throated Mango *A. nigricollis*[2].

Status and Distribution
Casual in autumn and winter (mid August to late January, mainly August–September) in lowlands of S Texas, N to Corpus Christi, with 7 accepted records (all apparently immatures) through 1999[10]; see DeBenedictis[3,4]; also once late May[7]. First North American record (September 1988) originally accepted only as Mango sp., but subsequently accepted as Green-breasted[6]. Presumably, however, Veraguan Mango can be eliminated only on probability.

Range

Tropical lowlands from E Mexico to NW Panama, disjunctly in N South America. Birds in E Mexico are migratory (present there mainly February to August[5]) and the species has wandered north to Texas.

Field Identification

Structure

Large and powerfully built hummingbird. Bill fairly thick, medium length, and arched. Primaries medium broad with P10 slightly narrower and more tapered. Tail large, broad, and squared to slightly cleft (males) or squared to slightly rounded (females). At rest, male wing tips < tail, female/immature wing tips ≤ tail.

Similar species

No similar species recorded from North America but closely related and similar taxa occur to the south. Other mango species seem unlikely to occur naturally in North America, but might be kept in captivity and could occur as escapes. Thus, any vagrant mango should be scrutinized carefully.

The most similar species are Veraguan Mango (whose limited native range makes it an unlikely aviary bird?) and widespread Black-throated Mango (ranging from Panama to Argentina). Adult male **Veraguan Mango** has chin and throat wholly iridescent green (velvet-black in adult male Green-breasted); females and immatures probably not safely distinguishable in field from Green-breasted but chin white (n = 4) rather than black on 65% of adult female Green-breasted (n = 24), median throat stripe of adult female blacker and mixed with blue-green (typically solid sooty black on Green-breasted), black on median underparts of immature liberally mixed with blue-green. Adult male **Black-throated Mango** has broad, velvet-black median stripe on throat and chest, bordered laterally with deep turquoise-blue. Female Black-throated Mango has median stripe on underparts all-black (or with scattered dull bluish-green spots unlikely to be visible in the field); 95% show extensive purple in tail (n = 90). Immature Black-throated lacks extensive brick-rufous below but can show some brick-rufous flecks in malar; rectrices more narrowly tipped buffy white than Green-breasted. Immature **Antillean Mango** A. *dominicus* of eastern Greater Antilles suggests female Green-breasted, with variable dark median stripe below (especially on throat), but underparts overall whitish without extensive green on sides, white tail tips may be narrower.

Voice and Sounds

Mostly silent, although feeding and perched birds at times give fairly hard ticking chips that can be repeated steadily, *chik chik chik....* Also gives a high, sharp *sip* or *sik*, mainly in flight, and high, shrill, slightly tinny twitters in interactions.

Habitat

In Mexico favors semi-open country with scattered tall trees, such as hedges in farmland, gardens with tall trees, and residential areas.

Behavior

Feeds mainly at mid to upper levels, and often perches conspicuously on tall bare branches and twigs. Flight quick but relatively heavy and not dashing. Feeds with tail in, or cocked slightly above, body plane and held rigid or quivered; tail flashed in maneuvers and interactions. Most North American records have been at feeders[6].

Molt
Mostly September to January in N populations, i.e., during non-breeding season.

Description
Adult male (some adult females): often looks all dark. Crown, nape, and upperparts deep golden green to emerald green, the crown sometimes duller. Median throat velvet-black, bordered laterally by broad, iridescent turquoise-green malar stripes. Chest blue-green, sides/flanks and belly bronzy green with white vent band, undertail-coverts dusky purplish, narrowly tipped cinnamon. **Tail:** R1 dark bronzy green with blue-black shaft streak, R2–R5 coppery purple to violet with narrow dark edging and tips. Some adult females exhibit apparently full adult male plumage[5,9] although some may be distinguishable by narrow whitish tips to R3–R5[11]. Bill black, feet blackish.
Adult female: head and upperparts bronzy green to golden green, often with duller crown. Throat and central underparts white with a broad dark median stripe that is black on the throat and becomes glittering deep green to blue green on the chest and belly where often irregular and slightly broken; black throat stripe continues to bill base on 80% of birds with extensive violet-purple in tail (n = 20), on 50% of birds lacking obvious purple in tail (n = 10; subadults?). Sides and flanks bronzy green, vent band white, undertail-coverts dusky bronzy green, tipped pale gray. **Tail:** R1 bronzy green, R2–R5 mostly violet-purple with bronzy-green edgings to bases of outer webs, variable blue-black subterminal band, white tips to R3–R5, and fine white tip to R2 when fresh. Up to 20% of birds have R2–R5 mostly blue-black with little or no purple (n = 30); these, including occasional birds with scattered brick-rufous flecks in the malar, may be subadults.
Immature: resembles female but chin and upper throat white, blackish median 'stripe' on underparts often consists of two oily greenish-black patches on lower throat and lower chest, and malar and sides of white median stripe on underparts have distinct brick-rufous mottling and edging.

Hybrids
None reported (?).

References
[1] AOU 1983, [2] AOU 1998, [3] DeBenedictis 1991, [4] DeBenedictis 1994, [5] Howell & Webb 1995, [6] G. W. Lasley pers. comm., [7] NAB 53:300,343 (1999), [8] Olson 1993, [9] Stiles & Skutch 1989, [10] TBRC unpubl. data, [11] USNM specimen no. 102793, [12] Wetmore 1968:294.

2.1 Adult male Green-breasted Mango. Unmistakable relative to regularly occurring North American hummingbirds (see text for differences from other mango species). Note relatively thick, arched bill, velvet-black throat stripe bordered bluish, mostly purple tail. Painting by Sophie Webb. Reproduced courtesy of National Geographic Society.

2.2 Adult female Green-breasted Mango, fresh plumage. Note the thick, slightly arched black bill and blackish median throat stripe. J. Dunning (VIREO). Isla Cozumel, Quintana Roo, Mexico, January 1974.

2.3 Immature Green-breasted Mango. Note the thick, slightly arched black bill; the cinnamon markings below indicate an immature. Greg W. Lasley. Corpus Cristi, Texas, 9 January 1992.

2.4 Immature Green-breasted Mango. Unmistakable relative to regularly occurring North American hummingbirds (see text for differences from other mango species). Note relatively thick, arched bill, white median underparts with black-and-green central stripe, cinnamon lateral borders. Painting by Sophie Webb. Reproduced courtesy of National Geographic Society.

Emeralds Genus *Chlorostilbon*

These emeralds comprise a genus of about 18 species (taxonomy remains unresolved) ranging from Mexico and the Caribbean to Brazil, and are named for the overall glittering-green plumage of the males. They are small hummingbirds with medium-length to medium-short, straightish bills, and tails that typically are cleft to deeply forked, more strongly so in males. Bills often have some reddish or pink, at least on the mandible base. Casual vagrant to North America: one species (Cuban Emerald) has been reported from Florida.

3 Cuban Emerald

(*Chlorostilbon ricordii*)

9.5–10.5 cm (3.7–4.2 in) (male > female). Bill 15–17 mm.
Pics 3.1–3.6.

Identification summary

Small size. Tail long and deeply forked with broad rectrices, bill medium-length and straight. Male intense emerald-green overall with white undertail-coverts, reddish mandible base. Female has whitish post-ocular stripe and dark auricular mask, pale grey underparts with glittering green sides. Casual vagrant to S Florida.

Taxonomy

Two subspecies have been described: *ricordii* (Cuba and Isle of Pines) and *aeneoviridis* (Bahamas). The latter differs from nominate birds in its slightly shorter and less deeply forked tail. Confusion between *aeneoventris* and the extinct *Chlorostilbon bracei* was clarified by Graves and Olson[5].

Status and Distribution

Fourteen sight records (all months except February and December, mainly June–October[8]) from southern Florida, none substantiated by a specimen or photo[2,4,8], although Cruickshank[3] described a male Cuban Emerald (at Cocoa Beach in October 1963[1]) to the exclusion of other species (e.g., the 'deeply-lobed tail' and 'white triangle under tail,' in combination with other points of the description, eliminate other similar *Chlorostilbon*).

Range

Cuba, Isle of Pines, and NW Bahamas (primarily Grand Bahama, Abaco, and Andros).

Field Identification

Structure
Small size. Bill medium length and straightish to very slightly decurved (especially on female). Tail long and deeply forked (more so on adult male), rectrices broad and rounded. Primaries broad with P10 slightly narrower. At rest, wing tips fall well short of tail tip.

Similar species
Unlikely to be confused with any regularly occurring North American species although smaller male Ruby-throated Hummingbird facing away often looks solidly emerald-green and has distinctly forked tail, but tail much shorter and rectrices more tapered than Cuban Emerald, voice and habits distinct.

Other *Chlorostilbon* species occur in Mexico[6] and the Caribbean[7] and any vagrant should be studied carefully to establish its identification; also beware the possibility of escapes and hybrids. Female suggests **Broad-billed Hummingbird** in overall plumage and face pattern but smaller with much longer and more deeply forked tail, different voice.

Hispaniolan Emerald *C. swainsonii* averages slightly larger with slightly longer bill. Male has emerald-green gorget contrasting with blackish chest, remaining underparts dark greenish, including undertail-coverts; female has whitish post-ocular spot, not line, bold whitish tips to outer rectrices, and pale gray base to R5 (underside of closed tail appears whitish with broad black median band). **Puerto Rican Emerald** *C. maugeus* slightly smaller and shorter billed. Male tail all blue-black and less deeply forked, with narrower and more tapered rectrices, undertail-coverts dark; female has short, cleft tail (projecting only slightly beyond wings at rest) that is black distally with bold white tips and pale grayish bases to outer rectrices, bill all-black. **Canivet's Emerald** *C. canivetii* of eastern Mexico smaller overall with shorter and less deeply forked tail with narrower rectrices; male tail blue-black with grey-tipped inner rectrices, undertail-coverts dark, bill red with black tip; female tail cleft with white tips and whitish median band on outer rectrices; dry chattering call quite different from Cuban Emerald.

Voice and Sounds
Male call in flight an abrupt, cicada-like or 'electric' buzz, *dzzzih* or *bizzz,* usually singly or doubled; from perch gives more prolonged and often slightly quieter series, *zzi zzi zzi-zzi zzih* or *zzi zzi zzi-zzi zzi zzi zzi-zzi zzi-zzi zzi...;* chase call (?) in flight a rapid-paced, buzzy *dizz-i-zzih* or *dizz-iz-it.* Female call usually slightly quieter, a buzzy *zzzir,* often doubled or trebled, e.g., *zzi-zzih* and *chi-di-dit* or *zhi-zhi-zhit,* and longer series in flight and from perch, overall with more rattled and less buzzy quality than male.

Habitat
On Bahamas occurs widely: in understory of open pine woods, edge and clearings of coppice woodland, second growth, and gardens.

Behavior
Feeds mainly at low to mid levels and regularly visits feeders. Perches low to high, males often on fairly exposed bare twigs, females more often low and less conspicuous, at edges and 'inside' bushes; tail usually held closed or only slightly spread when

perched. Feeds and hovers with active wagging of slightly spread and fanned tail; male's wings make a fairly loud buzz that often draws attention, while female has an unremarkable, quiet wing hum.

Molt
Breeding may occur year-round but details poorly known, and may vary among islands, such that molting birds might be encountered in any month.

Description
Adult male: intense, glittering emerald-green overall (duller on crown and often with bluish highlights below), with distinct white post-ocular spot; longest uppertail-coverts bronzy green, like central rectrices; vent band fluffy white; undertail-coverts white or with faint dusky centers to lateral feathers. **Tail:** R1–R2 bronzy green, R3–R5 blackish with variable bronzy-green sheen on basal 70–80% of outer webs. Bill black above, reddish below with black tip (can appear all-black unless seen from underneath), feet blackish.

Adult female: face and underparts pale gray with dark auricular mask and white post-ocular spot that runs into whitish post-ocular stripe; sides/flanks mottled glittering green; vent band fluffy white; undertail-coverts pale gray. Crown, nape, and upperparts glittering emerald-green with duller crown, bronzy-green longest uppertail coverts. **Tail:** R1–R2 bronzy green, R3–R5 blackish with variable bronzy-green sheen on outer webs. Bill black, at times showing some pinkish basally from below (often looks all-black unless seen from directly underneath).

Immature: Not well known. Juvenile apparently resembles female but R4–R5 tipped pale gray to whitish; male may have more deeply forked tail than adult female. Subadult (?) male like adult male but throat and chest less solidly glittering emerald, belly relatively dark bronzy green with fine buffy to pale gray tips, rectrices may average slightly narrower.

Hybrids
None reported.

References
[1]AFN 18:26 (1964), [2]AOU 1998, [3]Cruickshank 1964, [4]DeBenedictis 1991, [5]Graves & Olson 1987, [6]Howell & Webb 1995, [7]Raffaele *et al.* 1998, [8]Stevenson & Anderson 1994.

3.1 Adult male Cuban Emerald. The long and deeply forked tail is usually held closed and projects well beyond the wing tips on perched birds. Small size, overall emerald-green color and medium-length straight bill with some reddish below are also distinctive. The white undertail-coverts eliminate other potentially similar emeralds from the Caribbean and Mexico. Kevin T. Karlson. Abaco, Bahamas, March 1999.

3.2 Adult male Cuban Emerald. Note the deeply forked blackish tail with broad and rounded rectrices, and medium-length straight bill with reddish below. Greg W. lasley. Port Lucaya, Bahamas, 5 March 1997.

3.3 Adult male Cuban Emerald. The apparent bluish-green coloration might suggest larger male Broad-billed Hummingbird, but note black maxilla and, especially, the diagnostically long and deeply forked, bronzy-green tail. Bruce Hallett. Grand Bahama, Bahamas, 2 March 1998.

3.4 Female Cuban Emerald. Note the long and deeply forked tail with bronzy-green central rectrices and lack of distinct white tips to outer rectrices. Bruce Hallett. Grand Bahama, Bahamas, February 1999.

3.5 Female Cuban Emerald. The long and deeply forked tail is usually held closed and projects well beyond the wing tips on perched birds. The face pattern suggests female Broad-billed Hummingbird but the shorter bill is more slender and mostly black. Kevin T. Karlson. Abaco, Bahamas, March 1999.

3.6 Female Cuban Emerald. The long tail is striking in flight, when it is often wagged. The most similar North American species is Broad-billed Hummingbird but the emerald has a much longer tail and very indistinct pinkish on the mandible base. Kevin T. Karlson. Abaco, Bahamas, March 1999.

Broad-billed Hummingbirds
Genus *Cynanthus*

A small genus of from two to four species (species limits are vexed) largely endemic to Mexico. One species (Broad-billed Hummingbird) occurs north into the southwestern U.S. These are lightly built, medium-sized to medium-small hummingbirds with medium-long, straightish bills that are broad across the base. Their broad tails are cleft to forked and often wagged by hovering birds. The bills of males are bright red with a black tip, while females and immatures have reddish mostly restricted to the mandible. The male Broad-billed is bright green overall, the female is pale grayish below with a broad dark mask. By virtue of structure, plumage, and habits, this species is distinctive in North America.

4 Broad-billed Hummingbird

(Cynanthus latirostris)

9–10 cm (3.5–4 in). Bill 18.5–23.5 mm.
Pics I.19, 4.1–4.11.

Identification summary
Medium to medium-small and lightly built. Tail fairly broad and cleft, often fanned and wagged by hovering birds. Distinctive male appears deep green overall with blue throat, whitish undertail-coverts, and bright red, black-tipped bill. Female pale gray below with broad dark or dusky auricular mask bordered above by whitish to pale gray post-ocular stripe; bill reddish at base (mainly below). Dry chattering call suggests Ruby-crowned Kinglet *Regulus calendula*.

Taxonomy
Birds recorded in North America are of the northern subspecies *magicus*, weakly differentiated from nominate *latirostris* of central Mexico. Other closely related taxa in Mexico are variably treated as subspecies of Broad-billed Hummingbird or as separate species, e.g., *lawrencei* of the Tres Marias Islands and *doubledayi* of southwestern Mexico[6,7].

Status and Distribution (Map)
Common to fairly common summer resident (mainly March to September) in SE Arizona and SW New Mexico; rare, at least formerly (mainly April to September) in W Texas[14]. Rare during winter (mainly at feeders) in S Arizona, and casual to rare in fall

and winter (mainly September to March) in S California and Texas. Casual (mainly September to November) NW to Oregon[9] and Utah, and NE to Michigan (June[3]), S Ontario, and New Brunswick[2]. Casual (mainly October to February) E to Louisiana, Mississippi[8], and South Carolina (July[1]).

Range SW U.S. to central Mexico.

Field Identification

Structure

Medium to medium-small and lightly built hummingbird. Bill straightish and medium-long, becoming laterally expanded towards base. Tail fairly broad and cleft (more strongly so in male). Primaries fairly broad, with P10 narrower and more tapered. At rest, wing tips slightly < tail tip on male, ≤ tail tip on female and immature.

Similar species

Combination of plumage, call, and behavior should identify this species readily in North America but some pitfalls can be encountered by observers unfamiliar with Broad-billed and other southwestern hummingbirds. Adult male Broad-billed should be unmistakable, but with vagrants always check features carefully to rule out possibility of hybrids or escapes of species that might be similar. Problems may occur with females and immature males.

Blue-throated Hummingbird. Immature male Broad-billed with blue concentrated on throat might suggest much larger Blue-throated Hummingbird (juveniles of which can even have pinkish on mandible) but size of latter should be obvious (dwarfing any other species except Magnificent). Blue-throated is a mountain species with overall slightly rounded blue-black tail that has bold white distal corners. It also has no green spotting on underparts, different behavior, and very high-pitched squeaking call.

White-eared Hummingbird. Female is stockier and proportionately shorter billed than female Broad-billed, with much bolder white post-ocular stripe, blacker auricular mask, and green throat spotting. Feeding White-eared typically has tail closed and rigid, in or near body plane, and not wagged and spread. Call a clipped, smacking tick, often doubled.

Black-chinned Hummingbird. Dullest female Broad-billed Hummingbirds can suggest Black-chinned Hummingbird, or *vice versa*. The two species often occur side-by-side at feeders, are of similar size, and both habitually tail-wag. Broad-billed has broad inner primaries, pinkish mandible base (can be hard to see), and emerald-green spotting on chest sides of adult female. Dusky auricular mask and pale post-ocular stripe of Broad-billed typically distinct but most poorly marked birds approach most strongly marked (usually immature) Black-chinneds. Also note distinctly different calls, and more extensive white tail corners of Black-chinned.

Voice and Sounds

Call a dry *ch* or *cht*, given singly or doubled and trebled, and chattering series suggest call of Ruby-crowned Kinglet, *ch-cht* and *ch-ch-cht*, etc. Also a rolled chattering *trrit* or *chirr-rrt*, and in interactions a high squeaky chippering. Song apparently a high, sharp *sing* repeated 3–5 times[12].

Habitat

Favors arid to semi-arid brushy woodland, scrub, and semi-open areas in general, especially in riparian situations, e.g., desert washes, suburban gardens, etc. Small numbers range upslope into mountain canyons.

Behavior

Feeds and perches low to high, sings from perch. Hovering and feeding birds often wag their spread tail persistently, at times almost frenetically. At other times, simply feeds with tail loosely cocked (usually slightly above body plane) and quivered, but without the strong wagging or fanning that is often considered habitual of this species.

Molt

Primary molt starts between April and September (later in some immatures?), ends mainly July to January or February; averages later in immatures. Molt of adults and early-hatched young occurs mainly on breeding grounds. Late-hatched young and perhaps some adults may suspend primary molt and complete on non-breeding grounds, while some immatures may molt after autumn migration.

Description

Adult male: crown, nape, and upperparts glittering bronzy green to bluish emerald-green, duller on crown, and usually with whitish post-ocular spot or short line. Throat iridescent blue, underparts glittering blue-green; undertail-coverts white with variable dusky centers, and vent white (crissum typically appears whitish). **Tail** blue-black with broad grayish tips to R1 and R2, and narrower grayish tip to R3. Bill bright red with variable black tip most extensive along tomia of maxilla. Feet blackish.

Adult female: crown, nape, and upperparts glittering bronzy green to bluish golden green, averaging duller and bronzier than male and usually dullest on crown. Face and underparts dingy gray with broad, dark dusky-gray auricular mask bordered above by whitish to pale gray post-ocular stripe; post-ocular spot sometimes contrastingly whiter. Chest sides spotted glittering green, and limited green mottling on sides/flanks usually covered by wings; undertail-coverts whitish with variable dusky centers, vent white. Some may have a few glittering bluish throat feathers[11] but confirmation of this desirable. **Tail**: R1 green to blue-green with variably darker and typically blue-black subterminal band, R2 green basally, blue-black distally, and R3–R5 blue-black with blue-green (on R3) to grayish (on R5) base, distinct whitish tips to R4 and R5, small white tip to R3. Closed tail often looks dark with variable amount of bluish green visible at base; worn tails more uniformly dark or very dull two-tone (poorly contrasting greenish base to R1). Bill black above with reddish-pink at gape and, rarely, limited reddish on culmen base; reddish pink below with dark tip.

Immature male: resembles adult female overall but in fresh plumage upperparts have variable buff tipping, and dark mask may average blacker, with more contrasting whitish post-ocular line. Most individuals have blue feathers on throat, often concentrated as median patch of variable extent. **Tail**: blue-black overall with pale gray tips to R1–R3, narrow whitish tips to R4–R5. Bill like adult female but usually with some reddish at base of culmen. Attains adult plumage over fall and winter, during which time bill also attains adult color.

Immature female: resembles adult female but in fresh plumage upperparts have variable buff tipping, underparts have glittering green spotting reduced to absent. Bill averages less extensively and duller pinkish at base. **Tail:** similar to adult female but whitish tips to outer rectrices may average narrower, and R1 emerald green with no dark tip. Attains adult plumage over first fall and winter.

Hybrids
Presumed with Violet-crowned Hummingbird[5,10] and Magnificent Hummingbird[10,13].

References
[1]AB 40:99 (1986), [2]Bain & Shanahan 1999, [3]Binford 1997, [4]S. N. G. Howell unpubl data, [5]S. N. G. Howell pers. obs. (Patagonia, Arizona; July 1997), [6]Howell & Webb 1995, [7]Navarro-S. & Peterson 1999, [8]NAB 53:64 (1999), [9]NAB 53:96,117 (1999), [10]Phillips *et al.* 1964, [11]Pyle 1997, [12]W. C. Russell pers. comm., [13]Short & Phillips 1966, [14]TOS 1995.

4.1 Adult male Broad-billed. The overall green and blue color, bright red bill, and strongly cleft blue-black tail are diagnostic of an adult male Broad-billed. Mark M. Stevenson. Near Tucson, Arizona, September 1999.

4.2 Adult male Broad-billed. The overall deep-green color and bright red bill are distinctive among North American hummingbirds. Charles W. Melton. Madera Canyon, Arizona, 21 May 1999.

4.3 Adult male Broad-billed. Whitish undertail-coverts contrast on deep blue and green underparts, and the broad-based bill is shown well here. Ralph Paonessa. Madera Canyon, Arizona, June 1995.

4.4 Female Broad-billed. Note relatively dull face pattern, plain gray throat and longish bill (cf. White-eared Hummingbird), reddish mandible and green-mottled sides (cf. Blue-throated Hummingbird); primary molt has been suspended at P3. Charles W. Melton. Madera Canyon, Arizona, 21 April 1993.

4.5 Female Broad-billed. With whitish restricted to a post-ocular spot, dull female Broad-billeds may suggest a Black-chinned Humingbird. Note reddish mandible base and evenly broad primaries with new feathers out to P6, and P7 shed. Charles W. Melton. Madera Canyon, Arizona, 17 August 2000.

4.6 Female Broad-billed. The whitish post-ocular stripe, dusky mask, pinkish mandible base, plain greyish underparts, and tail pattern identify this bird to species and sex. P1–5 are new, P6–P7 growing, and P8–10 old. Charles W. Melton. Guadalupe Canyon, Arizona, August 1991.

4.7 Adult female Broad-billed. Note face pattern and reddish mandible. Charles W. Melton. Madera Canyon, Arizona, 14 May 1999.

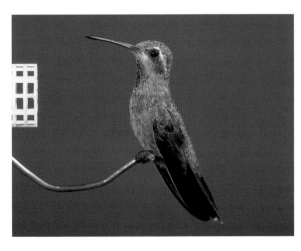

4.8 Immature male Broad-billed. Even fresh-plumaged juveniles can have large blue throat patches (cf. Pic. 4.9). From Blue-throated Hummingbird by smaller size, lighter build, behavior, call, brighter red bill base, and small white tail corners. Charles W. Melton. Guadalupe Canyon, Arizona, August 1991.

4.9 Immature male Broad-billed. Fresh plumage indicates an immature, and a combination of face pattern, bill color, and tail pattern indicate species and sex, cf. tail pattern of immature female (Pic. 4.11). Larry Sansone. Miller Canyon, Arizona, 5 September 2000.

4.10 Immature male Broad-billed. Throat and neck pattern could suggest White-eared Hummingbird but face pattern duller, bill proportionately longer, and call and behavior different. Note primary molt, with P7–P10 still unmolted. Greg W. Lasley. Patagonia, Arizona, 21 August 1993.

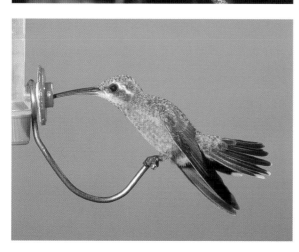

4.11 Immature female Broad-billed. Broad buff tipping to upperparts indicates age. Told from immature male by distinct white tips to R4–R5, distinct green bases to outer rectrices, lack of blue in throat. Charles W. Melton. Madera Canyon, Arizona, 25 August 1998.

White-eared Hummingbirds
Genus *Basilinna* ('*Hylocharis*')

Typical *Hylocharis* comprise a fairly distinct group of about six species known as sapphires, which occur mainly in tropical lowlands from southern Mexico to northern Argentina. Two other species (White-eared and Xantus' hummingbirds), typical of temperate habitats in northern Middle America, are also sometimes placed in *Hylocharis*[3]. These two are distinct in several ways, however, and consequently have been separated in the genus *Basilinna*[6,8,9]. *Basilinna*, then, are two species of fairly stocky, medium-sized to medium-small hummingbirds with medium-length, straightish bills that are broad across the base. Their broad tails are squared to slightly notched, and are held mostly rigid by feeding birds. The bills of males are bright red with a black tip, while females and immatures have restricted reddish at the bill base. All age/sex classes have a boldly contrasting white post-ocular stripe and blackish auricular mask, and both are striking species unlikely to be mistaken if seen well.

5 White-eared Hummingbird

(*Basilinna leucotis*)

9–10 cm (3.5–4 in). Bill 15–18.5 mm.
Pics I.25, 5.1–5.10.

Identification summary
Medium-sized and fairly stocky. All plumages have thick white post-ocular stripe contrasting strongly with broad blackish auricular mask; whitish underparts spotted and mottled glittering green. Male has bright red bill, tipped black. Female/immature bill has some reddish at base. Rare summer visitor to mountains of SW U.S.

Taxonomy
U.S. records are of the northern subspecies *borealis*, weakly differentiated from nominate *leucotis* of central and southern Mexico by slightly larger average size. A third and slightly smaller subspecies, *pygmaea*, occurs in Central America. Sometimes placed in the genus *Hylocharis*[3].

Status and Distribution
Rare and local summer visitor (April to October, with most records during June to August) to mountains of SE Arizona, where has bred[5]; casual in summer in SW New Mexico and W Texas. Casual in winter (November to March) in SE Arizona[1]. Vagrant to S Texas (July[10]) and Mississippi (November to January[4]).

Range Highlands from Mexico to Nicaragua.

Field Identification

Structure
Medium-sized and fairly stocky. Bill straightish and medium length, becoming laterally expanded towards base. Tail fairly broad and squared to slightly cleft. Primaries broad overall, P10 slightly narrower and more tapered. At rest, wing tips about equal with, or slightly shorter than, tail tip.

Similar species
Boldy contrasting, thick white post-ocular stripe in combination with stocky shape and relatively short bill distinctive in normal range. Face pattern shared with congeneric Xantus' Hummingbird but that species has bright rufous in tail, cinnamon belly.

Broad-billed Hummingbird. Female more lightly built and longer billed with less striking face pattern (narrower whitish post-ocular stripe and dusky auricular mask), unspotted dingy-gray underparts, note tail-wagging behavior and call.

Voice and Sounds
Common call a clipped, fairly hard, ticking chip, given singly or, more often, trebled or doubled, *tik* and *ti-ti-tik* and *chi-tik chi-tik...* or *tchi-chip,* etc. Calls given often in flight and also from perch whence may be repeated steadily with slightly clipped rhythm. Song from perch a rapid-paced, rhythmical, at times fairly prolonged chipping interspersed with rapid-paced, fairly quiet gurgling and squeaky warbling; also simply a steady, high tinny *tik tik tik....*

Habitat
Mountain forests. In Mexico favors pine-oak and oak forest in highlands, where often common at banks of flowers along roadsides and in clearings. In U.S. most often seen in mountain canyons.

Behavior
Feeds low to high and perches mainly at low to mid levels. In U.S. seen mostly at feeders. Common feeding behavior may suggest Anna's Hummingbird: White-eared tends to hold its tail in or slightly above the body plane, and its closed tail is broad, and often quivered or flashed. Male sings from perch at mid-levels, often 'inside' a bush or tree, i.e., not necessarily from a prominent perch.

Molt
Primary molt starts mainly between June and August (possibly later in some immatures), ends mainly September to February; averages later in immatures. Molt of adults and early-hatched young occurs mainly on breeding grounds. Late-hatched young and perhaps some adults may suspend primary molt and complete on non-breeding grounds.

Description
Adult male: Thick white post-ocular stripe contrasts boldly on dark head. Iridescent violet forecrown and chin and iridescent turquoise-green throat often look simply black and merge with broad blackish auricular mask. Underparts pale grayish, mottled heavily with golden green on chest and flanks; vent band whitish, undertail-coverts dusky greenish with whitish edgings. Nape and upperparts golden green, often becoming bronzier on rump; uppertail-coverts tipped rufous. **Tail:** R1 bronzy green to golden green (looking

dark oily green when worn), R2 to R5 blue-black with bronzy-green outer edging widest on R2; R3 to R5 with fine whitish tips when fresh; R4–R5 occasionally with distinct pale gray to whitish tips (subadults?). Bill bright red with black tip, feet blackish.

Adult female: thick white post-ocular stripe contrasts with blackish auricular mask and dark green (to brownish when worn) crown. Throat and underparts whitish, spotted golden green to bronzy green on throat and mottled more coarsely with green on neck sides, chest, and flanks; vent band whitish, undertail coverts whitish with dusky greenish centers. Nape and upperparts similar to male. **Tail:** R1 bronzy green to golden green; R2 green on outer web, blackish on inner web, on some with blackish extending to tip of outer web; R3 to R5 blackish with variable green basally, mainly on outer webs, narrow white to pale gray tip to R3 and R4, and distinct white to pale gray tip to R5. Bill blackish above, reddish pink below with dark tip. Some adult females may show occasional glittering violet feathers on forehead and chin[7]; needs confirmation.

Immature male: resembles adult female overall (including tail) but upperparts with distinct cinnamon tips when fresh; crown dark oily green with variable cinnamon tips that wear off, sometimes with one or more violet spots; throat overall with lines of dusky flecks, chin with variable lines of blue to bluish-violet spots, and throat with variable emerald to turquoise-green spots that often form a fairly solid patch. Maxilla black, but soon shows some reddish at base. Apparently attains adult-like plumage by early winter.

Immature female: resembles adult female but upperparts with distinct cinnamon tips when fresh; crown dark brownish; throat with lines of dusky bronzy flecks and no solid patch of emerald-green on neck sides (but with a few small blue-green spots); chest and sides with smaller and sparser green spots; outer rectrices may average larger whitish tips that can be tinged buff when fresh. Apparently attains adult-like plumage by early winter.

Hybrids Apparently with Broad-tailed Hummingbird[2].

References
[1]AB 47:285(1993), [2]AMNH specimen no. 754805 (Huachuca Mountains, Arizona), [3]AOU 1998, [4]AFN 50:181(1996), [5]AFN 50:979(1996), [6]Howell & Webb 1995, [7]Pyle 1997, [8]Ridgway 1911, [9]Schuchmann 1999, [10]TOS 1995.

5.1 Adult male White-eared. Unmistakable in this portrait, which shows the rarely seen colors of a male's head. Sid & Shirley Rucker. Divisadero, Chihuahua, Mexico, 10 September 1998.

5.2 Adult male White-eared. A typical view, the head looking 'black' with a thick white post-ocular stripe. Jim & Deva Burns (Natural Impacts). Miller Canyon, Arizona, 11 July 1998.

5.3 Adult female White-eared. Note the bold face pattern and green-spotted underparts typical of this species. The all-black maxilla, dull crown, and relatively extensive green throat spotting indicate an adult female. Greg W. Lasley. Davis Mountains Resort, Texas, 1 July 1993.

5.4 Adult female or immature male White-eared. Note broad-based red mandible, bold face pattern, and green-spotted throat and sides diagnostic of this species. Without a better view of throat and crown pattern, plus maxilla color, the age/sex of this individual is difficult to determine. Jim & Deva Burns (Natural Impacts). Miller Canyon, Arizona, 11 July 1998.

5.5 Immature male White-eared. Bold face pattern and green-spotted underparts indicate species. The red maxilla base, fresh plumage, and throat pattern (purplish-blue spots above a green median patch) point to immature male. The postjuvenal molt of this species starts quickly: P1–P2 already have been replaced. Ralph Paonessa. Miller Canyon, Arizona, July 1998.

5.6 Immature male White-eared. Same bird as Pic.5.5, and note oily blue-green centers visible to cinnamon-tipped crown feathers. Ralph Paonessa. Miller Canyon, Arizona, July 1998.

5.7 Immature male White-eared. Note steep forehead, bold face pattern, rufous-edged uppertail-coverts, and broad tail that appears all-green when closed. Red maxilla base and mottled throat indicate immature male; inner primaries have been molted. Greg W. Lasley. Davis Mountains Resort, Texas, 18 August 1997.

5.8 Immature male White-eared. Bold face pattern and green-spotted underparts diagnostic of species. Postjuvenal molt of primaries almost complete, and head and throat attaining adult-like male colors. Larry Sansone. Miller Canyon, Arizona, 5 September 2000.

5.9 Immature female White-eared. Bold face pattern and green-spotted underparts diagnostic of species. Extensive cinnamon tips to upperparts indicate a fresh-plumaged immature, and sparsely marked whitish throat a female. P1–P2 have been replaced, with P3–4 shed. Ralph Paonessa. Miller Canyon, Arizona, July 1998.

5.10 Immature female White-eared. Same features apply as Pic. 5.9 (perhaps the same individual?); P6 has been renewed by this date. Charles W. Melton. Miller Canyon, Arizona, 13 August 1998.

6 Xantus' Hummingbird

(Basilinna xantusii)

8–9 cm (3.3–3.8 in). Bill 16–19 mm.
Pics 6.1–6.6.

Identification summary
Medium-sized to medium-small and fairly stocky. All plumages have thick white post-ocular stripe contrasting strongly with broad blackish auricular mask; cinnamon belly; mostly rufous tail. Male has bright red bill, tipped black. Female/immature bill has some reddish at base. Casual vagrant from Mexico's Baja California peninsula.

Taxonomy
No subspecies described. Sometimes placed in the genus *Hylocharis*[2].

Status and Distribution
Casual vagrant to S California (two records, December to March) where nested[3] and British Columbia (November 1997 to September 1998[1,5,6,7]).

Range
Endemic to central and southern Baja California, Mexico, perhaps with northward dispersal in fall and winter[4].

Field Identification

Structure
Medium-sized to medium-small and fairly stocky. Bill straightish and medium length, becoming laterally expanded towards base. Tail fairly broad and squared to slightly cleft. Primaries broad overall, P10 slightly narrower and more tapered. At rest, wing tips about equal with tail tip.

Similar species
Nothing really similar, note face pattern shared by congeneric White-eared Hummingbird and superficial color pattern shared with plain-faced Cinnamon Hummingbird. As usual, when confronted with any vagrant, check identification carefully and consider hybrid combinations and possible escapes.

Voice and Sounds
Common call a low, fairly fast-paced, dry to slightly wet rattle, *trrrrr* or *trrrt*, often given in short series by feeding birds, e.g., *turrrr, turrrr, turrrr turrrt*, etc.; may suggest certain *Amazilia* hummingbirds such as Cinnamon, and is faster-paced and lower than kinglet-like chatter of Broad-billed Hummingbird. Warning call (from perch) and longer, aggressive chase calls (in flight) are series of high, thin, slightly tinny to slightly squeaky chips, *ts tii-tii-tii,* or *tsi-ti ti-ti-ti-ti-ti-ti,* and variations. Less often a metallic *chi-ti* or *ti-tink* and *chi ti-tink* that may be given two or three times in series and which suggests White-eared Hummingbird, and a single high *tiik*. Song from perch apparently a quiet, rough, gur-gling warble, at times interspersed with rattles and high, squeaky notes.

Habitat

In Baja breeds mainly in arid subtropical scrub, oak, and pine-oak woodland on upper slopes of southern mountains, ranging to sea level in desert scrub and gardens.

Behavior

Feeds low to high, and perches mainly at low to mid levels, at times on exposed twigs. Males sing from low to mid levels in bush, at times atop bush on a prominent twig. While feeding, tail mostly closed and appears fairly broad, held rigid in or near body plane, and often quivered or flashed, the latter mainly when hovering in windy conditions. Also feeds at times with tail cocked above body plane and flipped about, again mainly when maneuvering.

Molt

Adult primary molt mainly March to September (completing June to October), but presumed to vary with time of local breeding[4]; immature molt may average later.

Description

Adult male: Thick white post-ocular stripe contrasts boldly with black auricular mask. Forehead and chin black, and iridescent green throat often looks blackish also. Underbody cinnamon, with variable green mottling on chest and flanks, white vent band; undertail-coverts pale cinnamon with whitish edgings. Crown, nape, and upperparts golden green to emerald green, with rufous-tipped uppertail-coverts. **Tail:** rufous-chestnut overall. R1 broadly edged green to mostly green with rufous-chestnut patch along basal shaft; R2–R5 finely edged green. Bill bright red with black tip extending proximally along tomium of maxilla. Feet blackish.

Adult female: Thick whitish to pale buffy post-ocular stripe contrasts boldly with dull greenish crown and dark auricular mask. Throat and underparts pale cinnamon to cinnamon with white vent band, whitish edgings to undertail-coverts. Crown, nape, and upperparts golden green, with rufous-tipped uppertail coverts. **Tail:** R1 golden green with rufous shaft-streak; R2–R4 dark rufous, paler distally, with broken black and bronzy-green subterminal band; R5 slightly paler rufous, especially distally, sometimes with dark spot on inner web. Bill blackish above, pinkish red below with dark tip; some birds may have red on maxilla base.

Immature male: resembles adult female overall but usually with some reddish at maxilla base; auriculars blacker; crown blackish green with rufous-cinnamon edging when fresh; rump and uppertail-coverts more broadly edged cinnamon; rectrices average narrower and less truncate; R1 usually bronzy green with narrow rufous shaft streak, rarely like adult male R1; black and bronzy-green subterminal band on R2–R5 broader and more often continuous across shaft on R2–R3; chin streaked dusky; variable number of iridescent blue-green spots on lower throat. Apparently attains adult plumage by complete molt within first year, but 'adult' male with blackish and bronzy-green band on R2–R5 might represent second-year plumage; confirmation needed from known-age birds.

Immature female: resembles adult female overall but green crown broadly tipped cinnamon when fresh; rump and uppertail-coverts more broadly edged cinnamon; rectrices average narrower and less truncate; R1 bronzy green with narrow rufous shaft streak; black and bronzy-green subterminal band on R2–R5 broader and more often continuous across shaft on R2; underparts average paler cinnamon. Apparently attains adult plumage by complete molt within first year.

Hybrids None reported.

References [1]AFN 52:5 (1998), [2]AOU 1998, [3]Hainebach 1992, [4]Howell & Howell 2000, [5]Marven 1999, [6]NAB 53:93 (1999), [7]Toochin 1998.

6.1 Adult male Xantus'. Unmistakable. In this view suggests congeneric White-eared Hummingbird (cf. Pic. 5.2) but underparts cinnamon and tail mostly chestnut. Kimball Garrett. Los Dolores, Baja California Sur, Mexico, 11 January 1997.

6.2 and 6.3 Adult male Xantus'. Unmistakable. Steve N. G. Howell. Sierra de San Francisco, Baja California Sur, Mexico, 28 September 1999.

6.3

6.4 Adult female Xantus' (same bird as Pic. 6.5). Note diagnostic bold face pattern and pale cinnamon underparts. Larry Sansone. Ventura, California, 4 February 1988.

6.5 Adult female Xantus' (same bird as Pic. 6.4). Combination of bold face pattern, cinnamon throat, and coppery tail are diagnostic. Brian E. Small. Ventura, California, February 1988.

6.6 Female Xantus'. Unmistakable. D. True (VIREO). Mulege, Baja California Sur, Mexico, 24 March 1993.

Amazilia Hummingbirds Genus *Amazilia*

This genus comprises what have been termed 'typical' hummingbirds in Middle America, where about half of the 30 or so species of *Amazilia* occur. The slender-billed species with dark maxillas and darker tails (including Berylline) have been separated in the genus *Saucerottia* (e.g., Ridgway 1911, Schuchmann 1999). *Amazilia* are medium-sized to medium-large hummers with medium to medium-long, straightish bills and 'average' to fairly large and broad tails that are cleft to squared at the tip. The bills show at least some reddish at the base and typical *Amazilia* have bright red bills, tipped black. Underparts range from all-white to cinnamon to green. Four species (Berylline, Buff-bellied, Cinnamon, and Violet-crowned hummingbirds) are known from North America, north of Mexico.

7 Berylline Hummingbird

(Amazilia beryllina)

9.5–10 cm (3.7–4 in). Bill 18.5–21 mm.
Pics 7.1–7.6.

Identification summary
Medium-sized. Bright green overall with dingy pale buffy belly, copper-purplish uppertail-coverts and tail (looking more rufous when worn), and rufous wing patch (often striking in flight). Casual summer vagrant to SW U.S. from Mexico.

Taxonomy
North American records refer (presumably) to the northwestern subspecies *viola*, distinguished from nominate *beryllina* of central Mexico by averaging less rufous in the wings and a slightly dingier belly. Berylline Hummingbirds from south and east of the Isthmus of Tehuantepec (the races *devillei*, *lichtensteini*, and *sumichrasti*[10]) are perhaps different enough to be considered specifically distinct, as Deville's Hummingbird[6]. Has been placed in the genus *Saucerottia*[6,8].

Status and Distribution
Casual to rare summer visitor (late April to mid September, mainly June to August[7]) to mountains of SE Arizona, where has bred[2]. Casual in SW New Mexico (May[1]) and W Texas (late May, August to September[9]).

Range
Mexico to Honduras, mainly in foothills.

Field Identification

Structure
Medium-sized, with 'average' proportions. Bill medium length, straightish, and slender. Tail medium-length, fairly broad, and slightly cleft (more strongly so on males). Primaries fairly broad with P10 narrower. At rest, wing tips about equal with tail tip.

Similar species
Nothing similar in normal U.S. range but as always identify birds with caution and check for hybrids.

   Buff-bellied Hummingbird (south Texas lowlands, wintering to Florida) superficially similar but lacks rufous flash in wings, tail more strongly cleft, bill wider based (with obvious red on maxilla of adults) uppertail-coverts mostly green, rufous rectrices broadly edged and tipped green, and call different.

Voice and Sounds
Common call in flight and from perch a distinctive, fairly hard, buzzy *dzirr* or *dzzrit;* warning call a slightly higher, more trilled or drawn-out, buzzy *siirrr* or *dzzzir* usually given one to a few times. Flight chase call a high, slightly buzzy, fairly fast-paced chitter or rapid, fairly hard ticking chatter, *ji-ji ji-ji-ji,* and *ti ti-ti-ti-ti-ti-ti* and *chi ti-ti ti-ti-ti,* etc. Song from perch varies from a short, varied, jerky to squeaky phrase, repeated, e.g., *ssi kirr-i-rr kirr-i-rr,* or *ssir, ki-tik ki-dik,* etc., to a more prolonged squeaky warbling and chippering; also from perch a high, thin, even-paced, insect-like series, *siip-siip-siip-siip...,* etc.

Habitat
In Mexico favors oak-dominated and subtropical woodlands, mainly in foothills, but also ranges to temperate highlands and locally to tropical lowlands. In SW U.S. found mainly in mountain canyons.

Behavior
Feeds and perches low to high and visits feeders. Feeding flight often fairly quick, darting from flower to flower. Feeds with tail held in body plane or slightly cocked, and quivered with occasional flashes and flicks. Feeding birds often aggressive to smaller hummers (at least in Mexico). Sings from perch on bare twig, often in subcanopy.

Molt
Primary molt of *viola* (adults) starts mainly March to June, ends July to October; no data for immatures.

Description
Adult male: throat and chest solidly iridescent emerald-green, contrasting with dusky vinaceous to dusky buffy-gray belly; whitish vent band usually inconspicuous, undertail-coverts dusky cinnamon, edged whitish. Head and back emerald-green to golden green, brightest on crown, with small whitish post-ocular spot and variable, usually indistinct, narrow pale eye-ring; rump dull bronzy to brownish, becoming coppery purple on uppertail-coverts. Wings have rufous flash across bases of secondaries (usually $\geq$ 50% of exposed portion of secondaries) and primaries, noticeable at rest and often quite striking in flight when accentuated by rufous under primary-coverts. **Tail:** coppery purple overall, grading to coppery chestnut on outer rectrices; closed tail can look almost blackish from above and is more purplish when fresh, overall more

rufous-chestnut when worn. Bill blackish, with pinkish red at mandible base often hard to see. Feet blackish.

Adult female: resembles adult male but throat and chest less intense and less solidly iridescent green with chin mottled pale gray to whitish; crown duller, bronzy green; belly averages paler and grayer, pale vinaceous gray to dusky grayish buff; rufous in wings slightly less extensive (usually < 50% of exposed portion of secondaries); tail averages more coppery or bronzy, less purplish.

Immature (sexes similar): resembles female overall but throat and chest dingy pale vinaceous-buff, mottled emerald-green at sides and often with some glittering turquoise-green down center of throat and chest; belly dingy pale vinaceous-buff to grayish cinnamon; rump, and especially uppertail-coverts, tipped cinnamon; tail like adult but rectrices narrower.

Hybrids

Presumed with Magnificent Hummingbird[4] (see Pics I.4–I.5) and possibly with Azure-crowned Hummingbird *Amazilia cyanocephala*[3]. Reported hybridization with Blue-tailed Hummingbird *A. cyanura* in Central America unverified[5].

References

[1]AB 47:441,466 (1993), [2]Anderson & Monson 1981, [3]Berlioz 1932, [4]Heindel & Howell 2000, [5]Howell & Webb 1995, [6]Ridgway 1911, [7]Rosenberg & Witzeman 1998, [8]Schuchmann 1999, [9]TBRC unpubl. data, [10]Weller 1998.

7.1, 7.2 and 7.3 Male Berylline. Rufous wing patch, relatively slender bill, and dark uppertail-coverts all distinct from Buff-bellied Hummingbird. Solid green throat and chest, plus cinnamon-buff belly indicate adult male; coppery-looking tail suggests worn plumage (cf. Pic. 7.4) but may be an artefact of the photo. Kelly B. Bryan. Davis Mountains Resort, Texas, 17 August 1997.

7.2

7.3

7.4 Berylline Hummingbird. Molt has completed recently of wings and tail, while still finishing on head and neck. Tail is purple in fresh plumage, becoming more coppery when worn (cf. Pic. 7.3). Sid & Shirley Rucker. Divisadero, Chihuahua, Mexico, 10 September 1998.

7.5 Berylline Hummingbird. The fairly bright buffy belly suggests Buff-bellied Hummingbird but note diagnostic rufous bases to secondaries, also the all-black maxilla, dull brownish lower back, and wing tips falling about equal with tail tip. Whitish scalloping on throat and reduced rufous in secondaries suggest adult female, but brightness of belly (perhaps an artefact of the photo?) more typical of adult male. Narca Moore-Craig. Guadalupe Canyon, New Mexico, 25 May 1993.

7.6 Berylline Hummingbird. Irregular whitish mottling on throat and chest indicates adult female or immature, while relatively extensive rufous in secondaries (diagnostic of species) suggests immature male. Jim & Deva Burns (Natural Impacts). Ramsey Canyon, Arizona, August 1997.

8 Buff-bellied Hummingbird

(Amazilia yucatanensis)

10–11 cm (3.8–4.3 in). Bill 19–22 mm.
Pics 8.1–8.7

Identification summary
Medium-sized to medium-large. Bright green overall with buffy belly, mostly rufous tail, and bright red bill, tipped black. Breeds S Texas, rare to casual winter migrant around Gulf of Mexico to Florida.

Taxonomy
North American records refer to the duller northern subspecies, *chalconota*. Populations from Chiapas (*cerviniventris*) and the Yucatan Peninsula (*yucatanensis*) have a brighter cinnamon belly (see Howell and Webb[3]).

Status and Distribution
Fairly common summer resident (nests mainly April to August) in S Texas from Lower Rio Grande Valley N locally to Victoria County[7]; more local and generally less common in these areas during winter (October to February). Ranges more widely during mid August to early May (mainly late October to March) when occurs rarely but in increasing numbers N and W to N Texas and E to SE U.S., mainly around Gulf coast lowlands; casual to S Florida[1,6]. Veracity of 1891 specimen labeled New Mexico[5] has been questioned[4].

Range
South Texas to Yucatan Peninsula of Mexico and adjacent Belize, in winter to SE U.S.

Field Identification

Structure
Medium-sized to medium-large with 'average' proportions. Bill medium-long and straightish with broad base. Tail medium-length, fairly broad, and cleft (more strongly so in males). Primaries fairly broad with P10 narrower and tapered. At rest, wing tips fall short of tail tip (more so on males).

Similar species
Nothing similar in its normal U.S. range, but when confronted with a vagrant always identify birds with caution and check for hybrids.
   Berylline Hummingbird (summer vagrant to mountains of SW U.S.) superficially similar but has slender dark bill, more coppery and less strongly cleft tail, rufous wing patch (often striking in flight), and dull rump blending into darker, coppery-purple uppertail-coverts, distinct voice.
   Rufous-tailed Hummingbird *Amazilia tzacatl*, a widespread neotropical species that occurs N to SE Mexico, unlikely to occur in North America (an old record from Texas is questionable[2]). Told from Buff-bellied by grayish belly contrasting more with darker, cinnamon-rufous undertail-coverts, less strongly cleft (more squared) tail with narrower green edgings, and rufous lores[3].

Voice and Sounds

Common calls are a clipped to slightly smacking chip, *tik* or *tk*, at times run into a harder, rolled *tirr*, and a short, rattled *tsirrr* or *trirrr*. Calls usually given singly while feeding, and can be repeated from perch in prolonged, fairly fast-paced series of chips and rattles alternated and at times paired, e.g., *tk-tk-tk-tk-tk-tk-tk tirrr-tirrri tk-tk...*, *or tirrrítirrr tirrrítirrr tk tk tirrr tirrr...*, etc. Also a single, slightly buzzy *sssir* in warning; longer, variable, and usually fast-paced series of buzzy to lisping calls in chases, *sssirr chi-chi chi-chir*, or *ssi-ssi ssi-ssi ssi-ssi ch-chí*, etc.; and a high, sharp *tísi* or *siik* given in series by chasing birds and by single birds in wide-ranging and erratic (display?) flight. Song varied, an arrangement of one or more high, thin, slurred whistles and chip notes, *t'siiiie t'siiiie tk-tk-tk*, or *t'swiiin tk-tk tk-tk tk-tk*, etc., or series of chips alternated with short, wheezy, creaky notes.

Habitat

Brushy woodland and edge, thickets, suburban areas with trees and bushes.

Behavior

Feeds and perches low to high, mainly at low to mid levels, and readily visits feeders. Flight quick, moving rapidly among flowers. Feeds by hovering with tail held in or near body plane, usually slightly spread and quivered, and flashed during maneuvers. Sings from perch on bare twig, often in subcanopy.

Molt

Primary molt starts in adults mainly from June to August (ending September to November?); in immatures not until January or later, usually ending by June or July.

Description

Adult male: throat and chest solidly iridescent emerald-green, contrasting with pale vinaceous-cinnamon belly; undertail-coverts slightly darker, cinnamon; vent band whitish. Head and upperparts golden green to bronzy green, duller and bronzier on crown, with whitish post-ocular spot and variably distinct pale gray to buffy-gray eyering; uppertail-coverts edged rufous. **Tail**: bright rufous overall. Inner rectrices broadly edged and tipped green to bronzy green (rufous base of R1 may be covered by uppertail-coverts), outers with narrower bronzy-green tips and edging becoming very reduced or even absent on R5. Bill bright red, tipped black and with black stripe along tomium of maxilla, feet blackish.

Adult female: Resembles male but throat and chest less intense and less solidly iridescent green with chin mottled buffy white, tail less strongly cleft with R1 mostly to all-green, often lacking visible rufous at base. Bill may average duller and pinker with more black on maxilla.

Immature: resembles adult of respective sex but throat and chest pale grayish buff, mottled bronzy green at sides and often with some glittering, adult-like green down center of throat and chest (can be extensive on some males); belly often paler than adult, pale buff to grayish buff and contrasting slightly more with undertail-coverts. Maxilla mostly to all-black, reddish at base developing over fall and winter, mandible pinkish red. **Tail**: rectrices narrower than adult. Bronzy-green R1 can have fine cinnamon-rufous tip when fresh and on some males may show limited rufous basally, R2–R5 rufous with variable bronzy-green subterminal edgings (at times almost forming a subterminal band on R2–R4) and slightly paler, cinnamon-rufous tips.

Hybrids
None reported.

References
[1]AOU 1998, [2]DeBenedictis 1992, [3]Howell & Webb 1995, [4]Hubbard 1970, [5]MVZ specimen no. 107011, [6]Stevenson & Anderson 1994, [7]TOS 1995.

8.1 Adult (male) Buff-bellied. Lack of rufous in wings, tail pattern, and red on maxilla of broad-based bill rule out Berylline Hummingbird. Solid bronzy-green tips to rectrices and bright red on maxilla indicate adult, and intensity of green on chin and throat suggest male. Steve Bentsen. San Benito, Texas, April 1995.

8.2 Adult (male) Buff-bellied. All-dark wings and distinctly cleft tail with rufous and bronzy-green pattern are distinct from Berylline Hummingbird. Bright throat, bill, and deeply cleft tail indicate male. Larry Ditto. McAllen, Texas, April 2000.

8.3 Adult (female) Buff-bellied. All-dark wings and red on maxilla are distinct from Berylline Hummingbird. Small buff area on chin and apparently all-green R1 indicative of female. Charles W. Melton. Rio Hondo, Texas, 12 May 1994.

8.4 Adult female Buff-bellied. Note all-dark wings, reddish on maxilla, cf. Berylline Hummingbird. Charles W. Melton. Near Harlingen, Texas, 26 May 1994.

8.5 Immature Buff-bellied. Broad-based bill, lack of rufous in wings, and tail pattern rule out Berylline Hummingbird. Mostly black maxilla, relatively pale and grayish belly, and relatively narrow rectrices with rufous tips indicate immature. Larry Ditto. McAllen, Texas, September 1999.

8.6 Immature (female?) Buff-bellied. Lack of rufous in wings rules out Berylline Hummingbird. Into first winter, throat and chest are pale buff or buffy gray, similar to belly but with variable green spotting. Cinnamon-rufous tips to rectrices and relatively shallow tail cleft indicate immature and female, respectively. Robert A. Behrstock. Houston, Texas, 7 January 1996.

9 Cinnamon Hummingbird

(Amazilia rutila)

10–11.5 cm (4–4.5 in). Bill 20.5–23.5 mm.
Pics 9.1–9.4.

Identification summary
Medium-sized to medium-large. All ages have plain green head and upperparts, wholly cinnamon underparts. Bill bright red with black tip. Casual vagrant to SW U.S. from Mexico.

Taxonomy
North American records most likely refer to the NW Mexican race *diluta*, which differs from more southerly races in its paler underparts. Three other subspecies occur in Mexico and Central America, with the larger and duskier *graysoni* of the Tres Marias Islands[2] sometimes considered specifically distinct, as Grayson's Hummingbird[4].

Status and Distribution
Casual vagrant to SW U.S., with single records from SE Arizona (July 1992[1,5,6]) and SW New Mexico (September 1993[7]).

Range
Mexico to Costa Rica, mainly in arid tropical lowlands.

Field Identification

Structure
Medium-sized to medium-large, recalling Violet-crowned Hummingbird in size and shape. Bill medium-long and straightish with broad base. Tail fairly broad and cleft to slightly cleft. Primaries fairly broad with P10 narrower. At rest, wing tips < tail tip.

Similar species
Should be unmistakable in North America. Smaller and stockier Xantus' Hummingbird superficially similar in color but has bold face pattern. Beware the possibility of hybrids and escapes when confronted with vagrants.

Voice and sounds
Feeding birds give hard ticks with a buzzy or rattled quality, *tzk* or *dzk*, and which can be run into buzzy rattles. Perched birds give a hard rattled *trrrt* or *dirrr* that may be repeated steadily, at times in rapid-paced series. In interactions, high squeaks run into an excited chatter, and in flight chases a fairly hard chipping *chi chi-chi-chi-chi-chi*, etc. Song comprises short, varied series of slightly squeaky chips, repeated from perch, e.g., *si ch chi-chit* or *tsi si si-si-sit*, etc.

Habitat
In northwest Mexico favors thorn forest and tropical semi-deciduous forest and edge, ranging into semi-open areas and gardens. Has turned up at feeders in North America.

Behavior
Feeds low to high and often aggressive to smaller hummers. Feeds mostly with tail in or near body plane; often hovers fairly vertically with tail held slightly depressed, and slightly fanned and quivered. Perches low to high, mainly at mid levels and often on prominent bare twigs.

Molt
Primary molt (adults) mainly during April/May to October/November in NW Mexico, ending on some birds by July.

Description
Adult (sexes similar): throat and underparts cinnamon; whitish vent band usually inconspicuous. Head and upperparts bronzy green with longest uppertail-coverts tipped rufous, face often shows narrow pale eye-ring. **Tail:** deep rufous overall, rectrices fairly broadly tipped and narrowly edged bronzy green. Bill bright red with black tip (perhaps more extensive on female?) extending back along tomium of mandible; feet blackish.

Immature: similar to adult but underparts average paler, upperparts duller with cinnamon tips to rump, more extensive rufous on uppertail-coverts, narrow cinnamon tips to secondaries. Rectrices average narrower, with broader bronzy-green edging and cinnamon tips (narrowest on R1). Bill mostly to all-black above, reddish at base developing over first year.

Hybrids
Presumed with Rufous-tailed Hummingbird[3].

References
[1]DeBenedictis 1994, [2]Howell & Webb 1995, [3]Howell & Webb 1995:412 (SD/RA under Buff-bellied Hummingbird), [4]Ridgway 1911, [5]Rosenberg & Witzeman 1998, [6]Stejskal & Rosenberg 1992, [7]Williams 1994.

9.1, 9.2 and 9.3 Adult Cinnamon. Relatively extensive black on bill may indicate female. This bird provided the second record for North America. Unmistakable. Kelly B. Bryan. Santa Teresa, New Mexico, 20 September 1993.

9.2

9.3

9.4 Adult Cinnamon. Unmistakable. Steve N. G. Howell. Puerto Vallarta, Jalisco, Mexico, 9 January 2000.

10 Violet-crowned Hummingbird

(Amazilia violiceps)

10–11.5 cm (4–4.5 in). Bill 21–24 mm.
Pics 10.1–10.6.

Identification summary
Medium-sized to medium-large. All ages have bright white underparts, unique among North American hummingbirds. Crown glittering bluish violet, bill bright red with black tip. Immature duller above, with less red on bill (maxilla mostly blackish).

Taxonomy
North American records pertain to the northern subspecies *ellioti*, which differs from nominate *violiceps* of central Mexico mainly in its duller tail (bronzy green versus coppery bronze; see Howell and Webb[3]).

Status and Distribution
Uncommon to rare and local summer resident (mainly April to September) in SE Arizona and extreme SW New Mexico; casual to rare in winter (October to March) at feeders in SE Arizona. Casual (March, May, July to December) NW to N California[1] and E to E Texas[5].

Range
SW U.S. to central Mexico.

Field Identification

Structure
Medium-sized to medium-large. Bill medium-long and straightish with broad base. Tail fairly broad, squared to slightly cleft, averaging longer and more strongly cleft on male. Primaries fairly broad with P10 narrower and more tapered (most strongly on male). At rest, wing tips < (male) to ≤ tail tip (female).

Similar species
Nothing similar in North American range. With vagrants, check tail color for subspecies (nominate southern race might be kept in captivity, and unlikely to occur as wild vagrant).

Voice and Sounds
Common call a hard chip, *stik* or *tik*, often run into rattled short series, e.g., *tik ti-tik*, harder than chatter of Broad-billed Hummingbird. Chase call a rapid-paced, hollow, slightly squeaky chatter, e.g., *chuh tuh-tuh-tuh-tuh-tuh*. Song (?) simply a single plaintive chip, repeated by perched bird, *chieu chieu chieu....*

Habitat
Arid to semi-arid scrub, riparian woodland, semi-open areas with hedges and scattered trees.

Behavior
Feeds and perches low to high, mostly at mid to upper levels except at feeders. Feeds mainly with tail closed and held close to body plane, at times slightly cocked. Tail quivered and occasionally flashed or fanned while hovering, but not wagged.

Molt
Primary molt of *ellioti* (adults) starts mainly September to December, ends March to May; immatures molt later in first year, mainly from March to September. Adults molt mainly on non-breeding grounds, after migration, but some may start on breeding grounds and suspend to non-breeding grounds. Some immatures may start on non-breeding grounds and complete on breeding grounds.

Description
Adult (sexes similar): throat and underparts bright white (throat can be discolored yellowish by pollen). Dull bronzy green on sides/flanks usually covered by wings at rest; faint dusky centers to undertail-coverts on some birds (mainly females?) rarely noticeable. Crown and auriculars violet-blue (rarely turquoise-blue), typically with small whitish post-ocular spot. Rest of upperparts, including upperside of tail, dull bronzy greenish to brownish, at times with tail appearing bronzier green than duller and browner back. Rectrices have fine white tips when fresh. Bill bright red to pinkish red with black tip, feet blackish. Male bill may average brighter and redder than female, with smaller black tip that extends back less along tomium of mandible; needs confirmation.
Immature: crown mostly dull bronzy green to dark oily bluish with cinnamon feather tips in fresh plumage, and often with a few turquoise to violet-blue spots apparent. Upperparts have narrow buffy tips in fresh plumage, especially noticeable on rump and tail coverts. Pale rectrix tips tinged cinnamon-buff in fresh plumage. Bill mostly blackish above, pinkish red below with dark tip, red on maxilla developing over first year.

Hybrids
With Broad-billed Hummingbird[2,4].

References
[1]CBRC unpubl. data, [2]S. N. G. Howell pers. obs. (Patagonia, Arizona; July 1997), [3]Howell & Webb 1995, [4]Phillips *et al.* 1964, [5]TBRC unpubl. data

10.1 Adult Violet-crowned. Unmistakable. The longer tail projection beyond wing tip and small black bill tip may indicate a male, cf. Pic. 10.2. Brian E. Small. Patagonia, Arizona, July 1999.

10.2 Adult Violet-crowned. Unmistakable. The short tail projection beyond wing tips and extent of black bill tip may indicate a female, cf. Pic. 10.1. Charles W. Melton. Guadalupe Canyon, Arizona, August 1991.

10.3 Adult Violet-crowned. Unmistakable. The medium-large size of Violet-crowned can be appreciated here with a Black-chinned Hummingbird for scale. Brian E. Small. Patagonia, Arizona, July 1999.

10.4 Adult female Violet-crowned. Unmistakable. Brian E. Small. Portal, Arizona, August 1996.

10.5 Immature Violet-crowned. Dark oily blue of crown is tipped cinnamon in fresh plumage, white underparts are slightly dingy, and bill is much duller than adult with maxilla mostly to entirely blackish. Ralph Paonessa. Miller Canyon, Arizona, July 1998.

10.6 Immature Violet-crowned. A subadult (second calendar-year) bird in heavily worn plumage with little blue on head, red developing on bill; P7 is growing, P8–P10 unmolted. Rick & Nora Bowers. Ramsey Canyon, Arizona, June 1987.

This genus of about 6–10 species (taxonomy, again, is unresolved) is endemic to temperate and subtropical habitats in Middle America. Most *Lampornis*, but not the Blue-throated Hummingbird found in North America, are called mountain-gems. Think how a change in this species' common name would spice up birding in Arizona – 'Have you seen any Blue-throated Mountain-gems?' sounds a lot more exotic than 'just another hummingbird.' *Lampornis* are large to fairly large hummers with straightish, medium-short to medium-length black bills and fairly long and broad tails that are slightly double-rounded to cleft. They favor shady and often moist areas, and commonly feed 'inside' flower banks, rather than in the open.

11 Blue-throated Hummingbird

(Lampornis clemenciae)

12–13.5 cm (4.8–5.3 in). Bill 21.5–26 mm (female > male).
Pics I.24, 11.1–11.11.

Identification summary
Large size, with relatively short bill and large tail. Together with size, all ages can be identified by whitish double face stripes and very bold white corners on blue-black tail. Male's blue throat often looks simply dusky. Very high-pitched call note. Summer resident of mesic canyons in mountains of SW U.S.

Taxonomy
Arizona birds are of the subspecies *bessophilus*, averaging slightly duller above and paler below than nominate *clemenciae* of central Mexico. Texas birds have been described as the subspecies *phasmorus*, differing from Arizona birds by slightly greener (less bronzy) upperparts and average slightly shorter bill[4,10].

Status and Distribution
Uncommon to fairly common but local summer resident (mainly April to September) in mountains of SE Arizona and W Texas. In SE Arizona, very rarely ranges into lowlands, and also lingers rarely into winter in mountains. Rare and local summer resident (mainly May to September) in SW New Mexico where may breed[11]. Casual W (December to May[3]) to S-central California, N (mainly late June to September) to Utah[9] and Colorado[2], and E (mainly November to March) to central Texas[7] and S Louisiana[1,6].

Range　Mountains of SW U.S. to S Mexico.

Field Identification

Structure

Large size. Bill medium length but proportionately short, and straightish. Tail large, broad, and squared to slightly double-rounded (closed tail often appears broadly rounded). Primaries broad, with P10 slightly narrower and more tapered. At rest, wing tips slightly < tail tip on male, ≤ tail tip on female.

Similar species

Combination of large size, face pattern, tail pattern, relatively short bill, and call distinctive in North America. Only hummer of similar size in North America is Magnificent, which often occurs side-by-side with Blue-throated.

Magnificent Hummingbird has distinctly longer bill (especially female), more sloping forehead, less substantial and more distinctly cleft tail, and different call note. Female Magnificent further told from Blue-throated by white post-ocular spot (or at most a short post-ocular stripe) and reduced dark mask, indistinct and less extensive white moustache (so face lacks double-striped effect of Blue-throated), dusky-mottled throat, and overall greenish tail with narrower white tips. Male Magnificent usually appears all-dark with long bill and bold white post-ocular spot, unlikely to be confused with Blue-throated. Magnificent also often favors more open areas and perches more conspicuously.

Broad-billed Hummingbird. Immature male Broad-billed with blue concentrated on throat might suggest much larger Blue-throated Hummingbird but size of latter should be obvious (dwarfing any other species except Magnificent). Broad-billed is a medium-small, lightly built hummer favoring lowland habitats. It has a cleft tail with narrow white corners, and very different behavior and call from Blue-throated.

Voice and Sounds

Common call a high, thin, penetrating squeak, *siip* or *siik!*, given in flight and from perch. Less often a fuller *tsiuk*. Common song appears to be steady repetition of call by perched male, *siip siip siip ...*, etc., although more complex vocalizations have been reported[5].

Habitat

Favors shady canyons with running water in pine-oak and oak woodland, ranging into more open situations to feed at banks of flowers and feeders.

Behavior

Feeds and perches mainly at low to mid-levels, and often feeds 'inside' flower banks where it can be hard to see, although calls give away its presence. Birds near feeders may perch more prominently on fences or wires. Hovering and feeding birds mostly hold tail closed, in or near body plane, with occasional flashes when changing position. Tail wagged loosely and flashed by maneuvering birds.

Molt

Primary molt of adults in northern populations mainly starts October to December and ends March to May; occurs mostly on non-breeding grounds. Primary molt can suspend on immatures in their first year, completing on breeding grounds in first summer through fall.

Description

Adult male: white post-ocular stripe contrasts with green crown and dusky auricular mask; blue gorget typically bordered by short white moustache. Blue throat mostly fails to catch the light and often appears smooth gray, like underbody or slightly darker. Upperparts bronzy green to golden green with bronzier rump and dark bronzy-green to blackish longest uppertail-coverts. Underparts fairly smooth, dusky pale gray, washed green on sides of neck. Sides and flanks sparsely mottled and washed green (often covered by wings at rest); undertail-coverts dusky to sooty gray, edged whitish. **Tail**: blue-black with broad white tips to R5 and R4, and sometimes a white distal shaft streak or (subadults?) a small white tip to R3. Bill black, feet dusky to dark grayish.

Adult female: resembles adult male but throat dusky pale gray, similar to underparts, distal uppertail-coverts dark bronzy green, and R3 has distinct white tip; some birds have a few, scattered blue throat feathers.

Immature male: resembles adult male but blue throat patch less extensive and more irregular in shape, bordered laterally by broad grayish or green-washed band below narrow whitish moustache stripe; outer rectrices slightly rounded (less truncate) and averaging larger white tips, including distinct white tip to R3 (similar to female); upperparts in fall and winter fresh and with more distinct pale edgings (especially on rump). Attains adult-like plumage by complete or near-complete molt over first year, with some to all rectrices (especially R3) sometimes retained through first summer. Underside and tomium of mandible often pinkish, at least into fall, and feet can be flesh-pink.

Immature female: resembles adult female but plumage in fall and winter fresher, with more distinct pale edgings (especially on rump), white tail tips average larger. Bill and feet show pinkish, like immature male.

Hybrids

Probably with Anna's Hummingbird[3], possibly with Black-chinned Hummingbird[3], and possibly with Costa's Hummingbird[8].

References

[1]AB 47:106 (1993), [2]Andrews & Righter 1992, [3]Baldridge *et al.* 1983, [4]Browning 1978, [5]Ficken *et al.* 2000, [6]FN 49:263 (1995), [7]G. W. Lasley pers. comm., [8]Mayr & Short 1970, [9]NAB 53:82 (1999), [10]Oberholser 1974, [11]S. O. Williams pers. comm.

11.1 Adult male Blue-throated. Unmistakable. Note double white face stripes, neat blue throat, bold white tail tips. Charles W. Melton. Chiricahua Mountains, Arizona, 24 April 1993.

11.2 Adult male Blue-throated. Unmistakable. Note blue-black tail with bold white corners, dark uppertail coverts; limited white in R3 indicates full adult. Charles W. Melton. Chiricahua Mountains, Arizona, May 1993.

11.3 Adult male Blue-throated. Unmistakable; white fleck near tip of R3 indicates full adult. Sid & Shirley Rucker. Cave Creek Canyon, Arizona, September 1998.

11.4 Adult female Blue-throated. Sloping forehead in this posture suggests Magnificent Hummingbird but note bold white post-ocular stripe, plain gray throat and underparts, large white tail tips. Charles W. Melton. Cave Creek Canyon, Arizona, 18 August 1994.

11.5 Adult female Blue-throated. Note double white face stripes, plain throat, and rounded blue-black tail with bold white corners; relatively worn plumage may indicate a subadult (second calendar-year bird, cf. Pic. 11.10). John H. Hoffman. Southwest Research Station, Arizona, May 1993.

11.6 Adult female Blue-throated. Note diagnostic tail pattern and contrasting dark uppertail-coverts; also relatively fresh plumage cf. Pic. 11.5. Charles W. Melton. Chiricahua Mountains, Arizona, 23 April 1993.

11.7 Immature male Blue-throated. Neat and extensive pale scaly edgings to upperparts indicate immature. From Magnificent Hummingbird by relatively shorter black bill, bolder face pattern, and rounded black tail that hints of extensive white tips to outer rectrices. Greg W. Lasley. Portal, Arizona, 25 August 1993.

11.8 Immature male Blue-throated. Could suggest smaller and lightly built Broad-billed Hummingbird (e.g., pink mandible base) but note double white face stripes, dusky, white-edged undertail-coverts, blackish uppertail-coverts, and bold white tail tips. Cave Creek Canyon, Arizona, Brian E. Small. August 1996.

11.9 Immature male Blue-throated. Immature male has less blue on throat than adult, and R3 has distinct white tip like female (not visible here but cf. Pics 11.3, 11.10). Brian E. Small. Portal, Arizona, August 1996.

11.10 Immature male Blue-throated. The large blue-black tail with bold white tail corners, in combination with face pattern and blue-mottled throat (not catching the light in this photo) indicate a male Blue-throated Hummingbird. Note that primary molt has suspended or arrested, not having completed in the winter: P1–P8 are obviously fresh with P9–P10 contrastingly worn and old. Also note the generally worn plumage, including the outer rectrices. The distinct white tip to R3 is a character of immatures; this bird is therefore in its second calendar-year and has not molted its juvenal tail. Ian C. Tait. Madera Canyon, Arizona, May 1995.

11.11 Immature female Blue-throated. Fresh plumage, with extensive scaly buff tips to upperparts, and pale flesh mandible base indicate an immature. The diagnostic double face stripes and large blue-black tail with bold white tips are similar to an adult female, although the white tail tips average bigger. Alan Murphy. Portal, Arizona, 14 August 1996.

Magnificent Hummingbird
Genus *Eugenes*

This genus comprises a single species, the Magnificent Hummingbird (known formerly as Rivoli's Hummingbird), endemic to the mountains of Middle America and the southwestern U.S. As its name suggests, the 'Mag' is a large hummingbird. It has a long, straight, black bill, and a fairly long, broad, and cleft to slightly double-rounded tail. It often favors relatively open situations within woodland and perches prominently, at times making prolonged flycatching sallies. The Magnificent is often considered similar to the Blue-throated Hummingbird but, besides being very large, the two genera are distinctly different in structure, behavior, plumage, and voice.

12 Magnificent Hummingbird

(*Eugenes fulgens*)

12–13.5 cm (4.7–5.3 in). Bill 25.5–28.5 mm (male); 27.5–30 mm (female). Pics I.21, 12.1–12.11.

Identification summary
Large size with long, straightish bill. Together with size, main distinguishing features are relatively long bill, bold white post-ocular spot, and mostly greenish tail with relatively small white corners. Male head colors unmistakable but more often look simply black. Summer resident in mountains of SW U.S.

Taxonomy
North American birds are of the nominate Mexican subspecies *fulgens*, of which *aureoviridis*[8] is considered a synonym[5]. Two other subspecies occur south and east of the Isthmus of Tehuantepec, including *spectabilis* of Costa Rica and Panama, sometimes considered specifically distinct, as Admirable Hummingbird[6]. *Spectabilis* differs from northern Magnificent Hummingbirds mainly in average larger size and bronzy-green (versus blackish) underparts of male.

Status and Distribution
Fairly common to uncommon and local summer resident (March to October, mainly April to September) in mountains of SE Arizona, SW New Mexico, and W Texas; a few birds over-winter in these states, mainly in lower canyons of SE Arizona and SW New Mexico. Has also bred N to Colorado where occurs as rare to casual visitor (mainly

May to September[1]). Casual N (mainly July to August, rarely from mid April[4,7]) to Nevada, Utah, Wyoming, Kansas, and Minnesota; and E (mainly September to February[2,4]) to Alabama, Georgia, and Florida.

Range
Highlands from SW U.S. to W Panama.

Field Identification

Structure
Large size. Bill long (especially female) and straightish. Tail fairly large and notched in males, overall squared to slightly double-rounded in females. Primaries broad with P10 slightly narrower. At rest, wing tips < tail tip on male, about equal with tail tip on female.

Similar species
Often compared with Blue-throated Hummingbird but these two species are quite distinct, given a reasonable view and/or if heard. As likely to be confused with Plain-capped Starthroat. Other North American hummingbirds much smaller.

Blue-throated Hummingbird has shorter bill, more distinct whitish face stripes and larger dark auricular mask, more substantial and blue-black tail with bold white corners, and gives high-pitched squeak call. It also tends to have smoother gray underparts (especially throat) and favors damper and more shady areas.

Plain-capped Starthroat slighter overall in build with very long and straight bill and flycatching habits. Call more strongly recalls Black Phoebe *Sayornis nigricans*. Told from Magnificent by smaller body size with proportionately longer bill, blackish throat bordered by broad whitish malar, white patch on the lower back, (sometimes concealed) white flank patches, and white tips to R2.

Immature Anna's Hummingbird can suggest female Magnificent in plumage, and is relatively large compared to other small gorgeted hummers: Anna's is, nonetheless, much smaller and more compact than Magnificent, with proportionately much shorter bill, more smacking chip call, and often has reddish on throat.

Female Black-chinned Hummingbird might suggest female Magnificent with no size reference available, especially given Black-chinned's relatively long bill. Black-chinned is much smaller with quicker flight and fast wing-beats typical of small hummingbirds. It has narrow inner primaries and a proportionately longer tail (> wing tips on perched birds), its paler underparts often show a contrasting whiter forecollar, its tail is often wagged while feeding, and its call is a soft chipping.

Voice and Sounds
Common call, often given in flight or repeated steadily by a perched bird, a fairly loud, sharp *chik!* or *tsik!* that may suggest strong chip call of Broad-tailed Hummingbird or even a Black Phoebe (but less so than Plain-capped Starthroat). Also a higher *piik!* or *tiik!* mainly in flight and an abrupt *ch'tik*. Males at least also give a fairly hard, sharp, short rattle, *trrirr* or *trrrrr ch-chrr,* at times run into prolonged, squeaky, chattering rattles. In apparent aggression, a squeaky, slightly rippling or bubbling, accelerating chatter, *whee deedl-eedl-eu,* or *whee diu diu-diu-diu diu-diu-diu,* and variations, given in flight and from perch. Song apparently a fairly soft, slightly buzzy, gurgling warble, given by perched male.

Habitat

Pine-oak and oak highlands in general, also semi-open and open mountainous areas with flowering agaves, thistles, and cacti.

Behavior

Feeds and perches low to high, at times on prominent bare twigs and snags at edges of clearings and over streams, whence makes prolonged flycatching sallies, recalling a starthroat. Feeds mainly by trap-lining (i.e., visiting widely spaced flowers and feeders), rather than defending a feeding territory. Generally dominates smaller hummers (which rarely try to chase off Magnificent) but may yield to Blue-throated Hummingbirds. Feeds with tail mostly rigid or quivered slightly, held in or near body plane; hovering birds more often flash and fan tail, and flycatching sallies involve aerobatic, darting flight.

Molt

Primary molt starts June to August (on most adults, probably later on many immatures), ends November to March (later on some immatures?). Adults (and some immatures?) often start molt on breeding grounds, complete on non-breeding grounds. Some immatures may undergo complete molt on non-breeding grounds?

Description

Adult male: often looks all-dark with white post-ocular spot. Crown iridescent violet with small, dull bronzy forehead ('bill sheath'), gorget iridescent turquoise-green to emerald-green, auriculars dark with white post-ocular spot. Underparts mostly iridescent dark bronzy green (often looking black), becoming glittering bronzy green on sides/flanks, and smoky gray on lower belly; white vent band usually inconspicuous, and undertail-coverts dusky green with whitish edgings. Upperparts golden green to bronzy green, often with a pale gray patch on neck sides. **Tail:** wholly bronzy green and strongly cleft (fork 5–9 mm, n = 30[3]). Bill black, feet blackish.

Subadult male (?): two types of 'adult male' plumage are readily distinguishable, and this latter may represent a subadult (second-year) plumage. Confirmation from known-age birds is desirable. Resembles adult male (above) but more often with scattered gray feathers in gorget. **Tail:** bronzy green with variable blackish subterminal band and paler, grayish tips on R3–R5; weakly cleft (fork 2–5 mm, n = 21[3]).

Adult female: white post-ocular spot (or short streak) contrasts with dusky green crown and dark auriculars. Throat dirty whitish with lines of dusky spots, blending into dusky pale gray underparts that typically appear faintly mottled; bronzy-green spotting on sides/flanks often covered by wings at rest. White vent band often inconspicuous, and undertail-coverts edged whitish. Upperparts golden green to bronzy green. **Tail:** golden green to bronzy green, R2–R5 with fairly broad blackish subterminal band, and whitish tips broadest on R4 and R5, reduced to a pale fringe on R2.

Immature male: often looks superficially 'messy' or patchy, but fresh plumage very neatly scalloped. Crown, nape, and upperparts dull bronzy green, crown darker and often with a few iridescent violet spots (hard to see); scaly pale buff tips of fresh plumage soon abrade. Face dark with whitish post-ocular streak and often a short whitish moustache streak. Throat dirty pale gray with lines of dusky spots and variable (typically large) iridescent green central patch; underparts dusky gray to sooty gray (scaly pale tips of fresh plumage soon abrade), with chest mottled black; undertail-coverts dull bronzy green with whitish edgings. **Tail:** bronzy green, R2–R5 with variable, relatively diffuse blackish subterminal band and narrow, pale gray to whitish tips to R3–R5, fringes to R1–R2; black band and pale tips broadest on outer rectrices. *Immature female*: resembles adult female but underparts duskier with scaly pale edgings, tail bronzy green with dark subterminal tail band averaging less contrasting.

Hybrids
Presumed with Broad-billed Hummingbird[5] and Berylline Hummingbird (see Pics I.4, I.5).

References
[1]Andrews & Righter 1992, [2]G. Beaton pers. comm., [3]S. N. G. Howell unpubl. data (AMNH, CAS, MVZ specimens), [4]NAB, [5]Phillips *et al.* 1964, [6]Ridgway 1911, [7]Thompson & Ely 1989, [8]Van Rossem 1939.

12.1 Adult male Magnificent. Typical overall dark appearance with bold white post-ocular spot and medium-long black bill distinctive. Deeply cleft tail indicates adult male (apparent whitish on tail tip is light reflection). Charles W. Melton. Madera Canyon, Arizona. late May 1991.

12.2 Adult male Magnificent. Unmistakable. Deeply cleft tail indicates adult male (again, apparent white on outer rectrix edge is reflected light). Charles W. Melton. Madera Canyon, Arizona, 17 April 1995.

12.3 Subadult (?) male Magnificent. Unmistakable. Blackish at tail tip and shallowly cleft tail probably indicate subadult male. Brian E. Small. Portal, Arizona, May 1998.

12.4 Subadult (?) male Magnificent. Note blackish at tail tip and shallowly cleft tail. Brian E. Small. Portal, Arizona, August 1996.

12.5 Adult female Magnificent. With no scale, could suggest Anna's Hummingbird (e.g., Pic. 18.4) or Black-chinned Hummingbird, rather than similar-sized Blue-throated Hummingbird. From Anna's note long bill and relatively bold dark auriculars with bright white post-ocular mark and white sub-ocular streak. From Black-chinned note face pattern, green-mottled sides, and broad inner primaries. Blue-throated has plain gray underparts, black tail, etc. (apparent white tail tip on this bird due to reflected light). Also note dull pinkish feet (blackish on small gorgeted species). Charles W. Melton. Madera Canyon, Arizona, 22 August 1994.

12.6 Adult female Magnificent. Same comments apply as Pic. 12.5, but in flight relatively slow wingbeats, and thus large size, should be apparent. Note green tail with small white tips, cf. Pic. 11.6. Brian E. Small. Portal, Arizona, August 1996.

12.7 Adult female Magnificent. Same comments apply as Pic. 12.5 (note Black-chinned Hummingbird for scale); note advanced primary molt, typical of Magnificent (and Anna's) at this date. Matt Heindel. Miller Canyon, Arizona, 13 August 1999.

12.8 Adult female Magnificent. Note long bill, restricted white post-ocular mark, green tail with relatively small white corners, cf. Pic. 11.5. The tail is slightly raised such that the wing tips appear to project well beyond the tail tip. John H. Hoffman. Chiricahua Mountains, Arizona, May 1994.

12.9 Immature male Magnificent. Fresh scaly appearance, bold white post-ocular spot, and large green throat patch diagnostic of species and age/sex. Kelly B. Bryan. Davis Mountains Resort, Texas, 25 June 1993.

12.10 Immature male Magnificent. Note same characters as Pic. 12.9, plus relatively long but jagged white post-ocular mark and mostly green, distinctly cleft tail. Also note long bill and head profile. Larry Sansone. Miller Canyon, Arizona, 5 September 2000.

12.11 Immature female Magnificent. Note distinctive face pattern and head shape. The uniformly fresh and scaly, or mottled, plumage is typical of a juvenile, and distinct white rectrix tips and lack of green patches in the throat indicate a female. Mike Danzenbaker. Chiricahua Mountains, Arizona, 8 September 1987.

12.12 Immature female Magnificent. Uniformly fresh and scaly, or mottled, plumage is typical of a juvenile, and evenly spotted throat indicates a female. Larry Sansone. Miller Canyon, Arizona, 5 September 2000.

Starthroats Genus *Heliomaster*

Starthroats comprises four species of hummingbirds found in tropical lowlands from Mexico to Brazil and northern Argentina. They are large hummers with long to very long, straight bills, and squared to forked tails. At least the two Middle American species spend much time flycatching conspicuously, especially over streams. Only one (Plain-capped Starthroat) occurs as a casual vagrant north of the Mexican border, where it is unlikely to be confused except perhaps with female Magnificent Hummingbird.

13 Plain-capped Starthroat

(*Heliomaster constantii*)

12–13 cm (4.7–5 in). Bill 33–37 mm (female > male).
Pics 13.1–13.4.

Identification summary
Medium-large with very long, straight bill. Dark throat bordered by thick white moustache. White rump patch and white flank tufts. Black-Phoebe-like call. Casual summer and fall vagrant to SE Arizona.

Taxonomy
North American records presumably pertain to the NW race *pinicola*, distinguished from *leocadiae* of SW Mexico and nominate *constantii* of Central America by average paler coloration, especially on underparts.

Status and Distribution
Casual visitor (May to October, mainly June to early September) to SE Arizona, with one record N to Phoenix (October–November)[5,6]. Also two documented sight reports from New Mexico in August[1,2].

Range W Mexico to NW Costa Rica.

Field Identification

Structure
Medium-large size. Bill very long and straightish. Tail squared to very slightly double-rounded. Primaries medium width with P10 slightly narrower and more tapered. At rest, wing tips about equal with tail tip.

Similar species
Given a good view, this species is distinctive, but any identification should be made

carefully. Other starthroats unlikely to occur naturally in North America, but might be kept in captivity; see Howell and Webb[3] for comparison with Long-billed Starthroat of S Mexico.

Female **Magnificent Hummingbird** larger bodied and proportionately shorter billed (but still long billed), with white post-ocular spot (or, rarely, a short stripe), lacks starthroat's distinctive throat pattern, white back patches, and distinct white tip to R2.

Voice and Sounds
Common call, given mainly in direct flight and also while hovering, a sharp, fairly loud *peek* or *peek!* that may suggest Black Phoebe; also a quieter *sik* or *siik*. Song apparently a series of sharp chips interspersed with more varied notes, *chip chip chip chip pi-chip chip chip...*, etc., given from perch[4].

Habitat
In Mexico favors arid to semi-arid forest edge (from tropical lowlands up into lower pine-oak zone), riparian woodland, semi-open areas with scattered trees and hedges, especially near water.

Behavior
Feeds low to high, often perching high on exposed twigs or wires whence makes prolonged flycatching sallies with jerky, aerobatic movements. Flight generally quick and less heavy-bodied than Magnificent Hummingbird, with tail held in or near body plane to slightly cocked, and often slightly fanned and quivered. Visits feeders irregularly.

Molt
In NW Mexico, primary molt (adults, at least) starts mainly April to June, ends mainly July to October.

Description
Adult (sexes similar): whitish to pale gray post-ocular stripe (post-ocular spot often whiter) contrasts with dark green crown and dusky auriculars; broad whitish malar borders dark sooty throat patch which has variable iridescent pinkish-red to orangish-red mottling at lower edge. Underparts dusky pale gray becoming white on belly and vent; sparse green mottling on sides of chest. Undertail-coverts dusky with broad white edges. Upperparts dull bronzy green to coppery green with irregular-shaped white rump patch and semi-concealed white flank tufts (can be covered by wings at rest). **Tail:** R1 bronzy green with black tip; R2–R5 bronzy green to grayish green basally (paler and grayer on R5) with black subterminal band, bold white tip on R5, and smaller white tips on R2–R4 mostly on inner webs. Bill black, feet dark gray to blackish. *Immature*: resembles adult but crown, nape, and upperparts with buff tips; throat patch sooty gray with little or no iridescent red; pale malar and post-ocular stripe may be washed buff. **Tail:** like adult but R1 can lack black tip, subterminal black band averages narrower, and white tips of R3–R5 average bolder.

Hybrids
None reported.

References
[1]AB 45:138 (1991), [2]AB 48:138 (1994), [3]Howell & Webb 1995, [4]J. Kingery tape, [5]Rosenberg & Witzeman 1998, [6]Witzeman 1979.

13.1, 13.2 and 13.3
Adult Plain-capped
Starthroat. Diagnostic are
the very long and straightish bill, broad pale malar
between dark auriculars
and reddish throat, and
white back patch. Note
that molt of outer rectrices
makes tail shorter so wing
tips appear to project well
beyond tail (usually wing
tips fall about equal with
tail tip). James Lomax.
Portal, Arizona, 11 August
1992.

13.2

13.3

13.4 Adult Plain-capped Starthroat. The same bird as Pics 13.1–13.33. Combination of long straightish bill, broad whitish malar bordering dark throat patch, and white back patch diagnostic. Jim & Deva Burns (Natural Impacts). Portal, Arizona, August 1992.

Sheartails Genus *Calothorax*

The names 'sheartail' and 'woodstar' apply to sundry species in several genera of small to very small hummingbirds, males of which usually have long and deeply forked tails. Inter-generic relationships remain to be elucidated satisfactorily, to which end an appreciation of field characters appears useful. As defined here, *Calothorax* includes five species that share striking similarities in displays, flight behavior, vocalizations, plumage pattern, and structure, and which seem likely to comprise a monophyletic unit. I include in *Calothorax* the two species of *Doricha* (as done by Howell and Webb 1995) plus Bahama Woodstar, the latter recently placed in the genus *Calliphlox* (e.g., AOU 1998) but for many years included in *Doricha* and before that in *Calothorax* (see Ridgway 1911). All could be called 'sheartails' to set them apart from the mass of generic 'hummingbirds.'

Calothorax are small hummers with medium-long to long, arched to slightly arched black bills and tails that are forked, especially deeply in males. Sheartails are typical of open and semi-open areas, and the two species known from North America should not be confused with other hummingbirds in the region: Lucifer Hummingbird occurs in arid canyons of the SW U.S., while Bahama Woodstar is a casual vagrant to Florida.

14 Bahama Woodstar (Sheartail)

(*Calothorax evelynae*)

8.5–9.5 cm (3.4–3.7 in); male > female. Bill 16–17 mm.
Pics 14.1–14.7.

Identification summary

Small size. Bill medium-long and slightly arched, tail long and deeply forked (male) to double-rounded (female), usually held closed in a long, rounded point that projects well beyond wing tips at rest. Male gorget magenta-rose, sides and flanks dusky cinnamon-rufous, tail blackish with cinnamon inner webs to R3 and R4. Female sides and flanks dusky cinnamon-rufous, outer rectrices boldly tipped cinnamon.

Taxonomy

Two taxa are recognized: *evelynae*, which is widespread in the Bahamas, and *lyrura* of Inagua, the latter probably different enough to be treated as a separate species, Inagua Woodstar (or Sheartail), as done by Ridgway[5]; adult male *lyrura* has iridescent magenta-rose forehead and narrower rectrices than *evelynae*. The subspecies *salita* has been described from the Caicos Islands but was synonymized with *evelynae* by Buden[1]. On geographic grounds, *evelynae* is most likely to occur in Florida, and the single North American specimen is of this taxon[4].

The displays[2], vocalizations[3], behavior[3], structure, and plumage pattern of this species are all much like *Calothorax* (including *Doricha*) and unlike Middle American woodstars (Sparkling-tailed *Philodice [=Tilmatura] dupontii* and Magenta-throated *Philodice [=Calliphlox] mitchellii*). For this reason I merge *evelynae* into *Calothorax*, and recommend the English name be changed to Bahama Sheartail to avoid misleading association with the quite different woodstars.

Status and Distribution
Casual vagrant to S Florida, with four records: January 1961 (found dead), August to October 1971, April to June 1974, and July–August 1981[4,6].

Range
Endemic to the Bahamas (see Taxonomy, above), but uncommon to rare on islands nearest Florida.

Field Identification

Structure
Small size. Bill medium-long and slightly arched. Male tail long and deeply forked, female tail long and deeply double-rounded. Primaries fairly broad with P10 narrower (falcate on male). At rest, wing tips fall well short of tail tip.

Similar species
The only hummingbird common in Florida is Ruby-throated, although increasing numbers of western North American species are being found in Florida in winter (but mainly in the north and west). Ruby-throated has straighter bill and shorter tail that appears all-black in males, white-tipped in females and immatures, and always lacks cinnamon-rufous; male has ruby-red gorget. Ruby-throated has softer, more twangy chips and wags its tail less often. Female Bahama Woodstar suggests *Selasphorus* hummingbirds in chipping calls, cinnamon-rufous sides, flanks, and bases of outer rectrices, but told by slightly arched bill, plainer throat, longer and deeply double-rounded tail with cinnamon-tipped outer rectrices.

Voice and Sounds
Calls include a high, fairly sharp chipping *tih* or *chi*, given in flight and often repeated persistently from perch with doubled notes thrown in, *chi chi chi chi-chi chi...*; at times a more rapid-paced and harder chipping *tih-tih-tih-tih...*; and high, thin, *buzzi*er twitters in interactions, e.g., *si-chi ch-chi-chi-chi* and longer series.

Habitat
On Bahamas occurs widely: in understory of open pine woods, edge and clearings of coppice woodland, beach scrub, second growth, and gardens.

Behavior
Feeds mainly at low to mid levels and regularly visits feeders. Perches mainly at mid to upper levels, often on fairly exposed bare twigs and on wires, tail held closed or only slightly spread to reveal a notched tip. Flight quick and darting, not slow and

bee-like as in Middle American woodstars. Tail of feeding and hovering birds usually closed to slightly spread, and wagged noticeably but not deeply, held from slightly above body plane to distinctly cocked when feeding. Tail flashed and spread on occasions during hovering and maneuvering.

Molt
Breeding may occur year-round, but perhaps mainly October to April, as summarized by Johnsgard (1997) and nesting season probably varies among islands, so molting birds might be encountered in any month. In early December 1999, females on New Providence (n = 6) showed no signs of molt, females on Abaco (n = 3) were in active molt and had replaced 2–6 inner primaries[3].

Description
Adult male: gorget magenta-rose, offset by bold white forecollar; underparts dusky cinnamon, mottled green on sides/flanks, becoming bright cinnamon-rufous on underwing-coverts (visible in flight); vent band white, undertail-coverts pale cinnamon. Crown, nape, and upperparts dull golden green with distinct white post-ocular spot and narrow whitish sub-ocular crescent. **Tail:** R1 greenish, R2 blackish with some green distally and cinnamon-rufous basally, R3–R4 cinnamon-rufous with mostly black outer webs, R5 blackish. From below, tail often looks black with cinnamon-rufous median stripe. Bill black, feet blackish.

Adult female: crown, nape, and upperparts dull golden green with distinct white post-ocular spot and indistinct, dull pale gray post-ocular line above dusky auriculars, narrow pale buff supraloral, and blackish loral wedge. Throat dingy whitish to pale gray with faint duskier flecks visible at close range; white forecollar contrasts with throat and with underparts; sides and flanks dusky cinnamon-rufous, sparsely mottled green (mainly at chest sides), becoming dingy pale grayish down center; underwing-coverts brighter cinnamon-rufous, striking in flight; vent band white, undertail-coverts pale cinnamon. **Tail:** R1 greenish; R2 green basally with variable cinnamon-rufous at base of outer web, black distally; R3–R5 with cinnamon-rufous bases separated from broad black median band by narrow green band, and with bold cinnamon tips. Closed tail above looks green with broad black tip narrowly fringed cinnamon.

Immature male: resembles adult female but upperparts with narrow, faint, pale buffy to gray tips when fresh, throat dingy pale gray to dusky cinnamon with lines of faint dusky flecks and typically one to several iridescent magenta-rose spots. **Tail:** R1 greenish, R2 like female but may have small pale cinnamon tip, R3–R5 blackish with cinnamon tip and variable cinnamon basally; cinnamon tips to R3–R5 average smaller and paler than adult female. Outer rectrices slightly longer and narrower than adult female, R1 proportionately shorter, so tail more forked.

Subadult male: second stage immature plumage resembles adult male (including tail) but throat dusky cinnamon with no iridescent magenta-rose spots, or throat (worn plumage?) may be whitish with one or more iridescent spots.

Immature female: resembles adult female but in fresh plumage upperparts have narrow, faint, pale buffy to gray tips, and throat tinged buff; sides and flanks paler cinnamon to vinaceous-cinnamon without green spotting. **Tail:** resembles adult female but with reduced and paler cinnamon at base, R2–R5 tipped pale cinnamon (can look whitish, especially when backlit).

Hybrids None described.

References
[1]Buden 1987, [2]P. Dean pers. comm., [3]S. N. G. Howell unpubl. data, [4]Owre 1976, [5]Ridgway 1911, [6]Stevenson & Anderson 1994.

14.1 Adult male Bahama Woodstar. Unmistakable in North America. Note the very long and deeply forked tail with rufous inner webs, projecting well beyond the tail tip. Bruce Hallett. New Providence, Bahamas, January 1997.

14.2 Adult male Bahama Woodstar. Magenta-rose gorget and long tail more like Lucifer Hummingbird than any other species likely to occur in Florida. From Lucifer told by less elongated gorget, tail pattern, and shorter, less arched bill. Bruce Hallett. Great Exuma, Bahamas, 20 June 2000.

14.3 Adult female Bahama Woodstar. Note the diagnostic long and cleft tail with cinnamon-rufous bases and tips to outer rectrices. Bruce Hallett. Grand Bahama, Bahamas, February 1997.

14.4 Adult female Bahama Woodstar. Note the diagnostic long and cleft tail with cinnamon-rufous bases and tips to outer rectrices. Kevin T. Karlson. Andros, Bahamas, January 2000.

14.5 Immature male Bahama Woodstar. Young immature males are female-like in plumage (note the tail) but have scattered magenta-rose throat feathers. Bruce Hallett. Great Exuma, Bahamas, 20 June 2000.

14.6 Immature male Bahama Woodstar. Older immature males resemble adult male (note the tail) but have a dusky-cinnamon throat lacking magenta-rose spots; P7 is growing, P8–P10 old. Bruce Hallett. Great Exuma, Bahamas, 20 June 2000.

14. 7 Immature female Bahama Woodstar. This presumed immature female resembles a washed-out adult female; note the white-looking tips to R3–R5, caused largely by light passing through the tips (which are pale cinnamon, e.g., as seen from above), and reduced and paler cinnamon at tail base. Bruce Hallett. New Providence, Bahamas, March 1994.

15 Lucifer Hummingbird (Sheartail)

(Calothorax lucifer)

9–10 cm (3.5–4 in). Bill 19–23 mm (female > male).
Pics 15.1–15.7.

Identification summary

Small, with proportionately long and arched bill. Male has elongated magenta gorget and long, deeply forked tail (usually held closed in single point and spread mainly in display). Female and immature have buffy face and underparts with distinct dusky auricular stripe, rufous at base of outer rectrices. Very local in SW U.S. in summer.

Taxonomy

Monotypic. Closely related to very similar Beautiful Hummingbird *Calothorax pulcher* of S Mexico.

Status and Distribution

Very local summer resident (April to October, often with first arrivals in March) from SE Arizona to SW New Mexico and in W Texas, with occasional records in these states away from traditional sites. No records elsewhere in North America.

Range

SW U.S. to central and S Mexico.

Field Identification

Structure

Small size. Bill proportionately long and arched. Male tail long and deeply forked with narrow and sharply pointed outermost rectrices (tail usually held closed in single point). Female and immature tail double-rounded (more deeply cleft on immature male). Primaries fairly broad with P10 narrower (falcate on male). At rest, wing tips fall well short of tail tip.

Similar species

Adult male Lucifer should be distinctive in North America, note arched bill and long tail, elongated gorget. Male Costa's perhaps the most similar North American species, but note its shorter and straighter bill, short tail, and iridescent violet crown.

Other female and immature small gorgeted hummingbirds are sometimes misidentified as Lucifer but note Lucifer's arched bill, buffy face and underparts with dusky auricular stripe, and fairly long, notched and double-rounded tail with rufous basal corners. Female or immature **Black-chinned** and **Costa's** sometimes have slightly decurved bills, and some immature Black-chinneds may have extensively buffy sides/flanks, but both species lack rufous in tail. Black-chinned also has dark lores and broadly dusky auriculars with white post-ocular spot, softer chipping call.

Costa's has dingy face with whitish post-ocular stripe, short tail, and high, tinny to liquid twittering call. Immature and female *Selasphorus* have straighter bills, different face patterns, dark-flecked throats, etc.

Voice and Sounds

Call a fairly hard, slightly smacking *chih* or *chi!* (may sound intermediate between calls of Anna's and Broad-tailed hummingbirds) given by feeding birds and from perch, when can be repeated steadily and occasionally doubled into a slightly rolled *chi-ti*. Territorial (?) call a short, sharp, rapid-paced, slightly accelerating, rolled chipper, *chi-chi-chichichi* or *chi-ti-ti*, given from perch or in flight, approaching perch. Rapid-paced chase call in inter-specific interactions is a hard chipper run into a slightly squeaky, hollow chatter, *tirr-rr-rr chi-ti ti-ti-tih*, or *chi-rr-rrt chi-chi chi-chi-chi*, and variations. Male produces a fairly loud wing-buzz in shuttle display, which may attract attention.

Habitat

Arid scrub, especially in mountain canyons with flowering *Agave* plants, ranging to lower limits of oak and pine-oak woodland.

Behavior

Feeds and perches mainly at low to mid levels. Feeding and hovering birds mostly hold tail closed and quivered, in or slightly above body plane when feeding at near horizontal angle, or (females at least) cocked down below body plane when feeding up into flowers. Tail flashed and wagged loosely on occasions during hovering and maneuvering. In shuttle display, male buzzes loudly back and forth in convoluted, short-wavelength, rocking motion, his gorget flared to catch the light; in dive display male climbs to 20–30 m and stoops steeply, at times ending his dive with pendulum-like rocking[1,4].

Molt

Primary molt mainly September to April (averaging earlier on adults), occurs mostly on non-breeding winter grounds but adults can start on breeding grounds with inner 2 primaries and suspend to non-breeding grounds.

Description

Adult male: elongated gorget magenta to violet-magenta (occasionally with rose or bluish highlights), offset by whitish post-ocular stripe and broad white forecollar. Underparts mottled dusky green on buffy-washed background, typically showing a cinnamon flank spot and unmarked whitish median stripe; vent band and undertail-coverts whitish, or short undertail-coverts with bronzy-green centers. Crown, nape, and upperparts golden green to emerald green, duller on forecrown. **Tail:** R1–R2 golden green to blue green, elongated R3–R5 blackish, some birds with fine whitish tips to outer rectrices. Bill black, feet blackish.

Adult female: face and throat pale buff (may fade to whitish) with dusky auriculars offsetting pale buff post-ocular stripe; post-ocular spot often whiter. Underparts pale buff to buffy cinnamon, usually with paler forecollar below dingy throat and above narrow cinnamon band across chest; belly palest, buffy cream to whitish; undertail-coverts pale cinnamon to whitish. Some birds have one to a few magenta throat feathers[3]. Crown, nape, and upperparts golden green to emerald green, duller on crown. **Tail:** R1–R2 golden green, R3–5 with rufous base, broad black subterminal band (with variable green basal edge), and bold white tips.

Immature male: resembles adult female but plumage in fall fresher, with narrow cinnamon-buff tips on upperparts, especially rump and uppertail-coverts; tail slightly longer and more deeply double-rounded with slightly narrower and more pointed outer rectrices, more extensive rufous bases to outer rectrices. Some birds have scattered magenta throat feathers (as do some adult females, however). Complete or near-complete molt in first winter.

Subadult (first-year) males resemble adult male but some may have less solid and less elongated gorget, shallower tail fork with some pale on tip of R5[3].

Immature female: resembles adult female but fall plumage fresher, with narrow cinnamon-buff tips on upperparts; outer rectrices average slightly broader and blunter. Attains adult plumage by complete molt in first winter.

Hybrids
Presumed with Black-chinned Hummingbird[2].

References
[1]S. N. G. Howell pers. obs., [2]Lasley *et al.* 1996, [3]Pyle 1997, [4]Wagner 1946.

15.1 Adult male Lucifer. Unmistakable with a view like this, note long, slightly arched bill, long forked tail. Rick & Nora Bowers. Sonoita, Arizona, September 1997.

15.2 Adult male Lucifer (and adult male Black-chinned Hummingbird). In this typical view of a quick feeder visit note the long arched bill, long closed tail, expansive magenta gorget, and cinnamon flank spot. Matt. Heindel. Miller Canyon, Arizona, 13 August 1999.

15.3 Adult female Lucifer. A richly colored individual, with P1–P2 molted before migration; note long arched bill and buffy-cinnamon underparts with dark auricular mask. Rick & Nora Bowers. Sonoita, Arizona, September 1997.

15.4 Female Lucifer. A paler individual than Pic. 15.3, with P1–P3 shed at start of wing molt; note same distinctive features. Mark M. Stevenson. Tucson Desert Museum, Arizona, 8 September 1999.

15.5 Female Lucifer. The long arched bill, face pattern, and long narrow tail are diagnostic. Greg W. Lasley. Portal, Arizona, 25 August 1993.

15.6 Female Lucifer. Note face pattern, arched bill, and long tail. Peter E. Scott. Chisos Mountains, Texas, May 1981.

15.7 Immature male Lucifer. Note the arched bill, long narrow tail, cinnamon sides, and elongated magenta gorget streaks that in combination indicate species and age/sex. Greg W. Lasley (VIREO). Big Bend, Texas, 22 August 1986.

Small Gorgeted Hummingbirds

The genera *Archilochus*, *Calypte*, *Stellula*, and *Selasphorus* comprise North America's 'small gorgeted hummers,' a highly migratory group that involves the commonest and most difficult field identification challenges. Adult males of most small gorgeted species can be identified fairly readily (given a good view), although some green-backed male Rufous may not always be distinguishable from male Allen's. Identification of females and immatures, however, can be problematic, and under field conditions one should be content to call many birds *Archilochus* sp. (i.e., Ruby-throated/Black-chinned), or *Selasphorus* sp. (i.e., Rufous/Allen's). Females and immatures can be divided into four 'green-and-gray species' (Ruby-throated, Black-chinned, Anna's, and Costa's; Pics i-vii) and four 'green-and-rufous' species (Calliope, Broad-tailed, Rufous, and Allen's; Pics viii–x). The green-and-gray species typically lack any obvious rufous coloration (e.g., their tails have no rufous; **Figure 1**), and their underparts are dingy whitish or grayish (some female/immature *Archilochus* have a buffy wash to their flanks). The green-and-rufous species have distinct cinnamon or rufous coloration (e.g., their tails have rufous basally; **Figure 2**), and their underparts are strongly washed buffy to cinnamon, especially on the sides and flanks, which usually lack extensive green or dusky mottling. Narrowing a bird down to one of these pairs is a critical first step.

The green-and-gray species can be divided into two genera: *Archilochus* (Ruby-throated and Black-chinned) and *Calypte* (Anna's and Costa's). *Archilochus* (Pics i, ii, v) inhabit wooded habitats and have relatively narrow inner primaries, a smaller head and thinner neck, and a winter molt schedule. *Calypte* (Pics iii, iv, vi, vii) inhabit scrubby habitats and have broad inner primaries, a larger head and thicker neck, and a summer molt schedule. Although it takes practice to see, and a good view (a telescope is helpful), the width of the inner primaries is a very good field characteristic that should be determined on any problematic bird. Voices of the two genera also differ, and an experienced observer often finds a Costa's or Anna's among Black-chinneds simply by its call notes. The calls of Black-chinned and Ruby-throated, however, appear to be not safely distinguishable.

The green-and-rufous species comprise the monotypic Calliope Hummingbird and three *Selasphorus* (Broad-tailed, Rufous, and Allen's). All four can occur together in the west, and identification problems are not trivial. Calliope is very small (although without anything for comparison this can be hard to judge) but looks a lot like some Broad-taileds in plumage, while some bright Broad-taileds can resemble duller Rufous/Allen's hummingbirds. As well as being small, Calliope has a short, relatively squared-looking tail and should be identifiable by this structural feature (at rest the wing tips often project beyond the tail tip) (Pic. viii). Conversely, Broad-tailed is the largest of this quartet, and at rest its wing tips fall short of its relatively long and graduated tail (Pic. ix). To separate Broad-tailed from Rufous/Allen's (Pic. x) look first at the rump and tail – a lot of rufous coloration rules out Broad-tailed. Immature females are the most difficult, and features to concentrate on are tail shape (**Figures 2, 7**), contrast between forecollar and sides/flanks, tail pattern, primary shape, and P9/P10 projection. In general, Rufous and Allen's are not safely separated in the field unless a bird can be aged and sexed, and the relative width of its rectrices judged (which requires comparative experience), and even then many birds defy identification. With experience, calls are also useful for all but Rufous versus Allen's.

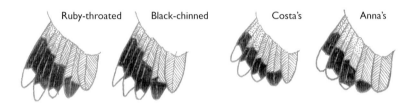

Figure 1. Tail shape and pattern differences in adult female *Archilochus* and *Calypte* hummingbirds. Hatching represents green, stippling pale grayish. Note longer and more deeply double-rounded tails of *Archilochus*, with broader black median band, shorter tails of *Calypte* with relatively more extensive pale bases to outer rectrices. Within *Archilochus*, Ruby-throated and Black-chinned essentially identical in pattern, note proportionately longer R4 of Ruby-throated and nipple-like tips of R5–R4 of Black-chinned. Within *Calypte*, Costa's tail relatively short and rounded (note proportionately short R5), Anna's tail relatively squared with broader rectrices than Costa's and averaging broader black median band, smaller white R3 tip.

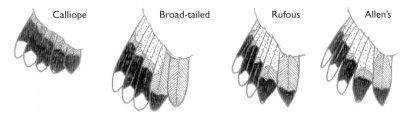

Figure 2. Tail shape and pattern differences in adult female Calliope and *Selasphorus* hummingbirds. Hatching represents green, stippling rufous. Note strikingly short and relatively squared tail of Calliope, with limited green at base (tail often looks mostly black); fine rufous edging to outer webs of bases of R1–R4 often hard to see. On Broad-tailed, note weak graduation of outer rectrices, relatively short R1 usually all-green, limited rufous on base of R2. Rufous and Allen's tails highly variable in pattern, particularly the extent of rufous basally (e.g., see Figure 9). Note narrower outer rectrices of Allen's, and more pinched-in tip of R2 on Rufous, but some birds defy identification, even in the hand.

Green-and-gray species: adult females perched

i Adult female Ruby-throated Hummingbird. Relatively narrow inner primaries and face pattern point to *Archilochus*. Notched inner webs to inner primaries (visible on the near wing) and relatively narrow and tapered P10 (visible on the far wing) indicate Ruby-throated. In worn plumage, such as this, upperparts often look darker and bluer than golden green of fresh plumage. Charles W. Melton. Martin, Tennessee, 4 July 1993.

ii Adult female Black-chinned Hummingbird. Relatively narrow inner primaries (with P7 distinctly broader) identify this as an *Archilochus*. The primaries are overall relatively blunt and broad, diagnostic of Black-chinned; note P10 visible on the far wing. Charles W. Melton. Madera Canyon, Arizona, 17 August 2000.

iii Adult female Anna's Hummingbird. Relatively broad inner primaries and lack of rufous or buff in plumage point to *Calypte*. From Costa's Hummingbird by more evenly dusky-spotted throat (extending up into malar region), more extensive dusky and green mottling on underparts. Also note relatively shorter bill, tail projecting slightly beyond closed wing tips, and loral pattern. Calls are also diagnostic. Charles W. Melton. Whittier Narrows Nature Center, California, 1 March 1996.

iv Adult female Costa's Hummingbird. Evenly broad primaries and lack of rufous or buff in plumage indicate *Calypte*. From Anna's Hummingbird by mostly plain throat with dark concentrated in center, and less extensive green mottling on underparts. Also note the relatively longer bill, wing tip about equal with relatively short tail, dark lores, and mostly whitish undertail-coverts. Calls are also diagnostic. Charles W. Melton. Borrego Springs, California, 25 March 1995.

Green-and-gray species: adult females on nests

v Adult female Black-chinned Hummingbird. To separate this bird from Anna's and Costa's note the relatively narrow inner primaries and broad outer primaries (especially the contrast in width between P6 and P7); the plain whitish undertail-coverts and relatively long bill also rule out Anna's, and the tail looks too long for Costa's. Rick & Nora Bowers. Catalina State Park, Arizona, May 1990.

vi Adult female Anna's Hummingbird. Evenly broad primaries point to *Calypte*; also note the black-tipped tail, unlike typical Black-chinned. Duskiness of face, dusky malar spotting, and dusky-centered undertail coverts indicate Anna's. William E. Grenfell. Near Sacramento, California, April 1990.

vii Adult female Costa's Hummingbird. The evenly broad primaries indicate *Calypte*; also note the black-tipped tail, unlike typical Black-chinned. The plain pale throat points to Costa's; also note the relatively short tail. The apparent glossiness of P7–P9 presumably is caused by differential light reflection. Brian E. Small. Los Angeles, California, June 1994.

Green-and-rufous species: immatures perched

viii Immature cf. female Calliope Hummingbird. Note broad, rounded primaries, relatively short and squared, mostly blackish tail, and extensive vinaceous-cinnamon wash on underparts, including sides of neck. Fresh plumage (in fall) and relatively lightly spotted throat (cf. Pic. 20.7) suggest immature female, although sex cannot be determined for sure from this photo. Charles W. Melton. Miller Canyon, Arizona, 22 August 2000.

ix Immature cf. female Broad-tailed Hummingbird. Long tail, evenly broad primaries, vinaceous-cinnamon sides, and fresh plumage (in fall) point to immature *Selasphorus*. 'Cold' face, lack of contrasting white forecollar, weakly graduated tail (with R1 slightly shorter than R2), and relatively short P9/P10 projection indicate Broad-tailed. The throat spotting, relatively tapered primaries, and relatively short tail projection beyond the closed wings suggest an immature female but many immatures, including this one, are difficult to sex in the field. Charles W. Melton. Miller Canyon, Arizona, 22 August 2000.

x Immature cf. male Rufous/Allen's Hummingbird. Fresh plumage in fall, throat pattern, contrasting white forecollar, and distinct rufous on uppertail-coverts and tail indicate immature Rufous/Allen's. Amount of rufous on uppertail-coverts/central rectrices and throat pattern are equivocal for determining sex based on this photo, although extent of rufous in tail suggests male. Charles W. Melton. Miller Canyon, Arizona, 22 August 2000.

Black-chinned Hummingbirds
Genus *Archilochus*

Two eastern and western counterparts – Ruby-throated and Black-chinned hummingbirds – comprise this genus. These are small hummers with medium to medium-long, straightish black bills, and tails that are forked in males, slightly double-rounded in females. The inner six primaries are proportionately narrower than the outer four, and the marked change in primary width between P5 and P7 is an excellent character to eliminate all other hummingbird species in North America. Adult male gorgets are shield shaped, ruby red to bluish violet, and chins of both species are black. Females and immatures have mostly plain underparts with an indistinct to distinct buffy wash on the flanks, and their tails lack rufous. Both sexes have a white post-ocular spot set off by dusky auriculars, and at rest the wing tips of all ages/sexes fall slightly to distinctly short of the tail tip.

16 Ruby-throated Hummingbird

(Archilochus colubris)

8–9 cm (3.2–3.7 in). Bill 14–19 mm
(female > male).
Pics I.13, I.15, I.30, i, 16.1–16.11.

Identification summary
Small size. Bill medium length and straightish (longer on female). Male's black chin and ruby-red gorget diagnostic, although gorget often looks black; note also dark face and white post-ocular spot (cf. male Broad-tailed Hummingbird), and primary shapes and longer tail (cf. male Black-chinned Hummingbird). Female and immature gray-and-white overall. Tail slightly forked to double-rounded with adult R4 ≥ R3 (R4 slightly < R3 on some immatures). Inner primaries relatively

Rare to casual in SE U.S. in winter, see text.

narrow (a feature shared with Black-chinned), P10 relatively narrow and tapered (broad and blunt-tipped on Black-chinned; **Figure 4**). Call a soft, twangy chip. Molts in winter.

Taxonomy
No subspecies described.

Status and Distribution
Summer resident (mainly April to October) in eastern North America, from E Texas and Florida N to S Canada, mainly N along E edge of Great Plains to the Dakotas, thence W through S Canada to central Alberta, and E to S Newfoundland[5]. Spring migrants (males precede females by 1–2 weeks) arrive in S U.S. starting mainly in March, reaching central states in mid to late April, and NW and NE ends of range in mid to late May or even early June. In fall, most depart N parts of breeding range by September (with birds lingering to December perhaps related to increased trend of wintering in SE U.S.; see below), with transient migrants in S U.S. through late October, rarely into November.

Rare migrant (both spring and fall) through W Texas and Great Plains. Casual W and NW (mainly May to July) as far afield as British Columbia[2] and Alaska[4], and SW (mainly August to September) to California[3].

Rare but perhaps increasing winter visitor (mainly November to March) at feeders in SE U.S., mainly along and near Gulf coast, S to S Florida and N locally to N Carolina[6,9].

Range
Breeds E North America, winters SE U.S. to Central America.

Field Identification

Structure
Small, with a straightish, medium-length bill (longer on female). Adult male tail fairly deeply forked (R4 longest; **Figure 3**), adult female tail slightly double-rounded (R4 $\geq$ R3; **Figure 1**). Immature male tail slightly longer and more forked than adult female, and R4 of immatures slightly > to slightly < R3; outer rectrices of immature male often with slightly pinched-in or nipple-like tips. At rest, wing tips < tail tip. Primaries relatively tapered, especially P10. Inner primaries of adults and of immature male have diagnostic notch, or step, on inner web (reduced to absent on immature female).

Similar species
Several other gorgeted hummers look similar to Ruby-throated but with prolonged, close-range views (especially of perched birds where details of wing structure can be studied), most individuals can be identified. In most of eastern North America Ruby-throated is the only hummingbird that occurs regularly, so other species should not be expected, and identification of summer birds is often by default range. The next most regular species of occurrence in the East is Rufous Hummingbird (the first fall migrants of which usually appear in July), all plumages of which are told readily from Ruby-throated by extensively rufous sides and rufous in the tail.

The most similar species to Ruby-throated is Black-chinned Hummingbird. These two occur together locally, mainly through the Great Plains (especially during migration) and, increasingly, in the SE U.S. in winter; see below for distinguishing characters.

Adult males

Adult male Broad-tailed Hummingbird (mainly Great Basin and Rocky mountains) slightly larger and stockier with magenta-rose gorget that lacks black chin. Eyes set in pale area that extends under chin, unlike black face and contrasting white post-ocular spot of Ruby-throated. Closed tail appears green and tapered, with R1 longest (versus forked black tip on Ruby-throated) and spread tail 'jaggedly squared,' with rufous edging on inner rectrices. Inner primaries broad, and P10 finely attenuate to create distinctive wing-trill in flight, very different from standard wing hum of Ruby-throated. Call a sharp chip.

Adult male Black-chinned Hummingbird (mainly W North America) very similar overall but has shorter and less deeply forked tail, averages longer billed, and black throat has broad bluish-violet band across bottom. Gorgets often look simply all-black, however. In such cases, note tail shape (assuming a bird is not molting): male Ruby-throated has longer and more deeply forked tail with R4 longest and three approximately equal-spaced tips visible beyond the green R1, male Black-chinned has 'double-rounded' fork (R3 longest) with shorter projection of only two approximately equal-spaced tips visible beyond R1 (**Figure 3**). At rest, wing tip falls at about tip of R1, so perched male Ruby-throated has longer tail projection. Also note narrower primaries of Ruby-throated, especially P8–P10: wing tip of Ruby-throated looks narrow and pointed versus broad and blunt on Black-chinned. On some birds in mid and late winter, tip of P10 can be so worn that shape cannot be determined; note that adult Black-chinned molts on average about a month earlier than Ruby-throated. Also, Ruby-throated tends to be deeper, more golden-green above, including the crown, Black-chinned duller, more bronzy-green or bluish-green above, with dusky crown. Dorsal colors vary with the light, however, and worn plumage tends to be bluer than fresh plumage. Adult male Black-chinned typically makes a distinct wing hum in flight (almost suggesting Rufous/Allen's at times), while Ruby-throated male has quieter and less noticeable wing noise. Male Black-chinned often wags its tail strongly, while Ruby-throated's tail is usually held more stiffly and quivered rather than wagged or pumped, but this is not diagnostic.

Adult male Anna's Hummingbird (mainly W North America) slightly larger, stockier, and bigger headed than Ruby-throated, with glittering rose-pink to orangish-red crown same color as somewhat elongated gorget. Anna's has broad inner primaries, relatively shorter and less deeply forked tail, and smacking chip call.

Females

When confronted with a problem bird in fall, determining its age is an important first step. Look for freshness of plumage (especially distinct buff tips to upperparts and secondaries) as an indicator of immatures, unlike the often duller metallic greens and more faded, browner primaries of worn-plumaged adults (but note that adults can retain narrow pale buff tips to tertials and rump through at least late summer).

Although some immature Ruby-throateds have the flanks washed quite strongly and extensively with buff or cinnamon, confusion with Rufous/Allen's hummingbirds should not be a problem: these have more distinct dusky throat flecking, brighter buffy-cinnamon to cinnamon-rufous flanks, distinct rufous in the tail, and sharper chipping calls.

Female Black-chinned Hummingbird (mainly W North America) very similar to Ruby-throated and under typical field conditions many birds best called *Archilochus* sp., without attempting to force an identification. Given good views, however, the two species can be distinguished. Best feature is wing shape, especially the shape of P10: Ruby-throated has relatively narrower and more tapered primaries throughout, often most noticeable on P8–P10 such that wing tip appears relatively narrow and tapered on Ruby-throated, broad and blunt-tipped on Black-chinned (**Figure 4**). On birds in mid to late winter, however, tips of outer primaries can be so worn and frayed that it is not possible to determine shape.

Subtleties in shape of inner six primaries may be useful given good views and/or sharp photos: these feathers are more acutely tapered on Ruby-throated, adult females of which have a notch on the inner web; (see figure 101 in Pyle[8]); immature female Ruby-throated, however, is more similar in this regard to adult and immature female Black-chinned.

Other useful features are tail shape and bill length. Adult female Black-chinned typically has nipple-like tips to the outer rectrices, unlike the more evenly tapered (or rounded) tips of adult female Ruby-throated and immature female Black-chinned, and Black-chinned's tail typically has R3 > R4 (versus R4 ≥ R3 on adult Ruby-throated; **Figure 1**). Black-chinned is longer billed than Ruby-throated and, while bill measurements overlap, the longest-billed Black-chinned and shortest-billed Ruby-throateds may sometimes be distinguishable with experience.

In general, Ruby-throated is deeper green above and whiter below, and typically appears more contrasting overall, than Black-chinned, which is duller green above and dingier below. Fresh primaries of both species are similarly dark but Black-chinned molts earlier and lives in more arid habitats which may help explain why its primaries often look browner and more worn than on an adult Ruby-throated at the same season.

Adult Black-chinned molts on average about a month earlier than Ruby-throated, such that the point reached by primary molt could be a useful identification character. Adults molt earlier than immatures, however, so adult female Ruby-throated might be at similar molt stage as immature Black-chinned, and perhaps only most advanced birds (adult female Black-chinneds) could be identified by molt timing. More work is needed on the reliability of molt timing as an aid to specific identification of winter hummingbirds.

Black-chinned often wags and spreads its tail frequently and at times persistently while hovering and feeding. Ruby-throated usually holds its tail rigid, quivering or flashing it only slightly (as does Black-chinned at times). While persistent tail-wagging suggests Black-chinned, any identification should be confirmed by unequivocal structural features.

Female Anna's Hummingbird (mainly W North America) slightly larger, stockier, and bigger headed than Ruby-throated, with broad inner primaries and more smacking call. Anna's tends to be dingier grayish below, and adults have splash of rose-pink to orangish red in center of throat. Anna's tail has similar pattern but tail more evenly rounded (R1 proportionately longer), rectrices slightly broader and more rounded, and black median band narrower, with relatively more extensive greenish gray visible at base of spread tail (**Figure 1**). In addition, most Anna's molt in summer and fall, so any bird with obvious wing molt in summer should not be Ruby-throated. Conversely, birds molting outer primaries in late winter should not be Anna's.

Female Costa's Hummingbird (W North America) smaller and shorter tailed, but overall stockier and relatively bigger headed, than Ruby-throated, with broad inner primaries and high, twittering call. Costa's tends to be duller, grayish green above with a plainer, less contrasting face that features a diffuse pale post-ocular stripe that wraps around smoothly pale gray auriculars; its underparts lack any buff or cinnamon that is often shown by Ruby-throateds. At rest, Costa's wing tips often project slightly beyond its short tail (versus wing tips shorter than tail tip on Ruby-throated), and hovering and feeding birds often wag and fan their tail. Costa's tail pattern superficially similar to Ruby-throated but black median band narrower, with relatively more extensive greenish and gray visible at base of spread tail, especially noticeable on outer rectrices (**Figure 1**). In addition, most Costa's molt in summer and fall, so any bird with obvious wing molt in summer should not be Ruby-throated. Conversely, birds molting outer primaries in late winter should not be Costa's.

Female Calliope Hummingbird (mainly W mountains) smaller and shorter tailed than Ruby-throated with broad inner primaries and a soft, chipping call. At rest, Calliope's wing tips project slightly beyond its short tail which typically has narrow rufous edging to bases of outer rectrices (often hard to see). Calliope consistently has the sides/flanks and undertail-coverts washed pale cinnamon (as do some fresh-plumaged juvenile Ruby-throateds) and this color often extends up into sides of neck, its throat is typically marked by lines of fine dusky flecks, and its 'softer' face has white lores with a dark loral crescent.

Female Broad-tailed Hummingbird (mainly Great Basin and Rocky mountains) slightly larger and stockier than Ruby-throated with larger and broader primaries and broad tail that has rufous at base (reduced or virtually lacking on some immature females). Broad-tailed also has cinnamon-washed sides/flanks and undertail-coverts, dusky-flecked throat, and sharp chip call.

Immature males
Immature male Ruby-throats can be distinguished from immature males and females of similar species by much the same combination of characters discussed for females, and note that immature male Ruby-throated's tail is proportionately longer than a female's, so its wing tips usually fall well short of the tail tip. Also note that immature males have shorter bills than females and often have a darker auricular mask and whiter throat and forecollar. The most similar species is again Black-chinned Hummingbird.

Some **immature male Black-chinned Hummingbirds** in fall can be deceptively bright emerald green above, with a green crown, relatively bright buffy flanks, and relatively short bill that all suggest Ruby-throated. Many immatures in fall have a few spots of diagnostic throat color but be especially aware of lighting when evaluating the color of single iridescent spots – ruby-red can easily appear black. Immature male Black-chinneds are best identified by shape of outer primaries (especially P8–P10): broad and blunt-tipped, versus tapered and relatively narrow on Ruby-throated (**Figure 4**). The inner primaries of Black-chinned also are relatively blunt and lack a distinct notch on the inner web. Differences in outer primary shape can be obscured in mid to late winter by feather wear, but by such time most birds show patches of diagnostic throat color – ruby-red in Ruby-throated, black and bluish violet in Black-chinned. Black-chinned also averages shorter tailed (with R4 < R3), and tail-wagging differences can be a useful clue, as noted for females.

Voice and Sounds

Calls all much like Black-chinned Hummingbird, and these two species typically not distinguishable by voice. Chase calls of Ruby-throated may average slightly buzzier overall, but note that male calls tend to be higher and buzzier than female calls. Common call a slightly twangy or nasal chip, *chih* or *tchih* and *tchew*, given in flight and perched, at times repeated fairly steadily by perched birds, with doubled notes interspersed. Also quick, short, slightly twittering series by feeding birds, *chi ti-ti* and *chi-ti ti-ti-ti*, etc. More varied and often stronger twitters in interactions, e.g., *chi ti-chi-chi-chi chi-chi*, and higher pitched chase calls often with wiry or slightly buzzy quality, *si chi-chi-chi* and *chih si-si-si-si si-chi* and *tssir ti-ti ssir-si*, etc. In general, calls lack strongly buzzy or sharp, smacking quality of Anna's and *Selasphorus*, and are also distinct from high, tinny to liquid chips and twitters of Costa's.

Male's wings make a quiet hum in flight, higher and softer than strong buzz of male Black-chinned Hummingbird, and loudest during shuttles. In dive display, male produces a relatively soft wing buzzing, and a rapid, slightly pulsating, sharp series of about 5 shrill, cricket-like notes at bottom point of dive[7,11].

Habitat

Deciduous and mixed woodland, parks, and gardens in general, also open and semi-open areas with hedges and flower banks; often in low coastal vegetation during migration. Winters mainly in humid second-growth habitats, hedges, forest edge, and weedy fields with flowers; less often in drier habitats where Black-chinned Hummingbird is most common.

Behavior

Feeds and perches low to high, and regularly visits feeders. Feeding birds typically hold their tail closed to slightly spread, in or near the body plane, with occasional quivers and dips but not wagged persistently as often done by Black-chinned Hummingbird. In windy conditions, however, Ruby-throat flips and spreads its tail more often, and at times wags it fairly persistently, similar to Black-chinned. Also, Ruby-throateds hovering (such as on approach to a feeder) and maneuvering among flowers spread and flip or wag their tail. Mostly seems not to occur in large concentrations in North America (as do Black-chinneds in much of the West), except for notable fall migration gatherings along Texas coast.

Displays appear broadly similar to those of Black-chinned Hummingbird but dive displays of both species require further critical observation and description across the species' ranges. Ruby-throated's dive trajectories are more often deeper than wide, i.e., more U-shaped than the shallower, pedulum-arc trajectories typical of Black-chinned. All ages/sexes of Ruby-throated make dive displays in aggressive context[10]: bird climbs to 3–15 m above subject and makes repeated U-shaped to pedulum-arc swoops about 3–10 m diameter over subject; swoops commonly repeated about 5–10 times, but only 1–2 times if successful in aggressive interactions, and rarely up to 15–20 times[7,9,10,11]. In shuttle display male flies back-and-forth rapidly in front of and over subject in short-wavelength (0.5 m or less) convoluted arcs.

Molt

Molt occurs on winter grounds. Primary molt starts October (rarely late September) to January, ends February to April, averaging later in immatures. Adult molt averages later than Black-chinned Hummingbird but immatures can have similar molt schedules. Male gorgets typically are last feathers to be molted, after primary molt has been completed, mainly during February to March in adults, March to April in immatures.

Description

All ages/sexes can show fairly large, round to oval white flank patches, especially obvious on hovering birds and apparently due to misarranged feathers.

Adult male: gorget ruby-red to orange-red (latter especially when worn, in winter) with black chin, separated from green-mottled underparts by white forecollar. Variable whitish median stripe down underparts, and fluffy white vent band; under-tail-coverts dusky to bronzy green with whitish edging. Crown, nape, and upperparts golden green to emerald-green, duller and darker when worn (mainly late fall into winter). White post-ocular spot (often small or lacking) contrasts with dark auriculars. **Tail:** R1 golden green to slightly bluish green, R2–R5 blackish with variable green edging mainly on outer webs, broadest on R2 which can be almost wholly green on some birds; R3–R5 typically look all-black in the field. Bill black, feet blackish.

Adult female: crown, nape, and upperparts golden green to emerald green (darker and bluer when worn), with the crown on some birds becoming worn and relatively dusky, mainly in fall and winter; pale buff tips to upperparts in fresh plumage can be retained on at least tertials and rump through late summer. Lores dark, and dusky auriculars offset white post-ocular spot; rarely shows a pale gray post-ocular line. Throat and underparts unmarked dingy whitish, often with paler forecollar extending back into sides of neck; sides/flanks washed dusky buff, usually with buffy-cinnamon spot on hind flanks where shows as buff spot posterior to legs on hovering birds (worn fall adults often lack buff on flanks). Throat often has lines of indistinct, fine dusky flecks, and exceptionally (in birds 5 years or older[10]) can have one to a few ruby-red feathers. **Tail (Figure 1):** R1 golden green (with blackish tip on up to 10% of birds), R2 green with broad black tip, (and fine whitish tip when fresh), R3–R5 mostly black with restricted green (tending to gray on R5) basally and bold white tips.

Immature male: resembles adult female overall but plumage in fall fresher, upperparts with neat, narrow buff to buffy cinnamon tips, and auricular mask often darker, in stronger contrast to whiter throat. Whitish throat typically has lines of distinct dark flecks; some birds have only a few lines of indistinct, fine dusky flecks, while others have overall whitish, unflecked throats but with relatively large splotches of ruby-red. Most, but not all, birds with flecked throats have one or more ruby-red feathers scattered, or concentrated, on the lower throat. The sides and flanks are often quite bright buffy cinnamon in fresh plumage, but by September can be relatively dull, dusky vinaceous. **Tail:** slightly longer and more forked than an adult female, rectrices slightly narrower and more tapered with slightly narrower and less contrasting blackish median band, and slightly smaller white tips to R3–R5. Adult plumage attained by complete molt over the winter, ending with the gorget in late winter and spring, although some first-summer birds can have fine white tips to outer rectrices[10].

Immature female: resembles adult female overall but fall plumage fresher, with face and primaries typically darker; upperparts with neat, narrow buff to buffy-cinnamon tips that can veil green of crown. Whitish throat typically unmarked or with faint dusky flecks. Sides and flanks often quite bright buffy cinnamon, at least in fresh plumage (through August). **Tail:** much like adult female but rectrices average slightly broader and more rounded at tips, R4 often slightly < R3. Adult plumage attained by complete molt over the winter.

Hybrids
Presumed with Black-chinned Hummingbird[1].

References
[1]Baltosser & Russell 2000, [2]Campbell *et al*. 1990, [3]CBRC unpubl. data, [4]Kessel 1989, [5]B. Mactavish pers. comm., [6]NAB, [7]B. Palmer-Ball pers. comm., [8]Pyle 1997, [9]Robinson *et al*. 1996, [10]R. R. Sargent pers. comm., [11]D. Sibley pers. comm.

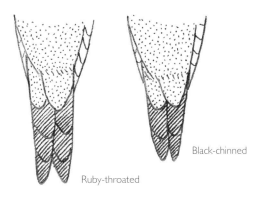

Figure 3. Comparison of tail shapes (as viewed from above) of adult male Ruby-throated and Black-chinned hummingbirds. R1 on both species is green (stippled), concolorous with the upperparts. Note Ruby-throated's longer, more deeply forked tail with 3 black (hatched) rectrix tips (R2–R4) visible beyond R1; Black-chinned has shorter, less deeply forked tail with 2 black rectrix tips (R2–R3) visible beyond R1.

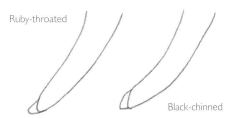

Figure 4. Comparison of wing-tip shapes in Ruby-throated and Black-chinned hummingbirds. Note more tapered tip of Ruby-throated, with P10 narrower than P9, blunter tip of Black-chinned, with P10 similar in width to P9.

16.1 Adult male Ruby-throated. Unmistakable in this view, note the black chin and face, and the deeply forked tail with R4 longest (cf. Pic. 17.1). Alan Murphy. Houston, Texas, September 1996.

16.2 Adult male Ruby-throated. With gorget colors not visible, note narrow P10, notched inner webs of the tapered inner primaries (which often get bunched up like this on *Archilochus*), long projection of tail beyond the wing tip, and glittering green crown (cf. Pic. 17.2). Charles W. Melton. Rio Hondo, Texas, 20 April 1994.

16.3 Adult male Ruby-throated. Beside the obvious gorget, note the diagnostic primary shapes with a narrow and pointed wing tip. Reflection from the gorget makes the mandible appear red, and the crown is dusted with pollen. Alan Murphy. Houston, Texas, September 2000.

16.4 Adult female Ruby-throated. Narrow inner primaries and face pattern point to *Archilochus*. Short bill and tapered primaries (creating tapered wing tip) indicate Ruby-throated. Note the dull crown (sometimes believed a character for Black-chinned; but see Pics 16.5–16.6) and the relatively blackish (fresh) primaries (cf. Pic. 16.5). Larry Sansone. Dry Tortugas, Florida, 15 April 1991.

16.5 Adult female Ruby-throated. Same features apply as Pic 16.4 but narrow P10 shows better; note the relatively faded (worn) primaries, perhaps exaggerated by the flash photo. Alan Murphy. Houston, Texas, September 2000.

16.6 Adult female Ruby-throated. Face pattern, buffy flank wash, whitish undertail-coverts, and tail pattern point to *Archilochus*. Short bill and relatively rounded tips to outer rectrices, with R4 longest, indicate Ruby-throated (cf. Pic. 17.6). Charles W. Melton. Carthage, Texas, 16 May 1998.

16.7 Immature male Ruby-throated. Face pattern and relatively long tail point to *Archilochus*, confirmed by relatively broad outer four primaries and narrow inner primaries. Fresh plumage in fall points to immature and dark-flecked throat with two ruby-red feathers indicates immature male Ruby-throated. Note also the notched inner webs of the inner primaries and narrow, tapered outer web of P10, both diagnostic of Ruby-throated. Structural features such as these are more important than field marks such as crown color – dull on this bird, a feature often associated with Black-chinned. Alan Murphy. Houston, Texas, September 2000.

16.8 Immature male Ruby-throated. Fresh plumage (buff-tipped upperparts, buff wash to sides) in fall indicates an immature, and dark-spotted throat and relatively long tail with narrow and tapered outer rectrices an immature male. Short bill and and long tail projection (at about its maximum on this bird) beyond tapered wing tips indicate Ruby-throated. Larry Ditto. McAllen, Texas, September 1999.

16.9 Immature female Ruby-throated. Fresh plumage (e.g., buff tips to crown and auriculars) indicates age, and narrow inner primaries point to *Archilochus*. The plain throat and vestigial notches on the inner webs of the inner primaries indicate a female. This bird looks atypically short billed, and note the relatively narrow and tapered primaries that end in a tapered rather than broad and blunt wing tip. Sid & Shirley Rucker. Rockport, Texas, September 1997.

16.10 Immature female Ruby-throated. Bright cinnamon flanks could suggest *Selasphorus* but note narrow inner primaries (with striking change in width from P5 to P7) diagnostic of *Archilochus*, and unmarked whitish throat. The short bill and relatively narrow and tapered P10 (look carefully) indicate Ruby-throated; fresh buff tipping to upperparts, short tail, and unmarked whitish throat indicate immature female. Larry Ditto. McAllen, Texas, September 1996.

16.11 Immature female Ruby-throated. Fresh plumage in fall (buff tips to upperparts, vinaceous-buff flanks) indicates immature. Face pattern and whitish undertail-coverts point to *Archilochus*, and also note the relatively broad outer four primaries. The relatively short bill, evenly tapering tip to outer web of P10, and bright, contrasting plumage all indicate Ruby-throated; a clean white throat indicates immature female, supported by lack of distinct notches on inner webs of inner primaries (cf. Pic. 16.7). Ralph Paonessa. Finger Lakes region, New York, August 1995.

17 Black-chinned Hummingbird

(Archilochus alexandri)

8.5–9.5 cm (3.3–3.8 in). Bill 16–22 mm (female > male).
Pics I.1–I.3, I.16, I.18, I.21–I.23, I.27–I.29, ii, v, 17.1–17.11.

Identification summary
Small size. Bill medium-long and straightish (longer on female). Male's black gorget with bluish-violet lower band diagnostic, although often looks black overall; note also dark face and white postocular spot (cf. male Broad-tailed Hummingbird), and primary shapes and shorter, less deeply forked tail (cf. male Ruby-throated Hummingbird). Female and immature gray-and-white overall. Tail forked to double-rounded with R3 ≥ R4 (**Figure 1**). Inner primaries relatively narrow (a feature shared with Ruby-

Rare to casual in SE U.S. in winter; see text.

throated), P10 relatively broad and blunt-tipped (narrow and tapered on Ruby-throated). At rest, wing tips fall short of tail tip. Call a soft, twangy chip. Molts in winter.

Taxonomy
No subspecies formally described. A 'diminutive race' was alluded to by Phillips[14] and Baltosser[2], with more information provided by Baltosser and Russell[3]. Black-chinneds breeding from S Texas south an undetermined distance into central Mexico average smaller than birds in most of North American range, e.g., male culmen 15.6–18.2 mm vs. 18.3–20.6 mm, female culmen 17.7–19 mm vs. 19–22.1 mm[3].

Status and Distribution
Summer resident (mainly March to September) in western North America, from S and W Texas N and W (mainly in drier interior areas) to S British Columbia, and W to S California. Spring migrants (males precede females by 1–2 weeks) arrive back in SW U.S. in late February and March, reaching coastal S California by late March or early April, Utah and Colorado by mid to late April, and British Columbia by late April or early May. In fall, most depart N parts of breeding range by late August, with migrants in the SW U.S. through late September, rarely into October.

Rare migrant (in spring and autumn) to coastal areas from central California N to S British Columbia, and through W Great Plains. Casual N (mainly June–July) to S Alberta and Saskatchewan, and E and NE (mainly late April to May, and

November) as far afield as Ontario, Nova Scotia[12], New Jersey[5], and Florida[18].

Rare but apparently increasing vagrant or winter visitor (mainly October to March) at feeders in SE U.S. (where apparently more numerous overall than Ruby-throated, based on numbers of birds banded; however, ratios vary regionally within the Southeast as well as between years and even within winters[13]). Winters mainly along and near Gulf coast and N locally to the Carolinas, occasionally W through E Texas to New Mexico[13]; also casual in winter (December to February) in S California[6].

Range
Breeds W North America to N Mexico, winters mainly in W Mexico.

Field Identification

Structure
Small, with a straightish, medium-long bill (longer on female). Adult male tail forked (R3 longest; **Figure 3**), female and immature male tail slightly double-rounded (R3 typically longest; **Figure 1**); outer rectrices of adult female and immature male often with distinctly pinched-in or nipple-like tips. At rest, wing tips fall short of tail tip (especially adult males) or may approach tail tip (some immature females). Primaries relatively broad and blunt-tipped, especially diagnostic on P10. Inner primaries of female and immature lack acute notch on inner webs.

Similar species
Several other gorgeted hummers look similar to Black-chinned but with prolonged, close-range study (especially of perched birds where details of wing structure can be seen), most individuals can be identified. While the most similar species to Black-chinned is its eastern North American counterpart, Ruby-throated Hummingbird, the breeding distributions of these two are mostly separate so many summer birds are identified by default range. The two species can occur together, however, mainly through the Great Plains (especially during migration) and, increasingly, in the SE U.S. in winter; see below for distinguishing characters. In western North America in summer, Black-chinned occurs side-by-side with Anna's and Costa's hummingbirds, females and immatures of which provide frequent identification problems.

Adult males
Adult male Black-chinned only similar to Ruby-throated Hummingbird and Broad-tailed Hummingbird (assuming gorgets do not catch the light). Male Anna's and Costa's have iridescent 'helmets,' not just gorgets, broad inner primaries, and distinctive call notes.

Adult male Ruby-throated Hummingbird (mainly E North America) averages shorter billed than Black-chinned, with ruby-red throat and black chin. Often the throat simply looks black, however, like a Black-chinned. In such cases, note tail shape (assuming a bird is not molting): male Ruby-throated has deeply forked tail with R4 longest and three approximately equal-spaced tips visible beyond green R1, male Black-chinned has 'double-rounded' fork (R3 longest) with shorter projection of only two approximately equal-spaced tips visible beyond R1 (**Figure 3**). At rest, wing tip falls at about tip of R1, so perched male Ruby-throated has longer tail projection. Also note narrower primaries of Ruby-throated, especially P8–P10: wing tip of Ruby-throated looks narrow and pointed versus broad and blunt on Black-chinned. On some birds in mid and late winter, tip of P10 can be so worn that shape cannot be determined; note that Black-chinned molts on average about a month earlier than Ruby-throated, and that point reached by primary molt may be a feature to support identification. Also, Ruby-throated tends to be deeper, more golden green above, including the crown, Black-chinned duller, more bronzy-green or bluish-green above, with dusky crown. Dorsal colors vary with the light, however, and worn plumage tends to be bluer than fresh plumage. Adult male Black-chinned typically makes a distinct wing hum in flight (almost suggesting Rufous/Allen's at times), while Ruby-throated male has quieter and less noticeable wing noise. Male Black-chinned often wags its tail strongly, while Ruby-throated's tail is usually held more stiffly and quivered rather than wagged or pumped, but this is not diagnostic.

Adult male **Broad-tailed Hummingbird** (mainly W mountains) slightly larger and stockier with magenta-rose gorget. Eyes set in pale area that extends under chin, unlike black face and contrasting white post-ocular spot of Black-chinned. Closed tail longer, green with broad, green, notch-tipped R1 covering closed tail (versus notched black tip on Black-chinned) and spread tail has rufous edging on inner rectrices. Inner primaries broad, and P10 finely attenuate to create distinctive wing-trill in flight, very different from lower wing buzz of Black-chinned. Call a sharp chip.

Females
When confronted with a problem bird in fall, determining its age is an important first step. Look for freshness of plumage (especially distinct buff tips to upperparts and secondaries) as an indicator of immatures, unlike the often duller metallic greens and more faded, browner primaries of worn-plumaged adults (but note that adults can retain narrow pale buff tips to tertials and rump through at least late summer).

In the west, Black-chinned occurs side-by-side with Costa's and Anna's hummingbirds, and females/immatures of these three are notoriously similar. Important features to check are face pattern, tail length, shape of inner primaries, call notes, and primary molt.

Rarely, some (mainly immature) Black-chinneds have the flanks washed quite strongly and extensively with buff or cinnamon, but confusion with Rufous/Allen's hummingbirds should not be a problem: these have brighter buffy-cinnamon to cinnamon-rufous flanks, distinct rufous in the tail, and stronger and sharper chipping calls.

Female Costa's Hummingbird superficially very similar to Black-chinned but smaller (noticeable in direct comparison) and shorter tailed, overall stockier and relatively bigger headed. Costa's has shorter, more strongly rounded tail (R5 proportionately shorter, often noticeable from below; **Figure 1**), more rounded outer rectrices, broad inner primaries (but P10 relatively narrower), and very distinct call a high-pitched, tinking and twittering. At rest, Costa's wing tips usually project slightly beyond the short tail (versus wings tips shorter than tail tip on Black-chinned). Costa's tail pattern superficially similar to Black-chinned but black median band narrower, with relatively more extensive greenish gray visible at base of spread tail, especially noticeable on outer rectrices (**Figure 1**).

Another excellent field identification character is molt timing: most Costa's molt in summer and fall, so any bird with obvious wing molt in summer should not be Black-chinned. Conversely, birds molting outer primaries in late winter are unlikely to be Costa's.

Most Costa's can also be distinguished from Black-chinned by relatively subtle plumage differences. While such differences may be apparent to observers familiar with both species, problem birds still occur, and structure, call, and molt timing should always be checked on such birds.

Costa's often looks plainer and duller overall, more washed out and grayish above than Black-chinned, and its face typically features a diffuse pale gray post-ocular stripe that wraps around smoothly dusky auriculars (versus a more contrasting white post-ocular spot and darker auriculars on Black-chinned) and a pale gray supraloral stripe (indistinct or absent on most Black-chinneds). The underparts of female Costa's often look dingier overall than Black-chinned, rarely with a distinct whitish forecollar, and Costa's lacks the contrasting (and long) white undertail-coverts and distinct buffy flank wash common on Black-chinned.

Feeding Costa's often wag and fan their tail, as does Black-chinned, but Costa's tail action looks weaker and more fluttery than the strong pumping tail action of Black-chinned. This is due to the latter's longer tail and, hence, it also has a more pronounced wag. Lastly, bill length and shape have been suggested as characters for separating female Costa's and Black-chinned, but these characters seem to overlap enough to make them little use for identification, although the longest-billed female Black-chinneds look distinct from any Costa's.

Female Anna's Hummingbird slightly larger (noticeable in direct comparison), stockier, bigger headed, and proportionately shorter billed and shorter tailed than Black-chinned, with broad inner primaries but relatively narrower and more tapered P10, and more smacking call. Feeding Anna's tends to hold the tail relatively rigid with occasional flicks and flashes, but on occasion hovers and feeds while wagging the tail strongly, like typical Black-chinned. Anna's has superficially similar tail pattern to Black-chinned but tail more evenly rounded (R1 proportionately longer), rectrices broader and blunter, and black median band narrower, with relatively more extensive greenish gray visible at base of spread tail (**Figure 1**).

Molt timing can be very useful in identification: most Anna's molt in summer and fall, so any bird with obvious wing molt in summer should not be Black-chinned. Conversely, birds molting outer primaries in late winter should not be Anna's.

Adult female Anna's typically is duskier below than Black-chinned, with green-mottled sides/flanks, and a splash of rose-pink to orangish red on throat. Immature female Anna's paler below than adult with little or no green mottling on sides/flanks, throat can lack color, and forecollar can be contrastingly paler (even whitish), thus much more similar to Black-chinned than is adult Anna's. Immature female Anna's lacks subtly contrasting whitish undertail-coverts often shown by female/immature Black-chinned, often has pale post-ocular stripe (versus white post-ocular spot typical of Black-chinned), distinct whitish supraloral stripe (usually indistinct or absent on Black-chinned), and wags its tail infrequently, all features that may be useful in drawing attention to a different bird. Identification should be confirmed by structure and voice.

Female Ruby-throated Hummingbird (mainly E North America) very similar to Black-chinned and under typical field conditions many birds are best called *Archilochus* sp., without attempting to force an identification. Given good views, however, the two species can be distinguished. Best feature is wing shape, especially the shape of P10: Ruby-throated has relatively narrower and more tapered primaries throughout, often most noticeable on P8–P10 such that wing tip appears relatively narrow and tapered on Ruby-throated, broad and blunt-tipped on Black-chinned (**Figure 4**). On birds in mid to late winter, however, tips of outer primaries can be so worn and frayed that it is not possible to determine shape.

Subtleties in shape of inner six primaries may be useful given good views and/or sharp photos: these feathers are more acutely tapered on Ruby-throated, adult females of which have a notch on the inner web; (see figure 101 of Pyle[15]); immature female Ruby-throated, however, is more similar in this regard to adult and immature female Black-chinned.

Other useful features are tail shape and bill length. Adult female Black-chinned typically has nipple-like tips to the outer rectrices, unlike the more evenly tapered (or rounded) tips of adult female Ruby-throated and immature female Black-chinned, and Black-chinned's tail typically has R3 > R4 (versus R4 $\geq$ R3 on adult Ruby-throated; **Figure 1**). Black-chinned is longer billed than Ruby-throated and, while bill measurements overlap, the longest-billed Black-chinned and shortest-billed Ruby-throated may be distinguishable with experience.

In general, Ruby-throated is deeper green above and whiter below, and typically appears more contrasting overall, than Black-chinned, which is duller green above and dingier below. Fresh primaries of both species are similarly dark but Black-chinned molts earlier and lives in more arid habitats which may help explain why its primaries often look browner and more worn than on an adult Ruby-throated at the same season.

Adult Black-chinned molts on average about a month earlier than Ruby-throated, such that the point reached by primary molt could be a useful identification character. Adults molt earlier than immatures, however, so adult female Ruby-throated might be at similar molt stage as immature Black-chinned, and perhaps only most advanced birds (adult female Black-chinneds) could be identified by molt timing. More work is needed on the reliability of molt timing as an aid to specific identification of winter hummingbirds.

Black-chinned often wags and spreads its tail frequently and at times persistently while hovering and feeding. Ruby-throated usually holds its tail rigid, quivering or flashing it only slightly (as does Black-chinned at times). While persistent tail-wagging suggests Black-chinned, any identification should be confirmed by unequivocal structural features.

Female Calliope Hummingbird (mainly W mountains) distinctly smaller, shorter tailed, and shorter billed than Black-chinned with broad inner primaries and soft, chipping call. At rest, Calliope's wing tips project slightly beyond its short tail which typically has narrow rufous edging to bases of rectrices (often hard to see). Calliope consistently has the sides/flanks and undertail-coverts washed pale cinnamon (as do some fresh-plumaged juvenile Black-chinneds) and this color often extends up into sides of neck, its throat is typically marked by lines of fine dusky flecks, and its 'softer' face has white lores with a dark loral crescent.

Female Broad-tailed Hummingbird (mainly Great Basin and Rocky mountains) slightly larger and stockier than Black-chinned with larger and broader primaries and broad tail that has rufous at base (reduced or virtually lacking on some immature females). Broad-tailed also has cinnamon-washed sides/flanks and undertail-coverts, dusky-flecked throat, and sharp chip call.

Dull **female Broad-billed Hummingbird** (SW U.S.) can suggest Black-chinned Hummingbird, or *vice versa*. The two species often occur side-by-side at feeders, are of similar size, and both habitually tail-wag. Broad-billed has broad inner primaries, pinkish mandible base (can be hard to see), and emerald-green spotting on chest sides. Dusky auricular mask and pale post-ocular stripe of Broad-billed typically distinct but most poorly marked birds approach most strongly marked (usually immature) Black-chinneds. Also note distinctly different calls, and less extensive white tail corners of Broad-billed.

Immature males
Immature male Black-chins can be distinguished from immature males and females of similar species by much the same combination of characters discussed for females; note that immature males have shorter bills than females and often have a darker auricular mask and whiter throat and forecollar. The most similar species is again Ruby-throated Hummingbird.

Immature male Ruby-throated Hummingbird has, on average, slightly shorter bill but is best identified by shape of outer primaries: tapered and relatively narrow on Ruby-throated versus broader and blunt-tipped on Black-chinned (see **Figure 4**). Many immatures in fall show one or more spots of diagnostic throat color; be especially aware of lighting when evaluating the color of single iridescent spots – ruby-red can easily appear black. The inner primaries of Ruby-throated also are relatively tapered, and show a distinct notch on the inner web. While differences in P10 shape can be obscured in mid to late winter by feather wear, by such time most birds show patches of diagnostic throat color – ruby-red in Ruby-throated, black and bluish violet in Black-chinned. Ruby-throated also averages longer tailed, and tail-wagging differences can be a useful clue, as noted for females.

Immature male Costa's Hummingbird has longer tail than female such that wing tips of perched birds can fall slightly short of tail tip, but tail still relatively short and more rounded (R5 proportionately shorter, and outer rectrices narrower than Black-chinned). Also note broad inner primaries, call, molt timing, and dingier upperparts. Tail patterns of immature males more similar than of females because immature male Black-chinned has narrower blackish subterminal band, more extensive greenish gray at base of outer rectrices. Many immature male Costa's have more contrastingly marked face than females, with darker auricular mask setting off the pale gray post-ocular stripe more strongly, and their whitish throat often has a central splash of purple, but it is not heavily flecked or spotted.

Voice and Sounds
Calls all much like Ruby-throated Hummingbird, and these two species typically not distinguishable by voice. Chase calls of Ruby-throated may average slightly buzzier overall, but note that male calls tend to be higher and buzzier than female calls. Common call a slightly twangy or nasal chip, *tchih* or *tchew*, given in flight and perched, at times repeated fairly steadily by perched birds, with doubled notes interspersed, *tchih, tchih, tchih, tchi-chih, tchih...,* or *chih chih chi-tih...,* etc. Also quick, short, twittering series by feeding birds, *chi-ti-ti,* or *chi-tih ti-ti-ti,* and variations. More varied and stronger twitters in interactions, *tchip-i-chi ti-chip-i-chi,* or *tchi-chi chi-chi-chi-chi,* and at times harsher and buzzier twitters, *chi ti ssi-ssi-ssi-chi* or *tssiuh chi-chi-chi-chir,* etc. In general, calls lack strongly buzzy or sharp, smacking quality of Anna's and *Selasphorus,* and are also distinct from high, tinny to liquid chips and twitters of Costa's.

Male's wings make a distinct low buzz in flight, notably stronger and lower than male Ruby-throated Hummingbird's wing hum, and loudest during shuttle display. In dive display, male produces two loud, abrupt buzzes, *zzt zzr,* at top points of arc (i.e., end points of U trajectory), and makes a short, stuttering whistled *whi-whi-whi-whi-*

whi or *wü-wü-wü-wü-wü-wü-wü-wü-wü* at bottom point of dive; stutter comprises about 5–10 notes[9,16].

Habitat

Brushy woodland and scrub, especially riparian groves and other areas near streams, open and semi-open areas with hedges and flower banks, gardens. Winters mainly in arid to semi-arid second-growth habitats, thorn-forest edge, less often in humid habitats where Ruby-throated Hummingbird is more common.

Behavior

Feeds and perches low to high, and regularly visits feeders where often a numerically dominant species at many interior western locations – literally hundreds, if not thousands, of Black-chins can be visiting batteries of feeders in SE Arizona on any day in late summer and autumn. Often wags or pumps tail strongly while hovering, e.g., on approach to a feeder, and also may feed while wagging spread to closed tail. At other times birds feed with tail mostly closed and held in or near body plane, with only slight quivering, and occasional dips or flashes, mainly when maneuvering.

Displays appear similar to those of Ruby-throated Hummingbird but dive displays of both species require further critical observation and description across the species' ranges. Black-chinned's dive trajectories more often wider than deep, i.e., shallower, pedulum-like arcs rather than U-shaped dives more typical of Ruby-throated. In Black-chinned, male climbs in shallow angle ascent to 3–20 m and makes repeated pedulum-arc to U-shaped swoops of about 3–30 m diameter over subject; arcs typically repeated 2–10 times in series[3,9,17]; in aggressive interactions male also swings back and forth through shallow-arc to level trajectory of 1–2 m above subject[7]. In shuttle display male flies back-and-forth rapidly in front of and over subject in short-wavelength (0.5 m or less) convoluted arcs.

Molt

Molt occurs mostly on winter grounds (rarely can start with inner primaries on summer grounds or during migration[8]). Primary molt mainly starts September (rarely from mid July[8]) to January, ends January to April, averaging later in immatures. Adult molt averages earlier than Ruby-throated Hummingbird (but immatures can have similar molt schedules), and much later than Costa's Hummingbird (but immature Costa's can molt at same time as adult Black-chinneds). Male gorgets typically are last feathers to be molted, after primary molt has been completed, mainly during February in adults, March in immatures. Observations of two July adults with contrastingly fresh P8–10 (male) and P9–10 (female), relative to distinctly worn and browner inner primaries, suggest primary molt may suspend on some birds in mid-winter[8] (see Pic. I.28).

Description

All ages/sexes can show fairly large, round to oval white flank patches, especially obvious on hovering birds and apparently due to misarranged feathers.

Adult male: gorget black with broad violet to violet-blue band across bottom, separated from green-mottled underparts by white forecollar. Variable whitish median stripe down underparts, and fluffy white vent band; undertail-coverts dusky to bronzy green with whitish edging. Crown, nape, and upperparts golden green to blue-green, darker and duller when worn (mainly late fall into winter), typically with the crown dusky. White post-ocular spot (rarely almost obsolete, and rarely a short white streak) contrasts with dark auriculars. **Tail:** R1 bronzy green to bluish green, R2–R5 blackish with variable green edging mainly on outer webs, broadest on R2 which can be almost wholly green on some birds; R3–R5 typically look all-black in the field. Bill black, feet blackish.

Adult female: crown, nape, and upperparts golden green to blue-green (duller when worn), typically with the crown dusky or duller green; pale buff tips to upperparts in fresh plumage can be retained on at least tertials and rump through late summer. Lores dark, and dusky auriculars offset white post-ocular spot; rarely shows a pale gray post-ocular line. Throat and underparts dingy whitish, often with paler forecollar offset by duskier sides/flanks that can be washed vinaceous-buff, especially on lower flanks and show as buff spot posterior to legs on hovering birds (worn fall adults often lack buff on flanks); some birds relatively plain dusky on underbody with whitish median stripe. Vent band white and undertail-coverts white with faintly duskier centers, often appearing as contrastingly whiter crissum. Throat plain on many birds, while others have lines of dusky flecks, often darkest and most concentrated on median throat. Some adult females can have one or more black and/or violet throat feathers[9]. **Tail (Figure 1):** R1 golden green to bluish green (with blackish tip on up to 10% of birds), R2 green with broad black tip (and fine whitish tip when fresh), R3–R5 mostly black with restricted green (tending to gray on R5) basally and bold white tips.

Immature male: resembles adult female overall but more variable. Plumage fresher in fall, upperparts with neat buff tips ranging from narrow to bold, often heaviest on head where can appear as buff to whitish blotches. Pale tips range from cinnamon-buff to whitish, some of the heaviest-veiled birds having relatively gray-looking upperparts, suggesting Costa's Hummingbird. On others, pale tips soon abrade to reveal bright emerald-green upperparts, suggesting Ruby-throated Hummingbird. Auriculars often mottled blackish, in strong contrast to white throat, and offsetting white post-ocular spot. Throat typically has lines of distinct dark flecks, varying from heaviest at sides to concentrated in center. One or more black and/or violet feathers often scattered, or concentrated, on lower throat. Exceptionally heavily marked birds have whole throat and auriculars dark with heavy whitish scalloping, creating 'hooded' effect. White forecollar often more contrasting than female. Flanks typically washed buff to pale cinnamon, this color often concentrated at rear where shows as buff spot posterior to legs on hovering birds. On some, sides/flanks heavily pigmented and dusky feather centers can appear as neat rows of dusky spots, suggesting mottled effect of Anna's Hummingbird. Undertail-coverts often appear as contrasting whiter crissum, like female, but on some birds have relatively strong dusky centers. **Tail:** slightly less rounded relative to adult female, rectrices with narrower and less contrasting blackish median band (so greenish basal area more extensive), R1 without black distally, and white tips to R3–R5 slightly smaller.

Immature female: resembles adult female overall but fall plumage fresher, with face and primaries typically darker; upperparts with neat buff tips ranging from narrow to bold (see immature male). More often shows pale gray post-ocular stripe (and whiter post-ocular spot) than adult, thus suggesting Costa's Hummingbird. Throat dingy whitish, unmarked or with lines of faint dusky flecks. On some, dingy throat appears to blend into auriculars with little contrast, especially when viewed head-on. Sides/flanks typically with some buffy wash, often showing as buffy-cinnamon spot posterior to legs on hovering birds. **Tail:** similar to adult female but outer rectrices average slightly broader and more rounded at tips. Adult plumage attained by complete molt over the winter.

Hybrids

With Anna's, Costa's, and Broad-tailed hummingbirds[4], Allen's Hummingbird[11]; presumed with Ruby-throated Hummingbird[3] and Lucifer Hummingbird[10]; possibly with Blue-throated Hummingbird[1].

References

[1]Baldridge *et al.* 1983, [2]Baltosser 1987, [3]Baltosser & Russell 2000, [4]Banks & Johnson 1961, [5]Crossley 1997, [6]Garrett & Dunn 1981, [7]S. N. G. Howell pers. obs., [8]S. N. G. Howell unpubl. data, [9]R. Hoyer pers. comm., [10]Lasley *et al.* 1996, [11]Lynch & Ames 1970, [12]McLaren 1999, [13]NAB, [14]Phillips 1982, [15]Pyle 1997, [16]Pytte & Ficken 1994, [17]W. C. Russell pers. comm., [18]Stevenson & Anderson 1994.

17.1 Adult male Black-chinned. Note the diagnostic tail shape versus Ruby-throated, with R3 longest (cf. Pic. 16.1). William E. Grenfell. Placer Co., California, June 1994.

17.2 Adult male Black-chinned. The narrow inner primaries (bunched up) and dark face with white post-ocular spot indicate *Archilochus*. With the gorget colors not visible, note broad P10, short projection of tail beyond the wing tip, and dusky crown (cf. Pic. 16.2). Brian E. Small. Miller Canyon, Arizona, July 1999.

17.3 Adult male Black-chinned. When it catches the light like this, the violet lower gorget band of male Black-chinned is diagnostic. Also note the short tail projection. Rick & Nora Bowers. Sonoita, Arizona, September 1997.

17.4 Adult female Black-chinned. The grayness of face and underparts, and even some dark on the throat, suggest Anna's Hummingbird but note the relatively long bill, small head, and, especially, the relatively narrow inner primaries (with P7 strikingly broader) which identify this as an *Archilochus*. The long bill and blunt P10 (plus the overall relatively broad and truncate primaries, lacking a notch on the inners) indicate Black-chinned. William E. Grenfell. Placer Co., California, June 1995.

17.5 Adult female Black-chinned. Adult females can retain buff on flanks into summer; together with face pattern and the long tail with plain whitish undertail-coverts, this rules out Anna's and Costa's. Separating this bird from Ruby-throated is problematic, based upon what is visible. The dull head suggests Black-chinned and the long bill would be another feature to check. Charles W. Melton. Madera Canyon, Arizona, 18 May 1997.

17.6 Adult female Black-chinned. Face pattern and relatively long bill and tail point to *Archilochus* (versus *Calypte*), and note also the small cinnamon flank spot. Tail shape, with R3 longest, and the nipple-like tips to R5–R4 are diagnostic of Black-chinned (cf. Pic. 16.6). Other pointers for Black-chinned (versus Ruby-throated) are the long bill, dusky spotting on the median throat, and overall dingy underparts. Ian C. Tait. Madera Canyon, Arizona, May 1997.

17.7 Immature male Black-chinned. A combination of face pattern, buffy flanks, tail length, and, most importantly, narrow inner primaries, indicate *Archilochus*. Fresh plumage at this season indicates an immature, and the heavily spotted throat and relatively long tail point to a male. The relatively blunt primaries and wing tip identify this bird as Black-chinned. Larry Sansone. Portal, Arizona, 5 July 2000.

17.8 Immature male Black-chinned. In fall, fresh buff tipping to upperparts indicates an immature; dark on the throat indicates a male; and face pattern and narrow inner primaries point to *Archilochus*. The relatively blunt primaries, especially P10, indicate Black-chinned. Compare this male's relatively short bill with Pic. 17.10, and note how the raised primaries accentuate the tail projection. John H. Hoffman. Madera Canyon, Arizona, September 1976.

17.9 Immature male Black-chinned. The relatively narrow inner primaries and face pattern point to *Archilochus*, and the fresh plumage an immature. The broad and truncate primaries and heavily marked throat indicate immature male Black-chinned. Charles W. Melton. Miller Canyon, Arizona, 14 August 2000.

17.10 Immature female Black-chinned. In fall, fresh buff tipping to upperparts, tertials, and primary coverts indicate an immature, and face pattern and relatively narrow inner primaries point to *Archilochus*. The relatively long bill and broad, blunt primaries suggest Black-chinned, and the widening outer web to P10 clinches the identification. Note how the slightly drooped and spread wings appear relatively close to the tail tip, and cf. Pic. 17.8. John H. Hoffman. Sonoita, Arizona, October 1990.

17.11 Immature Black-chinned (apparently female). Fresh plumage in fall and narrow inner primaries point to an immature *Archilochus*. The overall broad and blunt primaries are diagnostic of Black-chinned, and note also the poorly contrasting face and relatively broad and pale upperpart edgings, two features more typical of Black-chinned than Ruby-throated. Charles W. Melton. Miller Canyon, Arizona, 14 August 2000.

Helmeted Hummingbirds Genus *Calypte*

This genus comprises two western North American species: Anna's and Costa's hummingbirds. These are small (Costa's) to almost medium-sized (Anna's) and relatively stocky, large-headed hummers with medium-length, straightish black bills, and tails that are cleft in males, slightly double-rounded in females. The inner primaries are evenly broad, like the outers. Adult males have an iridescent rose-pink to violet 'helmet,' i.e., the gorget and crown, and the gorgets are elongated into 'tails' at the corners. Females typically have dark to dusky lores, a short whitish supraloral stripe, a whitish post-ocular spot or line; grayish to whitish underparts that lack buff on the flanks; and tails that lack rufous.

18 Anna's Hummingbird

(Calypte anna)

9–10 cm (3.5–4 in). Bill 16–20 mm (female > male).
Pics I.8–I.10, I.14, I.20, iii, vi, 18.1– 18.11.

Identification summary
W North America. Small to medium. Relatively stocky and large headed. Bill medium length, straightish, and proportionately short. Wing tips < tail at rest on adult male, ≤ tail at rest on female/immature. Adult male distinctive by virtue of brilliant rose-pink to reddish-orange helmet, i.e., gorget *and* crown. Female and immature can be confused with other western hummers, mainly Black-chinned and Costa's. Anna's larger and stockier than both, with underparts generally mottled dusky rather than plainer whitish, and adult females and many

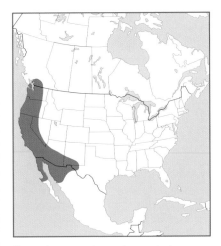

Seasonal movements complex, see text.

immature males have patches of rose-pink in throat. In addition, Anna's and Costa's share a summer and fall wing-molt schedule unlike the winter wing-molt of Black-chinned, and Anna's calls are distinct from both Black-chinned and Costa's.

Taxonomy

No subspecies described. *Calypte* has been merged into *Archilochus*[8].

Status and Distribution

Breeds and widely resident from SW British Columbia S to NW Baja California, E to S Arizona and, rarely, W Texas[1,12]. Main nesting season December through June, averaging earlier southwards (e.g., from mid October in Arizona[12]) and along the coast. In late summer, at least in California[5,6] and Arizona[12], there tends to be an upslope movement into the mountains, when flowering there peaks. Winters widely in milder areas, especially along and near Pacific coast but also locally in interior N to British Columbia. Local movements relatively complex; winter range and abundance show interannual variation related to harshness of winter conditions.

Rare to casual (mainly July to January) N to S Alaska and E to W Texas, and casual (mainly October to February) as far afield as Saskatchewan, Wisconsin, New York[9], North Carolina[10] and Florida[1]. Population and range have expanded greatly in historic times, attributed to widespread planting of non-native trees and shrubs, perhaps in combination with increased year-round use of hummingbird feeders[4,6,12,13,14,17].

Range

Western North America S to N Mexico.

Field Identification

Structure

Small to almost medium-sized, relatively stocky and large-headed, with a straightish, medium-length black bill that can appear proportionately short. Adult male tail moderately long and forked, with R5 slightly shorter than R4; at rest, wing tips fall well short of tail tip. Female tail medium-long, fairly broad, and slightly rounded (**Figure 1**), wing tips ≤ tail tip. Immature male tail very slightly double-rounded, wing tips ≤ tail tip. Female/immature rectrices relatively broad and truncate. Primaries broad out to P9 with P10 narrower and more tapered (most pronounced on adult male).

Similar species

Adult males

Adult male Anna's distinctive if seen well, and in North America a glittering helmet is shared only with Costa's Hummingbird of western deserts. If Anna's iridescent crown does not catch the light, however, confusion is possible with males of some other small gorgeted hummers.

Adult male Costa's Hummingbird (mainly W deserts) smaller and shorter tailed with violet crown and highly elongated gorget, and quite different calls and song-display (although some immature male Costa's may give song from perch suggesting Anna's). Also, Anna's and Costa's hybridize occasionally in S California[15]; presumed hybrids can look similar to Costa's but have calls more like Anna's or of intermediate quality[7].

Adult male Broad-tailed Hummingbird (mainly Great Basin and Rocky mountains) less thickset with smaller head, less elongated gorget corners, and bold white forecollar whose corners can be seen even from behind (**Figure 5**). Closed tail fairly long and tapered (rather than squared or cleft, depending on molt stage of Anna's; **Figure 5**), and wing molt occurs in winter. Call a higher, less smacking chip, and wing-trill diagnostic.

Broad-tailed   Anna's

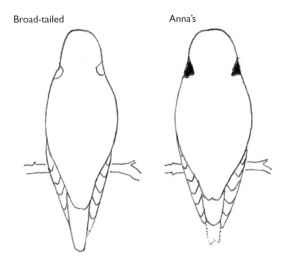

Figure 5. Comparison of adult male Broad-tailed Hummingbird and molting adult male Anna's Hummingbird in fall, as viewed from behind (e.g., on a feeder). Note slimmer build of Broad-tailed with white collar sides often visible, and long, all-green R1, wing tips short of tail tip. Anna's is stockier and larger headed, with dark gorget corners often visible, and short, all-green 'tail' with wing tips equal to or greater than tail tip (R1 only; with R2–R5 in molt – full tail shape indicated by dotted lines).

Adult male Black-chinned Hummingbird (W North America) slightly smaller but proportionally longer billed, and slimmer with smaller head that usually looks dark with white post-ocular spot and bold white forecollar. Gorget black and bluish violet. Call a soft, twangy chip. Wing molt in winter.

Adult male Ruby-throated Hummingbird (E North America) slightly smaller and slimmer with smaller head that usually looks dark with white post-ocular spot and bold white forecollar. Gorget ruby-red with black chin. Call a soft, twangy chip. Wing molt in winter.

Females

Anna's can be confused mainly with Black-chinned and Costa's hummingbirds, and these three species often occur side-by-side. Given prolonged, close-range study (especially of perched birds where details of wing structure can be seen), most individuals can be identified. Also note that typical call notes of Anna's separate it readily from Costa's and Black-chinned, useful even for a bird seen only briefly. However, presumed hybrids between Anna's and Costa's can look similar to Costa's but have calls more like Anna's or of intermediate quality[7]. Female Anna's told from female and immature *Selasphorus* and Calliope hummingbirds by larger size and bulk (although similar to Broad-tailed in this respect), duskier underparts with no distinct buffy on flanks, lack of rufous in tail. Its call is distinct from the soft chipping of Calliope, but more similar and not always easy to distinguish from chip notes of *Selasphorus*.

Female Black-chinned Hummingbird (W North America) slightly smaller, slimmer, smaller headed, and proportionally longer billed and longer tailed than Anna's, with narrow inner primaries and softer chipping call. Black-chinned has superficially similar tail pattern to Anna's but tail more double-rounded (R1 and R5 proportionally shorter), rectrices narrower and more tapered at tips, and black median band broader, with relatively reduced grayish green visible at base of spread tail (**Figure 1**).

Molt timing can be useful in identification: Black-chinned rarely starts primary molt before reaching winter grounds in September or October, while many Anna's molt in summer and fall. Thus, molting birds in the west in fall should not be Black-chinned, but birds not in primary molt may be either species.

Feeding Black-chins often wag or pump their tail persistently (Anna's do this rarely), which may draw attention. Black-chinned tends to be plainer and paler below than Anna's, without the strong dusky wash and green mottling on sides/flanks of adult female Anna's (but more like some immature female Anna's). Its throat is often plain whitish or pale gray, and the undertail-coverts often show as a contrastingly whiter crissum. Identification of problem birds should be confirmed by structure and voice.

Female Costa's Hummingbird (mainly W deserts) is smaller (usually obvious in direct comparison) but proportionately longer billed than Anna's, with shorter and more strongly rounded tail (R5 proportionately shorter, and at rest wing tips usually > tail tip on Costa's), narrower rectrices (**Figure 1**), and high, tinny *pit* call, often given in short twittering series (very different from smacking chip and buzzy twitters of Anna's).

Costa's tends to be paler and plainer below than Anna's, and lacks dusky wash and extensive green mottling on sides/flanks of adult female Anna's (but beware immature male Costa's molting in green on sides). Costa's throat is often plain whitish or pale gray and any color is violet, and its eye often looks beady and connected to bill by solid narrow black loral stripe (Anna's often has pale loral spot immediately forward of eyes).

Female Ruby-throated Hummingbird (E North America) differs from Anna's in much the same features as does Black-chinned Hummingbird, especially its plainer and whiter throat and underparts, narrow inner primaries, call, and later molt timing. Note, though, that Ruby-throated has a shorter bill than Black-chinned and also tends not to wag its tail so strongly while hovering.

Immature Males

Immature male Anna's distinguished from other species by much the same features as females, and most have some rose-pink splashes on their throat. Molting birds also have rose-pink patches about the head, and most molt into adult plumage from late summer or fall into early winter.

Voice and Sounds

Song (heard year-round) a varied, high-pitched, wiry to lisping or squeaky warble, often prolonged or with shorter phrases repeated in steady, at times slightly pulsating, succession. Often given by immature males in summer, when may be more prolonged and varied. Common call a slightly emphatic to fairly hard, chipping *tik* or *tih* and a more smacking *tsik,* given in flight and perched, and at times repeated steadily from a perch. Also, quick doubled notes, *ti-tik* or *tsi-sik,* given singly or in short series, and often interspersed amid prolonged series of single chips. Aggressive call of males in in-flight interactions, when physical contact can be made, a clipped, low buzzy *bizzt* or *bzzzt*. Flight chase call a rapid-paced, slightly buzzy twittering, *t-chíssi-chíssi-chíssi* or *chízzi-chízzi-chízzi-chízzi...*, and variations, this call often having a wiry quality reminiscent of the song. In dive display, male makes an abrupt, explosive, and variably metallic *dink!* or *kiip!* at bottom point of dive, which may suggest a ground-squirrel call.

Habitat

Breeding birds favor chaparral and other scrub habitats, open woodland, and urban areas with suitable trees and bushes. Migrants can occur anywhere around suitable food sources such as patches of tree-tobacco in the desert, or at feeders in any habitat.

Behavior

Feeds and perches low to high. Singing males often perch conspicuously on bare twigs atop bushes or in low trees, and on phone wires, holding their wings drooped under the tail. Feeding birds typically hold the tail close to the body plane unless probing up into hanging flowers from below, when tail may be held down, near vertically. Tail of feeding birds usually held closed but appears fairly broad, held fairly rigid and quivered, with occasional flicks; however, hovering and feeding birds also occasionally wag their tail strongly, suggesting Black-chinned Hummingbird.

In dive display, male usually starts from a vertical hover above subject with bill angled down, whence he gives short buzzy phrases, then towers (usually with bill angled down) near-vertically to 25–40 m, at times with one or more brief pauses in the climb, before power-diving down steeply, with helmet oriented into the sun, and pulling up in arc over subject and returning to near the initial hover position whence he may repeat the display or fly off to perch. In shuttle display, male rocks back and forth over subject in tight, low-wavelength arcs (0.5 m or less). Immature males can give full, adult-like dive displays, and variations, such as wider oval loops up to only 10 m or so high; two loops can run into each other without a pause after the first dive, and the dive pull-out is disconcertingly quiet, presumably because the immature lacks the modified adult rectrices.

Molt

Molts on breeding grounds or during post-breeding dispersal and migration, with some completing on non-breeding grounds. Primary molt mainly starts May to August, ends August to December; averages later on immatures but some early-hatched juveniles complete primary molt by August or September, i.e., potentially earlier than some late-breeding adults; some immature males do not attain full helmets till January but have adult-like wings and tail. Wing-molt timing overlaps broadly with Costa's Hummingbird, but earlier than Black-chinned Hummingbird.

Description

All ages/sexes can show fairly large, round to oval white flank patches, especially obvious on hovering birds and apparently due to misarranged feathers.

Adult male: crown, slightly expanded gorget, and post-ocular droplet iridescent rose to orangish red (latter mainly when worn). Distinct white post-ocular spot or short streak often runs into pale gray post-ocular line; many show short pale gray supraloral stripe. Nape and upperparts golden green to bluish green (brighter and more golden when fresh). Underparts mottled dusky and dull glittering green, with unmarked and often paler gray forecollar below gorget, and sometimes a narrow, unmarked, pale gray median line separating green-mottled flanks. Ventral band white, undertail-coverts bronzy green with pale grayish edgings. **Tail:** R1 golden green to bluish green; R2 green with black tip and narrow gray basal edging; R3–R5 dusky to pale gray with broad blackish tip and blackish shaft-stripe. Bill black, feet blackish.

Adult female: crown, nape, and upperparts golden green, duller and bluer when worn (mainly late summer and fall); some birds have scattered iridescent rose-pink feathers on crown[7,11,16]. Lores dark and auriculars dusky with white post-ocular spot or short streak, and usually a short, pale gray supraloral line and pale gray post-ocular line. Throat and underparts pale grayish, throat with central splodge of iridescent rose-pink to orange-red and variable lines of dusky spots. Some (perhaps first-year birds?) may lack iridescence on throat. Underparts mottled dusky, becoming dull glittering green on sides/flanks, often with paler and plainer forecollar; vent band white, undertail-coverts similar to male but duller. **Tail (Figure 1)**: R1–R2 golden green, with R2 broadly tipped black and occasionally some black distally on edges of R1; R3–R5 greenish to grayish-green (grayish mainly on R5) with black subterminal band, bold white tips to R4–R5, narrower white tip to R3.

Immature male: resembles adult female overall but upperparts in fresh plumage (mainly February to June) with pale buff tips, retained latest on secondaries and rump. Often has darker auriculars and whiter throat than adult female, creating more strongly masked look. Underparts vary from paler and plainer, pale gray to whitish, with variable dusky wash and limited dusky and green mottling on sides/flanks, to fairly heavily and coarsely mottled dusky below; rarely shows a very faint buff wash to belly and lower flanks. Some birds show paler forecollar that tends to contrast with dingier throat and grayish sides. Undertail-coverts dusky greenish with fairly broad pale gray to whitish edges. Throat with variable (often heavy) lines of dusky flecks and spots, and usually some iridescent rose-pink throat spots or patches. Molting birds soon attain spots and patches of color about head. **Tail:** similar overall to adult female but rectrices slightly less truncate. R1–R2 green to bluish green with black reduced to absent on R2 tip, blackish subterminal band more diffuse and narrower, white tips to R3–R5 narrower (R3 often lacks white tip, which can be very narrow on R4), and more gray visible on bases of R4–R5. Subterminal black on R5 typically forms distinct point into white tip, along shaft **(Figure 6)**. Attains adult plumage by complete molt from spring through late fall, but some year-old males may be distinguishable from adults by incomplete helmet (mixed with dusky greenish feathers) and less strongly elongated gorget corners[11].

Immature female: similar overall to immature male, differing from adult female mainly in paler and plainer underparts, pale edgings to upperparts in fresh plumage, and narrower white tips to outer rectrices (especially R3). Throat variably marked with lines of dusky spots that tend to be heaviest down center (some birds have almost plain throats), and usually lacks iridescent rose-pink feathers. **Tail:** similar to adult female but rectrices slightly less truncate. Averages less black on R2 and white tips to R3–R5 average narrower, sometimes absent on R3. Subterminal black on R5 typically does not form distinct point into white tip **(Figure 6)**. Attains adult plumage by complete molt from spring through late fall.

Hybrids
With Costa's Hummingbird[15], Black-chinned Hummingbird[3], Calliope Hummingbird[3], Allen's Hummingbird[3], possibly with Rufous Hummingbird[3] and Blue-throated Hummingbird[2]. Report of hybrid with Broad-tailed Hummingbird[11] apparently in error.

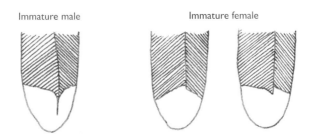

Immature male   Immature female

Figure 6. Pattern of R5 tip in immature male and immature female *Calypte* hummingbirds. Note that black extends in point into white tip in immature males, often visible from below on a perched bird.

References

[1]AOU 1998, [2]Baldridge *et al.* 1983, [3]Banks & Johnson 1961, [4]Contreras 1999, [5]Gaines 1992, [6]Grinnell & Miller 1944, [7]S. N. G. Howell, pers. obs., [8]Howell & Webb 1995, [9]NAB 53:37 (1999), [10]NAB 53:45 (1999), [11]Pyle 1997, [12]Russell 1996, [13]Shuford 1993, [14]Stiles 1973, [15]Wells *et al.* 1978, [16]G. Yanega unpubl. data, [17]Zimmerman 1973.

18.1 Adult male and immature male Anna's. Adult male's iridescent reddish helmet (looking relative dull and orangey due to wear; cf. Pic. 18.2) and extensively mottled underparts are distinctive; immature male starting to show diagnostic color on crown. Primary molt on bird in foreground (P1–P2 replaced) at this season also indicates a *Calypte* hummer, probably Anna's. Sid & Shirley Rucker. Sonoita, Arizona, September 1998.

18.2 Adult male Anna's. Unmistakable. Male's helmet when fresh is magenta-rose (cf. Pic. 18.1); note reflection of color on mandible. Brian E. Small. San Diego Co., California, February 1999.

18.3 Adult male Anna's. Note tail shape and extensive bronzy-green centers to undertail-coverts. Charles W. Melton. Whittier Narrows Nature Center, California, 27 March 1998.

18.4 Adult female Anna's. Relatively dusky underparts with extensive dark mottling, dusky-spotted malar region, and green mottling on sides indicate Anna's; also note loral pattern. Many show iridescent splodge in throat (cf. Pic. 18.5). Charles W. Melton. Whittier Narrows Nature Center, California, 1 March 1996.

18.5 Adult female Anna's. In fresh plumage following summer molt. Note lack of rufous coloration, face and throat pattern, and dusky mottled flanks and undertail-coverts (veiled and tipped with pale in fresh plumage). Brian E. Small. Portal, Arizona, August 1996.

18.6 Adult female Anna's. This bird shows classic Anna's shape with large head and thick neck, wings about equal with tail tip. From *Archilochus* note shape, especially the short tail and broad inner primaries, plus green-mottled flanks, face pattern, and, from Black-chinned, also relatively short bill. Separation from female Costa's more difficult, note extensively dusky-spotted throat (with spots extending faintly to malar region) extensive green mottling on underparts, relatively bright golden green upperparts (cf. Pic. 19.7), relatively shorter bill. Calls are also diagnostic. John Sorensen. Gonzales, California, April 1998.

18.7 Immature (probably male) Anna's. This recently fledged juvenile (note pinkish on mandible base) can be identified to *Calypte* by the lack of rufous plumage tones and relatively broad inner primaries. The extensive dusky mottling below, especially on the undertail-coverts, indicates Anna's (call would be another key feature), and the dark mask and dusky throat markings suggest a male (cf. Pics. 18.8–18.9 vs. Pics 18.10–18.11). Charles W. Melton. Montaña de Oro State Park, California, 27 July 1994.

18.8 Immature male Anna's. The same features apply as for ANHU 09. The extent of dark in the throat and black pointing distally into the white tip to R5 indicate a male. William E. Grenfell. Granite Bay, California, July 1994.

18.9 Immature male Anna's. The broad inner primaries and advanced primary molt (P7 new, P8 shed, P9–P10 old) indicate *Calypte* at this time of year. The relatively long projection of tail beyond wing tips indicates Anna's. Color of the iridescence on the head (rose versus violet) and call would be other key features. Note how worn and grayish the head feathers are, these being the last juvenal feathers replaced in the first complete molt. Brian E. Small. Kern Co., California, August 1997.

18.10 Immature female Anna's. A particularly dingy individual. Broad inner primaries, lack of any rufous tones, and relatively large-headed appearance indicate *Calypte*. The bright golden green upperparts typical of Anna's are here obscured by the grayish-buff tips of fresh juvenal plumage and, together with an indistinctly marked throat, suggest Costa's Hummingbird. The wing tips fall well short of the tail, however, indicating Anna's (cf. Pic 19.7), and note also the relatively oblique dark loral mark with a pale area immediately forward of the eye (cf. Pic. 19.7). Peter LaTourette. San Mateo Co., California, 3 June 1984.

18.11 Immature female Anna's. Evenly broad primaries and summer molt schedule immediately indicate *Calypte*. From Costa's by relatively long tail (longest rectrices apparently dropped in molt), extensive dusky throat spotting extending faintly into malar region; also note loral pattern with pale spot immediately forward of eyes. Limited dusky spotting on throat indicates an immature female. P7 is almost fully grown, P8–10 old. Brian E. Small. Kern Co., California, August 2000.

19 Costa's Hummingbird

(Calypte costae)

7.5–8.5 cm (3–3.4 in). Bill 15.5–18.5 mm (female > male).
Pics I.17, I.26, iv, vii, 19.1–19.12.

Identification summary
W deserts. Small size. Adult male distinctive by virtue of brilliant violet helmet, i.e., elongated gorget *and* crown. Female and immature can be confused with other western hummers, mainly Black-chinned and Anna's. Costa's call a high, tinny *pit*, often given in twittering series, and very distinct from calls of other North American hummers. Female/immature tail relatively short, so wing tips > tail tip at rest. Black-chinned longer tailed with white post-ocular spot, winter molt schedule. Anna's larger, bulkier, and slightly longer tailed, often with rose-pink on throat.

Seasonal movements complex, see text.

Taxonomy
No subspecies described. *Calypte* has been merged into *Archilochus*[6].

Status and Distribution
Breeding resident (mainly late January to June) in S California and SW Arizona, locally N (mainly March to July) to central California, S Nevada, and SW Utah; also breeds E to extreme SW New Mexico and has attempted to breed in S Oregon[5]. More widespread within general breeding range during migration (mainly February–May, June–July), and some birds present year-round locally in S California, extreme S Nevada[8], and S Arizona. Fall migrants (or vagrants) occur rarely in N areas through November, with occasional over-wintering records N to Oregon. Local movements relatively complex[1,2].

Casual N to British Columbia (mid-April to early July[4]) and S central Alaska (September–October[9]), and E (mainly late January to late March, September to December) to Texas[12] and Kansas[9], but no records in SE U.S.

Range
Western U.S. and NW Mexico.

Field Identification

Structure

Small size. Bill medium length and straightish (can appear slightly arched or decurved). Adult male tail medium-short and cleft, with R5 slightly shorter than R4. Female tail relatively short and distinctly rounded to slightly double-rounded (**Figure 1**). Immature male tail relatively short (slightly longer than female) and slightly double-rounded. Female/immature rectrices relatively narrow and rounded (e.g., **Figure 1**). At rest, wing tips ≤ tail tip on males (including some immatures), usually slightly > tail tip on females (and some immature males). Primaries broad with P10 slightly narrower. Hovering birds often look slightly pot-bellied, accentuated by short tail.

Similar species

Adult males

Adult male Costa's Hummingbird distinctive if seen well: note hunched posture, glittering violet helmet with elongated gorget tails. Larger Anna's Hummingbird has a rose-pink helmet with less elongated corners to gorget, longer tail, and different call. Anna's and Costa's hybridize occasionally in S California[13]; presumed hybrids can look similar to Costa's but have calls more like Anna's or of intermediate quality[7]. Adult male Lucifer Hummingbird (SW U.S. in summer) shares elongated violet gorget but note green crown, long arched bill, and very long tail, all quite different from Costa's.

Females

Female Costa's most often confused with Black-chinned and Anna's hummingbirds, and these three species occur side-by-side in some areas of the west. Given prolonged, close-range study (especially of perched birds where details of wing structure can be seen), most individuals can be identified. Note that typical call of Costa's separates it readily from Anna's and Black-chinned, useful for a bird seen only briefly. However, presumed hybrids between Anna's and Costa's can look similar to Costa's but have calls more like Anna's or of intermediate quality[7]; such birds can be puzzling when encountered.

Female Black-chinned Hummingbird (W North America) superficially similar to Costa's but longer tail more distinctly double-rounded (R1 proportionately shorter; **Figure 1**), rectrices more tapered, inner primaries narrow, and call a twangy chip. At rest, Black-chinned's wing tips fall short of tail tip (versus slightly beyond tail tip on female Costa's). Black-chinned's tail pattern superficially similar to Costa's but black median band broader, with relatively less extensive greenish-gray visible at base of spread tail, especially noticeable on outer rectrices (**Figure 1**).

Another excellent field identification character is molt timing: Black-chinned molts in winter, most Costa's molt in summer and fall. Thus, e.g., Costa's in Arizona in July and August often show conspicuous primary molt, whereas Black-chinned doesn't start molting primaries until September or later; conversely, birds molting outer primaries in late winter should not be Costa's.

Most Black-chinned can also be distinguished from Costa's by relatively subtle plumage differences. While such differences may be apparent to observers familiar with both species, problem birds still occur, and structure, call, and molt timing should always be checked on such birds.

In general, Black-chinneds look brighter and more contrasty than Costa's, which look dingy overall. Thus, Black-chinned is darker and brighter green above, its underparts often show a relatively contrasting whitish forecollar and contrasting (and long) whitish undertail-coverts. Also, fresh-plumaged Black-chinned often has buff wash to flanks. By contrast, Costa's is typically grayish-green above, underparts rarely show a distinct whitish forecollar and lack contrasting (and long) white undertail-coverts and distinct buffy flank wash. Adult female Black-chinned often has 'sterner' facial expression caused by blacker lores, darker crown, and darker auriculars with contrasting white post-ocular spot, versus 'softer' face of Costa's, with pale gray post-ocular stripe wrapping around smoothly dusky auriculars (but immature females more similar in face pattern than adults).

Feeding Black-chinneds often wag and fan their tail, as do Costa's, but Black-chinned's tail action looks stronger and more pumping than weaker and more fluttery action of Costa's. This is due to the former's longer tail and, hence, more pronounced wag. Lastly, bill length and shape have been suggested as characters for separating female Costa's and Black-chinned, but these characters seem to overlap enough to make them of little use for identification, although the longest-billed female Black-chinneds look distinct from Costa's.

Female Anna's Hummingbird (W North America) larger (obvious in direct comparison) and stockier than Costa's, with slightly longer and squarer tail (at rest wing tips ≤ tail tip), broader and blunter rectrices (**Figure 1**), proportionately shorter bill, and smacking chip call. Adult Anna's typically brighter green above, mottled extensively dusky gray and greenish on sides/flanks, and with rose-pink throat patch. Dark loral stripe of adult female Anna's tends to be more oblique than on Costa's, with pale spot immediately forward of eyes. Immatures plainer and paler below, but often more mottled-looking on sides/flanks than Costa's, and throat often with more distinct dusky flecks; note structure and call. Feeding Anna's tend not to wag their tails as much as Costa's. Anna's molts early, much like Costa's.

Female Calliope Hummingbird (mainly W mountains) also small and short-tailed, but has cinnamon-washed sides/flanks, brighter green upperparts, whitish post-ocular spot, and finely flecked throat. Calliope has a soft chipping call, quite distinct from Costa's, and molts in winter.

Female Ruby-throated Hummingbird (E North America) differs from Costa's in much the same features as does Black-chinned Hummingbird (see above), especially narrow inner primaries, call, face pattern, and later molt timing. Ruby-throated also tends to be more contrastingly colored, with bright emerald-green upperparts (unlike the washed out gray-green of many Costa's), and often has a buff wash to its sides/flanks.

Immature males

Immature male Costa's Hummingbird distinguished from other species by much the same features as are females, but immature male has shorter bill than female and often has a darker auricular mask and whiter throat and forecollar. Most have some purple spots or patches on central throat and older immatures also have purple patches about the head, and most molt into adult plumage from late summer to early winter.

Voice and Sounds

Common call a high, slightly tinny, fairly soft *tik* or *ti*, often run into short, slightly liquid or rippling twitters, *ti ti-ti ti ti-ti-ti*, or *ti ti-tik tik ti-tik*, etc., and at times slightly buzzier twitters. Warning call a high, slightly squealing *tssirr* or *tssir,* given singly or run into slightly buzzy twittering series in interactions, *tssir ti-ti-ti* or *tssir-ti ts-si-si,* and variations. Song a very high, thin, and drawn-out whining whistle, *tsi ssiiiiiiu,* given from perch. In dive-loop display male gives a louder, high, shrill, drawn-out whistle during descent and pull-up of high elliptical loops. Immature male Costa's give more varied, high twittering or slightly warbling songs from perch, which may suggest Anna's Hummingbird (especially immature male of latter).

Habitat
Breeds mainly in fairly open arid desert scrub, especially washes with *Ocotillo,* other cacti, and, in more northern areas, sage; locally in adjacent riparian areas where Black-chinned is commoner. Migrants occur in a variety of open and semi-open habitats, ranging in small numbers up into pine-oak zone of mountains.

Behavior
Feeds and perches mainly at low to mid-levels, although territorial males in breeding season often perch prominently atop tall bushes or on phone wires. Often wags and flips spread tail while hovering and feeding, at other times feeds with tail held closed to slightly spread, in or near body plane, and not wagged strongly. Tends to be dominated by Black-chinned and Anna's at feeders, but aggressive birds will challenge Magnificent Hummingbirds.

In dive-looping display, male climbs abruptly to 20–30 m or higher before power-diving down steeply (typically with helmet oriented into the sun), swooping up in abrupt arc over subject and continuing straight up for the next dive; dive-loops are usually repeated in steady succession, usually 5–10 times (exceptionally up to 39 times[2]), as male makes spectacular, high elliptical loops accompanied by high, shrill, whining whistles.

Molt
Molts on breeding grounds or during post-breeding dispersal and migration, with some completing on non-breeding grounds. Primary molt starts May to October, ends September to January; averages later on immatures. Timing overlaps broadly with Anna's Hummingbird, but earlier than Black-chinned Hummingbird.

Description
All ages/sexes can show fairly large, round to oval white flank patches, especially obvious on hovering birds and apparently due to misarranged feathers.
Adult male: crown and strongly elongated gorget iridescent violet (at times showing bluish highlights), typically with distinct whitish post-ocular stripe and white forecollar; many show short pale gray supraloral stripe. Upperparts relatively dull bronzy green to slightly bluish green. Underparts mottled dusky and dull glittering green, with variable, unmarked whitish median stripe and puffy-white vent band; undertail-coverts whitish with variable bronzy-green centers, strongest on short basal feathers.
Tail: R1 bluish green, R2 green with slight black tip, R3–R5 dusky to pale gray with broad blackish tip and blackish shaft-stripe. Bill black, feet blackish.
Adult female: crown, nape, and upperparts relatively dull gray-green to golden green (often duller on crown), duller and bluer overall when worn (mainly late summer), brightest golden green when fresh (mainly October to April); some birds have scattered iridescent purple feathers on crown[10]. Lores dark, and auriculars smoothly pale dusky with paler gray post-ocular stripe (post-ocular spot often whiter) and usually a

pale gray supraloral line. Head often looks fairly uniform and dingy overall with narrow dark loral stripe highlighting beady dark eye. Throat and underparts dingy whitish to pale grayish, at times with paler forecollar, and throat often has one or more violet feathers (typically concentrated as a central patch, exceptionally forming an extensive gorget). Sides washed slightly duskier, with sparse bronzy-green spots on sides/flanks typically covered by wings at rest, and rarely (if ever) with a faint buff wash; some shorter undertail-coverts can have small bronzy-green centers. **Tail** (**Figure 1**): R1–R2 bronzy green to bluish green, R2 with broad black tip (and fine white tip in fresh plumage); R3–R5 greenish to grayish green (grayish mainly on R5) with black subterminal band and bold white tips to R4–R5, narrower white tip to R3. *Immature male*: resembles adult female overall but tail averages slightly longer, and upperparts in fresh plumage (mainly February to July) have variable pale buff to whitish tips, on most heavily marked birds creating distinctive pallid, or 'floury' appearance; pale tips retained longest on secondaries and rump. Often has darker auriculars and whiter throat than adult female, creating more strongly masked look. Lower throat typically has lines of dusky flecks, often concentrated in center, and many birds also show some iridescent violet feathers, commonly concentrated in a central wedge. Hind flanks can have faint vinaceous-buff wash in fresh plumage, and undertail-coverts faint dusky to greenish centers. Older immature males show spots and patches of color about the head, and some attain fairly extensive violet on gorget and crown while retaining immature (female-like) tail. **Tail:** similar to adult female but rectrices narrower, black reduced to absent on R2 tip, blackish subterminal band more diffuse and narrower, white tips to R3–R5 narrower (R3 often lacks distinct white tip), and more gray visible on bases of R4–R5; in fresh plumage, R1–R2 finely tipped white. Subterminal black on R5 typically forms distinct point into white tip, along shaft (**Figure 6**). Attains adult plumage by complete molt from spring through late fall, but some year-old males may be distinguishable from adults by incomplete helmet (mixed with dusky greenish feathers) and less strongly elongated gorget corners[10].

Immature female: resembles adult female overall but upperparts in fresh plumage (mainly February to July) have variable pale buff to whitish tips, like immature male, and throat typically unmarked dingy whitish, rarely (if ever) with any violet feathers. Sides, flanks, and short undertail-coverts lack bronzy-green spots but hind flanks can have very faint vinaceous-buff wash in fresh plumage. **Tail:** similar to adult female but rectrices less truncate, R1 less bluish, blackish subterminal band less contrasting, and R1–R2 have fine white tip when fresh. Subterminal black on R5 typically does not form distinct point into white tip (**Figure 6**). Attains adult plumage by complete molt from spring through late fall.

Hybrids

With Anna's Hummingbird[13], Black-chinned Hummingbird[11], and Calliope and Broad-tailed hummingbirds[3].

References

[1]Baltosser 1989, [2]Baltosser & Scott 1996, [3]Banks & Johnson 1961, [4]Campbell *et al.* 1990, [5]Gilligan *et al.* 1994, [6]Howell & Webb 1995, [7]S. N. G. Howell pers. obs., [8]P. E. Lehman pers. comm., [9]NAB, [10]Pyle 1997, [11]Short & Phillips 1966, [12]TBRC unpubl. data, [13]Wells *et al.* 1978.

19.1 Adult male Costa's. The highly elongated gorget 'tails' and short tail readily identify this bird to species. Charles W. Melton. Borrego Springs, California, 10 April 1995.

19.2 Adult male Costa's. Unmistakable. The male's helmet with long gorget 'tails' rarely seem to catch the light, but the sight is memorable when they do. James Lomax. Big Morongo, California, 20 April 1994.

19.3 Adult male Costa's. Unmistakable. Note the relatively short tail. Charles W. Melton. Anza-Borrego Desert State Park, California, 14 March 1996.

19.4 Adult female Costa's. The short tail with narrow and strongly graduated outer rectrices indicates Costa's, as does the plain face pattern with pale gray post-ocular stripe and relatively reduced (cf. adult Anna's) green mottling on the sides and flanks. Call would be another key feature. Charles W. Melton. Borrego Springs, California, 25 March 1995.

19.5 Adult female Costa's. This bird approaches the extreme end of the spectrum with regard to adult female *Calypte* having iridescent throat patches (and some even have spots of purple on the crown). Also note the broad inner primaries and short tail. Charles W. Melton. Borrego Springs, California, 20 March 1997.

19.6 Adult female Costa's. Note the evenly broad primaries and wing tips extending slightly beyond the short tail. The hunched, 'neckless' posture is typical of *Calypte*, and the face pattern and dingy pale underparts further indicate Costa's. In fresh plumage the upperparts can be tipped pale gray (suggesting an immature) and overall look fairly bright green, often relatively bluer than the golden green of Anna's (cf. Pic. 18.6). Much of the time (in summer and fall) the upperparts are dingier and greyer. Rick & Nora Bowers. Tucson, Arizona, January 1999.

19.7 Adult female Costa's. A typical dingy and undistinguished-looking bird, in itself a pointer for Costa's. The evenly broad primaries and lack of rufous tones point to *Calypte*. Also note the beady eye standing out in the pale face, cf. Black-chinned Hummingbird. The straight dark loral stripe, dull upperparts (at this season), and wing tips projecting distinctly beyond the tail tip all indicate Costa's rather than Anna's (cf. Pic. 18.10). Call would another key feature. Mike Danzenbaker. Palm Springs, California, 15 March 1986.

19.8 Adult female Costa's. Another dingy looking bird. The evenly broad primaries rule out *Archilochus*; plain underparts and relatively narrow and strongly graduated outer rectrices indicate Costa's. Also note the dark lores and beady eye standing out in the pale face, and the whitish post-ocular stripe. Call would be another key feature. At this angle the wings held above the tail appear (misleadingly) to fall slightly short of the tail tip.) Brian E. Small. Riverside Co., California, May 1994.

19.9 Immature male Costa's. The dark mask and whitish post-ocular stripe are typical of young male Costa's (cf. Pic. 19.10). Note the plain whitish underparts and wings projecting beyond the tail tip, also diagnostic of Costa's. Brian E. Small. Riverside Co., California, May 1990.

19.10 Immature male Costa's. A dingy, thickset little hummer with broad inner primaries and no rufous tones, indicating *Calypte*. Dark auricular mask and throat markings indicate an immature male. Dinginess of upperparts and relatively short tail point to Costa's (throat color and call would be two other features to distinguish this bird from Anna's, and the outer rectrices also look relatively narrow); note that the wing tips project slightly beyond the tail tip. Mark M. Stevenson. Tucson Desert Museum, Arizona, June 1997.`

19.11 Immature male Costa's. The whitish post-ocular stripe and relatively short tail point to *Calypte*. The narrow outer rectrices, violet flecks on the throat and head, and mostly plain whitish underparts indicate Costa's. Call would be another key feature. Brian E. Small. Riverside Co., California, May 1991.

19.12 Immature male Costa's. This bird has mostly attained adult plumage (e.g., the tail and flanks); the head is the last area to molt and looks very worn and gray, with scattered spots of adult color. Sid & Shirley Rucker. Tucson, Arizona, September 1998.

Calliope Hummingbird Genus *Stellula*

The Calliope Hummingbird of western mountains is the single representative of this genus. It is a very small, relatively short-tailed and short-billed hummer that qualifies as the smallest North American breeding bird. At rest the wing tips of females and most immatures project slightly beyond the tail tip. Adult males have a cleft tail and uniquely streaked rose-magenta gorget elongated at the corners. Females and immatures are 'green-and-rufous' with a slightly rounded tail and distinctly buffy-cinnamon underparts.

20 Calliope Hummingbird

(Stellula calliope)

7.5–8 cm (3–3.2 in). Bill 12.5–16 mm (female > male).
Pics viii, 20.1–20.10.

Identification summary

W mountains. Very small with relatively short tail that often looks squared, or only slightly rounded. At rest, wing tips (except some adult males) usually slightly > tail tip. Adult male has uniquely streaked rose-magenta gorget and pale face. Female and immature green-and-rufous overall with throat finely flecked bronzy green, underparts washed cinnamon, tail inconspicuously rufous at base, and R1 broadly tipped black. Adult female (and some immatures) typically have diagnostic white line above bill 'lip.'

Casual to rare in SE U.S. in winter, see text.

Taxonomy

Monotypic. *A. c. lowei* described by Griscom[7] from Guerrero was based on winter migrants from North America. Some authors merge *Stellula* into *Archilochus*[9].

Status and Distribution

Summer resident (mainly April to August; males generally migrating 1–2 weeks earlier than females) in western mountains, from S California N to central British Columbia, E to W Alberta, W Wyoming, and central Utah. Spring migration (mainly late March to early May) mostly through foothills of California and W Arizona, casually E to Colorado, and with small numbers wandering to Pacific coast. Fall migration (mainly early July to late September) more easterly, with birds ranging through E Rockies and as far E as mountains of W and central Texas[10].

Traditional winter range W Mexico, but small numbers increasingly found in SE U.S. in winter (arriving in October–November, disappearing February–April), mainly along or near Gulf coast from Louisiana to Florida. Casual (mainly October–November) as far NE as Minnesota and New Jersey[1,11]. Sight records from SE Alaska[1] are unverified[5].

Range
Breeds W North America, winters W Mexico.

Field Identification

Structure
Very small size and relatively short tail. Bill medium length to medium-short, and straightish, at times appearing relatively slender. Adult male tail cleft (with R5 < R4). Female and immature tails slightly rounded (e.g., **Figure 2**). Primaries out to P9 broad and rounded with relatively wide outer web; P10 narrower and slightly curved (most strongly so on male). Rectrices relatively broad. At rest, wing tips ≤ tail on adult male, ≥ tail on female and immature. Hovering birds often look slightly pot-bellied, accentuated by short tail.

Similar species
Small size and short tail of Calliope are good field marks, as is its relatively low-key and quiet behavior (at least outside the breeding season). Adult males should not be confused, while females and immatures can suggest female *Selasphorus* hummers, especially Broad-tailed.

Adult males
Adult male Calliope's streaky rose-magenta gorget is diagnostic but can look solid, and beware immature males of other species in molt (although it is unlikely another species would replicate the rays of a male Calliope's gorget). Also note small size, short tail, relatively short and slender bill, extensively whitish face, and soft call.

Females
The female Calliope is fairly distinctive, but a lack of 'obvious' field marks seems to have made some observers uncertain about identification. Note that with longest tail coverts shed (on molting winter birds) Calliope can look deceptively long-tailed (or, at least, not characteristically short-tailed). Also see under **Bumblebee Hummingbird** (status in North America unclear).

Female Broad-tailed Hummingbird (mainly Great Basin and Rocky mountains) distinctly larger than Calliope with, like all *Selasphorus*, a longer and more graduated tail (**Figure 2**), and a relatively longer bill. Thus, at rest, wing tips of Broad-tailed fall short of tail tip, rather than extending slightly beyond (as on Calliope). In overall plumage and face pattern, however, Broad-tailed and Calliope are quite similar. Note that Broad-tailed lacks white-lored expression typical of adult female Calliope (which has white line above bill 'lip') but instead shows more of a whitish eye-ring, its longer and broader central rectrices are typically all-green to the tip (broadly black-tipped on Calliope), and adult females have more extensive rufous at tail base. Broad-tailed also has louder, sharp chipping call and, being a larger species, is more aggressive in feeding interactions (female Calliope tends to be chased away by most other hummingbirds).

Female Rufous/Allen's Hummingbirds (W North America) distinctly larger with longer, graduated tails with tapered central rectrices (**Figure 2**), and relatively longer bills. At rest, their wing tips fall short of tail tip. Rufous/Allen's also have brighter cinnamon sides/flanks with contrasting white forecollar, usually a more heavily spotted throat (often with spots or patches of flame iridescence), and obvious rufous in the tail. Their louder chip calls and typically aggressive behavior are also unlike Calliope.

Female Black-chinned Hummingbird (W North America) larger and longer tailed (wing tips fall short of double-rounded tail at rest) with longer bill, typically green-and-gray overall but some immatures have buff wash to sides/flanks. Note Black-chinned's narrow inner primaries, its louder, slightly twangy chipping, and that hovering and feeding birds often pump their tail strongly and are relatively aggressive. Black-chinned also has dark lores, its throat is often plain and unmarked, and its tail lacks any rufous.

Female Ruby-throated Hummingbird (E North America) larger and longer tailed (wing tips fall short of double-notched tail at rest), typically green-and-gray overall but some immatures have buff wash to sides/flanks. Note Ruby-throated's narrow inner primaries, its louder, slightly twangy chipping, and that feeding birds are relatively more aggressive. Ruby-throated also has dark lores, its throat is often plain and unmarked, and its tail lacks any rufous.

Female Costa's Hummingbird (mainly W deserts) also small and short-tailed, but duller and dingier, grayish green above and whitish below (with no buffy cinnamon), with diffuse whitish post-ocular stripe. Costa's also differs in its high, tinny twitters and summer molt schedule.

Immature males
The immature male Calliope is distinguished from other species by much the same features as are females, although most have more heavily flecked throats, often with a few streaks of rose-magenta (main molt of gorget is in late winter and spring). Tail averages proportionately longer than female (and can have reduced black at tip), so wing tips at times fall equal with tail tip. Like immature female, typically lacks adult female's white line above black bill 'lip.'

Voice and Sounds
Often quiet and rarely detected by sounds, except for displaying males. Common call a relatively soft, high chip, without strong hardness or buzziness, at times doubled, *chi* or *chi-ti,* and often repeated steadily from perch, less regularly when feeding, *chi chi-chi chi-chi chi chi...,* etc. High, slightly buzzier chippering series in interactions, *ssi ssi ssir or ssi ssi-ssi ssir* and *ti chi ssi-ssi,* etc.

Male's wing buzz not distinct except in displays, especially shuttle, when bursts of relatively loud, low, and insect-like wing-buzzing can attract attention. In dive display male produces an abrupt, slightly nasal *bzzt!* or *tzzt!* at pull-out of dive, followed immediately by a high, thin, drawn-out *zzing* that also may be given in shallower rocking flights and while perched.

Habitat
Breeds mainly in successional areas of conifer and mixed woodland, locally in narrow riparian corridors that descend into desert. Often near streams or other water, and with meadows and flower banks where males display. In winter (in Mexico) favors

brushy second-growth in oak and pine-oak foothills and highlands.

Behavior

Feeds and perches mainly at low to mid levels except for territorial breeding males which perch atop prominent look-outs, e.g., on bushes, conifers, dead snags. Often dominated at feeding sites by other hummers, although in Mexico usually dominates smaller Bumblebee Hummingbird[8]. Tail typically held closed while feeding, often cocked slightly above or below body plane, and quivered at times but not wagged or flashed strongly except perhaps when maneuvering or in aggressive interactions. Often feeds 'Inside' flower banks, probing up into flowers from below with tail cocked down almost vertically – presumably to avoid being seen and chased away by more aggressive hummers.

In dive display, male climbs to 10–30 m and power-dives down steeply, pulling up in arc over subject and at times continuing up in U-shaped trajectory to follow up with another dive; hover display starts from about 10 m above ground whence male alternates gradual descents with abrupt drops interspersed with bursts of hovering[3]. Male also makes short-wavelength shuttles in front of and slightly above perched subject (usually female).

Molt

Molts on winter grounds. Primary molt starts September (rarely August) to January, ends February (rarely January) to April; averages later on immatures.

Description

Adult male: elongated gorget formed by iridescent rose-magenta (to orange-red when worn, in winter) streaks that can look solid depending on the light and how the feathers are held); relaxed gorget often bordered by whitish lateral throat stripes, and lays over sides of white (to buffy white when worn, in winter) forecollar. Lores whitish with dark crescent forward of eyes, and white post-ocular spot contrasts with green crown and dusky auriculars. Underparts mottled green, with buff to cinnamon-buff wash on flanks, variable whitish median stripe, and fluffy white vent band; undertail coverts whitish, shortest feathers with small bronzy-green centers. Upperparts golden green to bluish emerald-green. **Tail** blackish, with R1–R4 edged rufous basally. Bill black with mandible often slightly paler and dull flesh-colored, feet blackish.

Adult female: crown, nape, and upperparts golden green to bluish emerald-green, duller and grayer when worn (mainly in winter). Lores white with dark crescent forward of eyes, and white line above bill 'lip.' White post-ocular spot (or short streak) contrasts with dusky auriculars (sparsely spotted bronzy green), and dull, pale gray post-ocular stripe often visible. Throat whitish with lines of bronzy-green flecks that vary from sparse to heavy, and some birds have scattered, short, iridescent rose streaks. Whitish forecollar forms poorly contrasting band below throat, and is often washed cinnamon on sides of neck, thus blending with cinnamon-washed underparts. Cinnamon darkest at sides of chest and typically extends in narrow band across center of chest, immediately below forecollar, and usually with a few iridescent green spots at chest sides; median underparts often whitish (but without strongly vested look typical of Rufous/Allen's), vent band fluffy white. **Tail (Figure 2)**: green basally with broad black tip to R1–R2, broad black subterminal band to R3–R5, and bold white tips to R4–R5, smaller white tip to R3; cinnamon edgings at bases of R1–R4 usually inconspicuous (and all-but-lacking on some birds). Closed tail often looks black, with base covered by uppertail-coverts. Bill black with mandible often slightly paler and dull flesh-colored.

Immature male: resembles adult female overall but plumage in fall fresher, upperparts with narrow, relatively inconspicuous cinnamon fringes most distinct on head and rump; throat typically flecked fairly heavily with bronzy green and often with some rose-pink spots or short streaks. Face washed buffy cinnamon and white line above bill 'lip' reduced to absent. **Tail:** looks blacker overall with duller, less contrasting bronzy green basally but R1 averages less black distally, R1–R3 average more cinnamon at base, and R1–R2 have fine white tip when fresh. Attains adult plumage by winter molt, but some year-old males may have sparser and shorter gorgets than adults[12].

Immature female: resembles adult female overall but plumage in fall fresher, upperparts with narrow, relatively inconspicuous cinnamon fringes most distinct on head and rump; throat typically flecked lightly with bronzy green and lacks iridescent rose feathers. Face washed buffy cinnamon and white line above bill 'lip' reduced to absent. **Tail:** similar to adult female, but cinnamon at base reduced (rarely[4]) to lacking (on most), and in fresh plumage has fine white tips to R1–R2.

Hybrids

With Costa's, Anna's, and Rufous hummingbirds[2,6], possibly with Broad-tailed Hummingbird[3]. Suggested with Bumblebee Hummingbird[13] but unlikely as these two species' breeding ranges are widely separated.

References

[1]AOU 1998, [2]Banks & Johnson 1961, [3]Calder & Calder 1994, [4]CAS specimen no. 46110 (15 August immature female), [5]D. Gibson pers. comm., [6]Graves & Newfield 1996, [7]Griscom 1934, [8]S. N. G. Howell pers. obs., [9]Howell & Webb 1995, [10]G. W. Lasley pers. comm., [11]Lehman 1997, [12]Pyle 1997, [13]Moore 1937.

20.1 Adult male Calliope. Unmistakable. Note elongated, streaked gorget, face pattern, and short cleft tail. Larry Sansone. San Bernadino Co., California, 4 June 1995.

20.2 Adult male Calliope. Unmistakable. Note relatively short tail and tail pattern, also dull flesh base to mandible. Charles W. Melton. Gila Cliff Dwellings National Monument, New Mexico, 4 August 1996.

20.3 Adult female Calliope. Note distinctive Calliope face pattern (e.g., white lores above bill 'lip'), a typical amount of throat flecking, and short tail. Ian C. Tait. Near Bridgeport, California, June 1984.

20.4 Adult female Calliope. Note distinctive Calliope face pattern (e.g., white lores above bill 'lip'), pale cinnamon sides, and short, mostly blackish tail. Some females have relatively plain whitish throats with very reduced bronzy-green spotting; the dark median throat spots on this bird were iridescent rose-magenta. Ian C. Tait. Near Bridgeport, California, May 1984.

20.5 Adult female Calliope. Note characteristic, slightly hunched pose, very broad wings with broad and rounded primaries projecting slightly beyond short, squared-looking, and black-tipped tail. Brian E. Small. Tucson, Arizona, August 1993.

20.6 Adult female Calliope. Note short, squared-looking (and mostly black) tail, cinnamon-washed underparts, and face pattern. Charles W. Melton. Turpin Meadows, Wyoming, June 1991.

20.7 Immature male Calliope. Note broad, rounded primaries, relatively short, mostly blackish tail, and extensive vinaceous-cinnamon wash on underparts, including sides of neck. Fresh plumage (in fall), distinct rufous at tail base, and heavily spotted throat indicate immature male. Charles W. Melton. Miller Canyon, Arizona, 21 August 2000.

20.8 Immature male Calliope. Short, squared, blackish tail (accentuating pot-bellied look) and vinaceous-cinnamon sides indicate Calliope, and relatively fresh plumage and heavily spotted throat suggest immature male (confirmed by banding). Bruce I Iallctt. Lilburn, Georgia (first state record), 9 November 1998.

20.9 Immature female Calliope. A typical 'feeder view' – note short, squared-looking black tail shorter than wing tips (cf. Pic. 22.5), and vinaceous-cinnamon wash below extending up into neck sides. That no primary molt has yet started suggests an immature bird. Greg W. Lasley. El Paso, Texas, 22 December 1995.

20.10 Immature female Calliope. Note short, slightly rounded tail with extensive black tip to R1 and little or no cinnamon at bases of outer rectrices. Jim & Deva Burns (Natural Impacts). Heber, Arizona, September 1995.

Rufous Hummingbirds Genus *Selasphorus*

This genus comprises eight species (including *Atthis*, merged by Howell and Webb 1995) of small to very small hummers that breed in temperate habitats from western North America to timberline in southern Central America. Three species breed in North America: Rufous, Allen's, and Broad-tailed hummingbirds, and a fourth (Bumblebee Hummingbird) may have occurred as a vagrant. Bills are black, straightish, and medium length in larger species to medium-short in Bumblebee. Tails are graduated (especially in males) to slightly double-rounded. P9 and P10 are about equal in length, so that P10 can be covered by P9 and almost completely hidden at rest. At rest, wingtips fall short of the tail tip. Males have solid gorgets slightly elongated at the corners and make a strong wing buzz in flight. Females have cinnamon-rufous sides and rufous in their tails.

21 Bumblebee Hummingbird

(Selasphorus [Atthis] heloisa)

7–7.5 cm (2.7–3 in). Bill 11–13 mm (female > male).
Pics 21.1–21.2

Identification summary

Status in North America enigmatic: known only from two 1896 specimens from SE Arizona. Very small size. Flight slow and bee-like, mostly silent and overlooked easily. Male distinctive, with elongated, 'shaggy' magenta-rose gorget, rufous base to rounded tail. Female from Calliope Hummingbird by smaller size, shorter bill, less rounded primaries, longer tail (at rest, wings < tail tip), and tail pattern.

Taxonomy

The two Arizona specimens were described originally as a new species, Morcom's Hummingbird *Atthis morcomi*[9] but *morcomi* was later merged into nominate *heloisa*[1,2]. On biogeographic grounds, however, one would expect the Arizona specimens to be *margarethae* of NW Mexico but this race was described in 1937[7], subsequent to the 1931 AOU checklist[1] and then presumably overlooked in the next AOU checklist[2].

Margarethae was originally ascribed to the Sierra Madre Occidental of NW Mexico[7], but later its range was defined as NW and central Mexico[4]. Several of the proposed characters of *margarethae* appear due to individual variation and plumage wear, but birds in NW Mexico may differ from other populations in slightly smaller size and male gorget color. A critical re-evaluation of Bumblebee Hummingbird subspecies, involving specimens in comparable plumage, is needed. Of interest is that the adult female from Arizona (USNM 153886) has a relatively lightly spotted throat much like an immature female from S Mexico; the probable immature female from Arizona (MVZ 10299) is more lightly marked on the throat and paler on the flanks than birds in S Mexico, and resembles Calliope Hummingbird in these regards.

Bumblebee Hummingbird is closely related to Wine-throated Hummingbird *S. ellioti* of northern Central America[6,11], with these two species often separated in the genus *Atthis*[3].

Status and Distribution

Known in North America from two female specimens collected on 2 July 1896 in the Huachuca Mountains, SE Arizona[8,9,10].

Range

Endemic to highlands of Mexico, north to SW Chihuahua (600 km or so S of Arizona).

Field Identification

Structure

Very small size. Bill medium-short, slender, and straightish. Male tail rounded, female tail slightly double-rounded (R1 < R2). Primaries moderately broad with male P10 finely attenuate and P9 narrow, female P10 narrow. At rest, wing tips < tail tip.

Similar species

Characters of NW Mexico birds not well known (see above under Taxonomy). Adult male Bumblebee should be unmistakable, female and immature could be confused with Calliope Hummingbird, and with other *Selasphorus*, which are quite similar in plumage.

Females (and Immature males)

Female **Calliope Hummingbird** is slightly larger with shorter and more squared tail (at rest, Calliope's wing tips slightly > tail tip, versus clearly < tail tip on Bumblebee), and quicker, darting flight (unlike slow, deliberate movements of feeding Bumblebee). Double-rounded tail of female Bumblebee means that closed tail often shows distinct white tip (can be obvious on closed tail of feeding birds), unlike black-tipped Calliope tail. Bases of all except R1 on all ages/sexes of Bumblebee are extensively rufous, striking on spread tail and much more obvious than dull and restricted rufous-cinnamon on Calliope's tail. Underparts of Bumblebee (at least in central Mexico) typically show distinctly dark-spotted throat, contrasting white forecollar, bright cinnamon-rufous sides (like immature Rufous/Allen's), but NW Mexico birds perhaps duller below with pattern more similar to Calliope (see Taxonomy).

Female/immature **Rufous/Allen's Hummingbird** overall similar in plumage to female Bumblebee but larger and longer billed (although size can be deceptive on a single bird); note more graduated tails of Rufous/Allen's with little to no pale tip on R2 and proportionately narrower outer rectrices (except perhaps immature female Rufous), and throat patterns: Bumblebee has evenly spotted throat, similar to immature Rufous/Allen's but distinct from adult females, and any iridescent feathers are magenta-rose versus flame-red. Note also aggressive behavior and quick hovering and feeding flight of Rufous/Allen's versus unobtrusive behavior and slow, deliberate feeding flight of Bumblebee.

Voice and Sounds

Mostly quiet except for loud insect-like wing buzz of adult male (strongest during shuttle display), but at times gives quiet, high chips when feeding. Female wing-buzz soft but stronger and buzzier than Calliope Hummingbird, unlikely to attract attention unless observer is keyed into the species. Song of male, given from perch, a very high, thin, whining whistle that may recall song of Costa's Hummingbird.

Habitat
Edges and clearings with flower banks in humid evergreen, pine-evergreen, and semideciduous oak forest, also adjacent shrubby growth with flowers.

Behavior
Feeds and perches mainly at low to mid-levels, often 'inside' flower banks (perhaps to avoid detection by other species). Feeding flight notably slow and deliberate, or 'beelike' (especially male), and quite distinct from relatively quick and 'nervous' flight of Calliope Hummingbird. Often hovers in a fairly horizontal plane with tail held cocked, closed, and rigid or with only slight quivering. Generally silent and overlooked easily, although male's wings make loud and distinctive buzz that can be hard to pinpoint. Typically dominated by other hummingbirds (even by Calliope[5]) so visits to hummingbird feeders seem unlikely if other hummers are present.

Molt
Presumably varies regionally depending on timing of breeding (cf. Howell and Webb[6]).

Description (see Taxonomy)
Adult male: elongated magenta to magenta-rose gorget offset by white forecollar. Underparts mottled bronzy green with cinnamon wash and whitish median stripe and vent band; undertail-coverts whitish with faint cinnamon centers. Crown, nape, and upperparts golden emerald-green with whitish to pale gray post-ocular line and dusky auriculars. **Tail:** R1 emerald-green to slightly bluish emerald-green with rufous basal edging, R2–R5 rufous basally with broad black subterminal band narrowly edged green basally, distinct white tips to R3–R5, smaller and buffy tip to R2. Bill black, feet blackish.

Adult female: crown, nape, and upperparts bronzy golden green to emerald-green, often slightly duller and bronzier on crown. Face with small whitish post-ocular spot and dusky, green-spotted auriculars. Throat whitish with lines of fine (to distinct, in Mexico) dusky to bronzy-green spots, underparts with contrasting whitish forecollar, cinnamon sides and flanks split by whitish median stripe, and pale cinnamon to whitish undertail-coverts. Some adult females may show one or more magenta-rose throat spots but this needs confirmation. **Tail:** R1 emerald-green to bluish emerald-green with indistinct rufous basal fringe and often a diffuse dark tip, R2–R5 rufous basally with broad black subterminal band narrowly edged green basally, bold white tips to R3–R5, slightly smaller and buffy tip to R2; relative to male, black subterminal band wider, white tips bolder, and rufous base more restricted.

Immature male: resembles adult female but throat with bolder bronzy-green spots and scattered magenta-rose feathers, cinnamon sides and flanks variably mottled green.

Immature female: resembles adult female but throat with finer bronzy-green flecks, sides and flanks paler cinnamon, contrasting less with whitish forecollar and median underparts, tips to R2–R5 washed buffy cinnamon when fresh.

Hybrids
None described. Suggested with Calliope Hummingbird[7] but this is unlikely as these two species' breeding ranges are widely separated.

References

[1]AOU 1931, [2]AOU 1957, [3]AOU 1998, [4]Friedmann *et al.* 1950, [5]S. N. G. Howell pers. obs., [6]Howell & Webb 1995, [7]Moore 1937, [8]Phillips *et al.* 1964, [9]Ridgway 1898, [10]Swarth 1904, [11]Zyskowski *et al.* 1998.

21.1 Adult male Bumblebee Hummingbird. Unmistakable in North America. Note small size, relatively short bill, 'female-like' tail with buffy tip to R2. Painting by Sophie Webb.

21.2 Female Bumblebee Hummingbird (based upon MVZ specimen 10299). From Calliope Hummingbird by longer tail (projecting beyond wing tips at rest) with more distinct rufous at base, cinnamon tip to R2, and all-green R1; also note lack of white line over bill 'lip,' and narrower and less broadly rounded primaries. In life, also note distinctively slow and deliberate, bee-like feeding flight. Painting by Sophie Webb.

22 Broad-tailed Hummingbird

(Selasphorus platycercus)

9–10 cm (3.5–4 in). Bill 16–20 mm (female > male).
Pics I.11, ix, 22.1–22.12.

Identification summary
Small to almost medium-sized. Male has relatively long, broad tail with 'jaggedly squared-off' tip, female/immature tail graduated but often with R1 slightly < R2. At rest, wing tips < tail tip. Adult male the only western hummer with green crown and rose gorget, and in flight outer primaries produce diagnostic, high, shrill, 'wing trill.' Female/immature have broad primaries, cold face with pale 'eye-ring,' finely flecked throat, cinnamon-washed underparts (typically lacking strongly white-collared and vested effect of

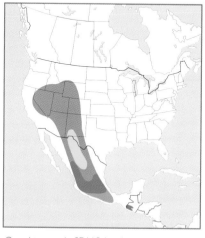

Casual to rare in SE U.S. in winter; see text.

Rufous/Allen's), relatively inconspicuous rufous at tail base, broad, green-based central rectrices, and less strongly graduated tail than Rufous/Allen's.

Taxonomy
North American populations are of the widespread nominate subspecies *platycercus*, which differs from *guatemalae* (of Guatemala and adjacent Chiapas, Mexico) mainly in its slightly larger size.

Status and Distribution
Summer resident (mainly April to August) of interior western mountains from W Texas and S Arizona N to E California, Idaho, S Montana, and Wyoming[2]; probably also breeds E Oregon[7]. Spring migrants reach S Arizona in March, and northern areas of breeding range by mid to late May[4]. Fall migration mainly August through September, ranging E rarely through western Great Plains.

Casual to rare N and W (mainly July to August) as far afield as British Columbia and Pacific coast of California. In winter (mainly November to April), casual in S California and S Arizona, casual to rare and perhaps increasing in SE U.S., mainly from Texas along Gulf coast to Florida[4,6,11], exceptionally north to Delaware[1].

Range
Breeds W U.S. to central Mexico, winters mainly Mexico; also resident Guatemala and adjacent SE Chiapas, Mexico.

Field Identification

Structure

Small to almost medium-sized. Bill medium length and straightish. Adult male has very slightly graduated tail that looks 'jaggedly squared' when spread, long and tapered when closed (usually covered by all-green R1). Female/immature tail slightly graduated (R3 ≥ R4), often with R1 slightly < R2 (**Figures 2,7**); R1 fairly broad and blade-like. P10 of adult male finely attenuated and slightly recurved, and P9 attenuated at tip; on perched birds, P10 usually lies mostly under P9 with attenuated tip looking like a sliver that is formed by a fork of the 'outer' primary. Primaries broad overall, with P10 narrower; P9/P10 project relatively short distance beyond P8. At rest, wing tips < tail tip.

Similar species

Adult males

In the west, adult male Broad-tailed distinctive among regularly occurring hummers by virtue of green crown and solid rose gorget (with white chin), and high, shrill, wing trill. On perched birds, where gorgets may not catch light, several features can be checked, including diagnostic, finely attenuated P10 and long, tapered, all-green closed tail of male Broad-tailed.

   Adult male Anna's Hummingbird (W North America) stockier and larger headed with more elongated gorget corners (often visible from behind as dark points, instead of white collar marks shown from behind by Broad-tailed; **Figure 5**), iridescent rose crown (often looks dark), lack of bold white forecollar, and summer molt schedule. On molting Anna's, closed tail often looks all-green but is short and squared (**Figure 5**), while full tail is cleft, with blackish outer rectrices projecting well beyond green R1. Anna's call a lower, more smacking chip, and lacks wing trill (although wings hum, and molting birds have labored wing rattle).

   Adult male Black-chinned Hummingbird (W North America) smaller and slighter in build with relatively longer bill, blackish face with contrasting white post-ocular spot, forked tail that lacks rufous edgings, narrow inner primaries, and twangier, less sharp call.

   Adult male Ruby-throated Hummingbird (E North America) superficially similar but smaller and slighter in build, with ruby-red gorget and black chin. Like Black-chinned, Ruby-throat has blackish face with contrasting white post-ocular spot, forked tail that lacks rufous edgings, narrow inner primaries, and different call.

Females

The most similar species in plumage is Calliope Hummingbird, but some Rufous and Allen's can look similar.

   Female Calliope Hummingbird (mainly W mountains) much smaller with shorter, slightly rounded but broad tail. At rest, wing tips of Calliope typically extend slightly beyond tail tip, rather than falling short of tail tip as on Broad-tailed. Calliope's closed tail looks short, squared, and broadly tipped black with little or no rufous visible; Broad-tailed has much longer and more strongly graduated tail with more extensive rufous bases to R3–5 (**Figure 2**). Adult Calliope's face typically has white lores including line above black bill 'lip,' and call soft and quiet. Calliope is a small species often dominated by other western hummers, something that happens less with larger and stockier Broad-tailed.

Female Rufous/Allen's hummingbirds (W North America) slightly smaller and slimmer in build with proportionately narrower tails that are more strongly graduated (R5 proportionately shorter, R4 obviously shorter than R3; **Figures 2, 7**), or tapered, when held closed (R1 with narrower, slightly notched tip), and slightly narrower and more tapered primaries, typically with longer and more tapered P9/P10 projection beyond P8. Rufous/Allen's typically have brighter rufous sides/flanks (most lack green spots at chest sides except *sedentarius* race of Allen's) contrasting with whiter forecollar and white median stripe on underparts, and all but some immature females show more obvious rufous at tail base. Throat typically more heavily marked, supraloral region and auriculars more strongly washed cinnamon in contrast to white post-ocular spot, and adults have flame-colored throat feathers. Dullest individuals can be similar in overall coloration to bright Broad-tailed. Note tail and rectrix shapes, tail pattern, primary shapes, and P9/P10 projection. Additonal clues may the bluer cast to upperparts of Broad-tailed (versus more golden green of Rufous/Allen's) and its later molt timing. Also, chip call of Broad-tailed is higher than Rufous/Allen's, useful with experience.

Female Black-chinned Hummingbird (W North America) slightly smaller and slighter in build with proportionately longer bill and narrow inner primaries. It has darker face, more contrasting white post-ocular spot, and often an unmarked whitish throat. Black-chinned lacks rufous in its tail and only a minority of bright immatures have sides/flanks distinctly washed buffy. Feeding Black-chinneds often wag their tail strongly, unlike Broad-tailed, and have a softer chipping call.

Female Ruby-throated Hummingbird (E North America) differs from Broad-tailed in much the same features as does Black-chinned Hummingbird, but is shorter billed and more often has buffy-washed sides/flanks, wags its tail less when hovering.

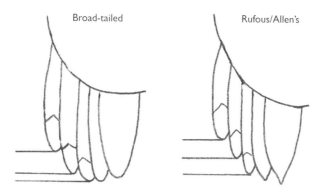

Figure 7. Comparison of tail graduation in female and immature Broad-tailed and Rufous/Allen's hummingbirds. Note more strongly graduated tail of Rufous/Allen's with proportionately shorter R5, and that R1 of Broad-tailed is often shorter than R2/R3. Shape of R1 varies with age/sex but typically broader and more blade-like on Broad-tailed, narrower and more tapered at tip on Rufous/Allen's.

Immature males
Immature male Broad-tailed distinguished from other species by much the same features as are females, although many have more heavily flecked throats, often with a few spots of rose. Some late-winter birds have adult-like wings, tail, and underparts, but throat still whitish with heavy lines of dark flecks, the rose gorget being the last feature to appear in first complete molt, usually during April–May. Others show bold splotches of adult-like rose in throat by mid-winter.

Voice and Sounds
Male calls tend to be higher than female calls. Common call a slightly metallic, fairly sharp *chip* or *chik*, higher than chip of Rufous/Allen's Hummingbirds. Given from perch and while feeding, and at times repeated steadily, mainly from a perch, with doubled notes thrown into series, *chi chi-chip, chip, chip...*, or *chik chik chik chi-tik chik...*, etc. Also simply doubled or trebled chip notes, *chi-tik* and *chi-ti-tik*; a fairly abrupt, clipped buzz, *tssir* or *tsssir*, mainly in warning; and longer, squeaky to slightly buzzy chippering series in interactions, e.g., *tssir-i chíp-i-chíp* or *tssir ti-chip chir*, with harsher and buzzier series at times. Chase calls typically higher and squeakier than Rufous/Allen's chase calls.

Adult male in direct flight (but not stationary hovering) produces diagnostic, high, shrill, somewhat cricket-like wing-trill, distinct from lower wing-buzz of male Rufous/Allen's and at times suggesting Cedar Waxwing (*Bombycilla cedrorum*) calls, but usually in shorter pulses. Male's wing-trill often reveals his presence in an area, even though he may avoid visual detection, but reduced to absent when P10 worn or molting (mainly in winter). Wing-trill loudest in accelerations, such as when leaving a perch or at top of power-dives in flight display, and male also produces (with his tail?) a short, typically trisyllabic, slightly buzzy rattle at bottom of power dive, *tr-tr-trt*.

Habitat
Breeding male territories mainly in shrubby areas and meadows within open, semi-arid conifer and mixed woodland where females nest; winters (in Mexico) mainly in fairly open, high-elevation conifer and pine-oak woodland with flower banks.

Behavior
Feeds and perches mostly at low to mid-levels, but territorial breeding males in breeding season often on prominent perch atop bush or tree. Feeds mainly with tail held closed, in or near body plane, and quivered, or occasionally flashed. Tail wagged and spread mainly in maneuvering and territorial interactions.

Flight displays include power-dive, hover-seeking, and shuttle. In typical dive display, male climbs steeply to 15–30 m, ending his climb with up to five or so short bursts, or pulses, of wing-trill that draw attention to display, and then flips over (making loudest wing-trill, or buzz, at this point) and power-dives down steeply to pull up in arc over subject and climb back to a similar height with pulses of wing-trill towards end of climb, i.e., repeating the pattern of the first climb and forming a U-shaped trajectory before turning and repeating the dive. Dives given one to several times in series which typically end with a deep J-shaped trajectory: male pulls up after last dive to a point about half the height of the U-shaped peak and often hovers there for a few seconds before flying off. Power-dives can feature a U-shaped trajectory, repeated over the same point, or can involve ranging over a wider area when trajectories can include looping over at the top points of climbs. Immature males probably give variations on adult power-dives, as in other *Selasphorus*.

Territorial males can also spend much time hover-seeking, i.e., hovering in one spot 5–40 m above their territory for up to a minute or longer, often with side-to-side swings; bill typically angled down, and tail varies from cocked above body plane to held near vertically downward. From stationary hover-seeking, birds often sink slowly in short steps and move short distances horizontally with deliberate progression, at times making shallow swooping dives or even loops between hover-seeking points, but without enough power to produce rattles at the bottom of dives. Male's short-wavelength shuttles appear much like Allen's Hummingbird (which see) but sound of Broad-tailed's wing-trill distinctive.

Molt

Molts on winter grounds. Primary molt starts October (rarely September) to January, ends February (rarely January) to May; averages later on immatures, and averages 1–2 months later than Rufous and Allen's hummingbirds. Some immature males in spring (through May, at least) still have juvenal outer primaries and splodges of gorget color on throat rather than a solid gorget (Pics 22.10, 22.11[10]). Exceptionally, P1–P2 of adult male can be molted in mid-July[8].

Description

Adult male: gorget iridescent rose to rose-red with narrow whitish chin stripe extending back into pale lores; dark crescent forward of eyes. White post-ocular spot contrasts with green crown and dusky to pale grayish auriculars border sides of gorget. White forecollar contrasts with gorget and green-mottled sides/flanks; variable whitish median stripe down underparts, white vent, and buff to cinnamon wash to axillars and lower flanks; undertail-coverts buffy white with variable dusky to bronzy-green centers. Upperparts relatively deep golden green to bluish emerald-green. **Tail:** R1–R2 bluish green to bronzy green with rufous outer web to R2. R3–R5 blackish with rufous basal edges to R3 and inner web of R4. Some birds (perhaps subadults?) have variable whitish on tip of R5 and rufous edgings to inner web of R5. Exceptionally, otherwise fully adult males can have female-like tails[9]. Bill black, feet blackish.

Adult female: crown, nape, and upperparts golden green to bluish emerald-green, darker and bluer when worn (so fall immatures look relatively golden green). Face typically has pale gray to pale buff supraloral stripe, dark loral crescent separated from eye by pale band, whitish post-ocular spot offset by dusky, green-spotted auriculars, and indistinct, dingy grayish post-ocular stripe. Throat whitish with lines of bronzy-green flecks that vary from sparse to heavy; some birds (up to 20–30%) have iridescent rose spots or splodges, mostly on center of lower throat. By fall, faded throat can appear unmarked dingy whitish with very faint dusky flecks hard to see. Whitish forecollar forms poorly contrasting band below throat, and is often washed cinnamon on sides of neck, thus blending with cinnamon-washed underparts. Cinnamon darkest at sides of chest and typically extends in narrow band across center of chest, immediately below forecollar, and usually with a few iridescent green spots at chest sides; median underparts often whitish (but without strongly vested look typical of Rufous/Allen's); vent whitish and undertail-coverts pale cinnamon. **Tail (Figure 2):** R1 wholly bluish-green to bronzy green (up to 5% can have dark distal marks, but lacks distinct dark tip), R2 green with black tip and variable to no rufous edging at base of outer web, R3–R5 with rufous bases (inner web of R3 green on some birds), black subterminal band bordered narrowly with green basally, and distinct white tips. Adult female tail pattern overlaps with both immature male and immature female.

Immature male: resembles adult female overall but plumage in fall fresher, upper-parts have narrow cinnamon to rufous tips most distinct on head and uppertail-coverts (often hard to discern in field), averages more green spots at chest sides; face washed cinnamon in fresh plumage (through fall migration) so lacks cold-faced adult expression with whitish eye-ring. Throat has lines of relatively heavy, bronzy-green spots, and up to 40% of birds show one to a few small rose feathers (often less than some adult females). **Tail:** similar to adult female but rectrices slightly narrower and more tapered, averaging more rufous at base: R1 can have rufous basal edging, R2–R3 often solidly rufous across bases, R2 in fresh plumage has fine white tip. Attains adult plumage by complete molt from first winter to spring or summer.

Immature female: resembles adult female overall but plumage in fall fresher, upper-parts have narrow cinnamon to rufous tips like immature male; face washed cinnamon in fresh plumage (through fall migration) so lacks cold-faced adult expression with whitish eye-ring. Throat has lines of small to moderate bronzy-green flecks and lacks rose spots; cinnamon sides lack green spotting. **Tail:** similar to adult female but rectrices slightly broader and blunter, averaging less rufous at base; R2 in fresh plumage has fine white tip. Attains adult plumage by complete molt over first winter through spring.

Hybrids
With Black-chinned and Costa's hummingbirds[3], possibly with Calliope Hummingbird[5]. Report of hybrids with Anna's, Rufous, and Allen's hummingbirds[12] appear unsubstantiated.

References
[1]AFN 52:309 (1998), [2]AOU 1998, [3]Banks & Johnson 1961, [4]Calder & Calder 1992, [5]Calder and Calder 1994, [6]Garrett & Dunn 1981, [7]Gilligan *et al.* 1994, [8]S. N. G. Howell pers. obs. (July 1999), [9]S. N. G. Howell pers. obs. (June 2000), [10]R. Hoyer pers. comm., [11]NAB, [12]Pyle 1997.

22.1 Adult male Broad-tailed. Note white chin and 'pale' face (cf. black-faced male *Archilochus*), broad primaries with diagnostic modified tips to P9 and P10 appearing as an oddly forked P10 (cf. Pic. 22.3). Charles W. Melton. Boulder, Colorado, June 1991.

22.2 Adult male Broad-tailed. Solid rose gorget with white chin is diagnostic. Also note pale face, rufous in tail. Sid & Shirley Rucker. White Mountains, Arizona, July 1995.

22.3 Adult male Broad-tailed. Note diagnostic shapes of P9 and P10 (producing unique wing trill), rufous in tail. Charles W. Melton. Boulder, Colorado, 14 July 1996.

22.4 Adult female Broad-tailed. The 'cold' face (lacking cinnamon tones) with a pale eye-ring, finely flecked throat, lack of a distinct whitish fore-collar, broad and truncate primaries, and lack of obvious rufous in tail all rule out female Rufous/Allen's and are much more like plumage of female Calliope. Note long tail with wing tips falling well short of tail tip (cf. Pic. 20.5), and lack of Calliope's white-lored expression. Nests are typically under some overhanging protection to reduce heat loss at night. Charles W. Melton. Boulder, Colorado, 13 August 1992.

22.5 Adult female Broad-tailed. A typical 'feeder view' – note wing tips short of relatively long tail tip with broad and all-green R1 (cf. Pic. 20.9), broad primaries, 'cold' face with pale eye-ring, finely flecked throat, lack of contrasting white forecollar. Mark M. Stevenson. Miller Canyon, Arizona, July 1999.

22.6 Adult female Broad-tailed. Long tail and cinnamon sides indicate *Selasphorus*. Weakly (not strongly) graduated tail, 'cold' face with pale eye-ring, pale vinaceous-cinnamon below extending across chest, and lack of contrasting white forecollar point to Broad-tailed. Lacks fresh plumage of fall immature (cf. Pics 22.7–22.8, 22.12); up to 20–30% of adult females have rose splodges (here looking black) on throat. Adult female Rufous/Allen's could match this face and throat pattern, and lack rufous in uppertail-coverts, but more strongly graduated tail would show more obvious rufous, face typically washed cinnamon and cinnamon-rufous sides/flanks more sharply demarcated from whitish forecollar and median stripe down underparts. Charles W. Melton. Walker Ranch, Boulder, Colorado, 10 August 1992.

22.7 Immature male Broad-tailed. Long tail, cinnamon sides, rufous in tail, and fresh plumage (in fall) point to immature *Selasphorus*. Relatively pale and not strongly contrasting cinnamon sides, 'cold' face, little or no rufous edging on uppertail-coverts, and R1 slightly shorter than R2 indicate Broad-tailed, and heavily spotted throat, relatively extensive rufous at tail base, and relatively long tail projection beyond wing tips all point to an immature male. Charles W. Melton. Miller Canyon, Arizona, 21 August 2000.

22.8 Immature male Broad-tailed. Same features apply as BrTHU 07 but flanks relatively bright and contrasting cinnamon, more like Rufous/Allen's, and note diagnostic rose spots of adult male gorget color. Jim & Deva Burns (Natural Impacts). Miller Canyon, Arizona, August 2000.

22.9 Immature male Broad-tailed. 'Cold' face, diffuse cinnamon below, and reduced rufous in long tail indicate Broad-tailed (the large dark throat patch was iridescent rose). Robert A. Behrstock. Houston, Texas, 7 January 1996.

22.10 Immature male Broad-tailed. Immatures can finish their postjuvenal molt relatively late and many molting males occur on spring migration. Appearance can suggest Anna's Hummingbird, cf. Pic. 18.9 (broad inner primaries and face pattern rule out *Archilochus*): note relatively clean white forecollar and median underparts, relatively long R1 (projecting well beyond wing tip), and equal-length P9 and P10 (a *Selasphorus* character). Molt timing could overlap with spring Anna's but immature male Anna's at this stage of primary molt would normally show more rose in throat and some on crown, or a much more worn grayish crown (cf. Pic. 18.9). Call is another useful feature. Charles W. Melton. Madera Canyon, Arizona, 17 April 1993.

22.11 Immature male Broad-tailed. In last stages of postjuvenal molt: note P10 and P9 growing, whitish tip to R5 (typical of many subadults), and incipient gorget. Charles W. Melton. Miller Canyon, Arizona, 12 May 2000.

22.12 Immature female Broad-tailed. Long tail, evenly broad primaries, vinaceous-cinnamon sides, and fresh plumage (in fall) point to immature *Selasphorus*. 'Cold' face, lack of contrasting white forecollar, weakly graduated tail (with R1 slightly shorter than R2), and relatively short P9/P10 projection indicate Broad-tailed. The throat spotting, relatively tapered primaries, relatively short tail projection beyond the closed wings, and reduced rufous at tail base point to an immature female. Charles W. Melton. Miller Canyon, Arizona, 13 August 2000.

Rufous/Allen's Hummingbirds
(Selasphorus rufus/sasin)

Probably no other species-pair of North American birds poses greater field identification problems than Rufous Hummingbird and Allen's Hummingbird, and observers should recognize that the majority of observations other than of rufous-backed adult males (at least outside the known breeding ranges and breeding seasons) are best lumped as 'Rufous/Allen's.' With comparative experience (preferably including extensive in-hand examination both of museum specimens and banded birds) some individuals (mainly males) can be identified in the field – those at the extreme ends of the bell-curve in terms of certain characters, particularly the width of R5 and emargination on R2. Still, many or most remain effectively unidentifiable under typical field conditions. Additional references that should be consulted on the identification of this problem pair are the seminal works of Stiles (1972) on identification and Phillips (1975) on migration routes and timing, plus the summary by Pyle (1997) and the analysis of adult males by McKenzie and Robbins (1999). Other useful sources of information include Kaufman (1990) and Heidcamp (1997). Nonetheless, the term 'Rufous/Allen's' (said as one word) should be a default option in the lexicon of hummingbird watchers.

23 Rufous Hummingbird

(Selasphorus rufus)

8–9 cm (3.2–3.7 in). Bill 15–19 mm (female > male).
Pics I.12, x, 23.1–23.13.

Identification summary
Breeds NW N America. Small size. Tail graduated. At rest, wing tips < tail tip. Adult male rufous overall with green crown, back ranges from all-rufous (typical) to all-green (rare; Pics 23.3, 24.4). Also note male's flame-colored gorget and wing buzz. Female/immature have variable throat markings (often with some flame-colored feathers), white forecollar, cinnamon-rufous sides/flanks, and rufous in tail. Tail and throat patterns important for age/sex determination. Often not distinguishable in field from Allen's Hummingbird.

Taxonomy
No subspecies described.

Status and Distribution

Summer resident (mainly March to July) from extreme N California, Idaho, and W Montana N and W to S central Alaska. Males typically arrive in S breeding areas by late February, in N areas late April or early May, and start to head S from mid to late June through July. Last fall migrants (immatures) leave breeding areas through September, with stragglers rarely into October including Kodiak Island, Alaska[16].

Rare in SE U.S. in winter, see text.

Spring migrant (mainly early February through early May) N from W Mexico through W Arizona and California, casually E through Colorado, and fall migrant (mainly late June through late September) S through western mountains (Coast Ranges/Sierra Nevada and Rockies, E to W Texas), in smaller numbers W to coastal California.

Rare but increasing (or increasingly detected?) vagrant or migrant (mainly July to November, with some lingering into winter, depending on the severity of cold weather) E to NE North America, exceptionally to the maritime provinces. Casual in spring (mainly April to early May) in E and central North America, N to Ontario[15]. Rare but apparently increasing fall and winter visitor (mainly October to March, with some arriving in late July and August) to SE U.S. [4,6], W to E Texas, e.g., 68 Rufous/Allen's hummingbirds (presumably almost all Rufous) reported in SE U.S. during 1909–1979, compared with 1643 birds during the 1990/91 to 1995/96 winters in the five states of Alabama, Georgia, Florida, Mississippi, and Tennessee[6]. Casual to rare and local (November to January) in S California[5], central California[18], and S Arizona[20]. Casual NW (June to August) to Bering Sea[11,14].

Range

Breeds NW North America, winters W Mexico, increasingly in SE USA.

Field Identification

Structure

Small size. Bill medium length and straightish. Tail distinctly graduated with R4 clearly < R3; R1 of female/immature tapered at tip; R2 typically with distinct emargination near tip (most pronounced in adults; Pic. 24.3, **Figures 2, 8**). At rest, wing tips < tail tip. Adult male P9 and P10 very narrow and sharply pointed. Female/immature P10 narrow and tapered (more so on immature male); P9/P10 project noticeably beyond P8.

Similar species

In North America, rufous in the tail and cinnamon-rufous sides/flanks essentially eliminate all but the other three species of green-and-rufous, small gorgeted hummingbirds: Allen's, Broad-tailed, and Calliope. (Bahama Woodstar, a casual vagrant to S Florida also has this plumage pattern, and some female/immature *Archilochus* have buffy-washed sides/flanks but all lack rufous in tail.)

Any identification in this group should start by determining the age and sex of a bird in question, because age/sex differences within a species can be greater than differences between the same age/sex of different species. Thus, immature female Allen's can have outer rectrices as wide as adult female Rufous, while immature male Rufous could have outer rectrices as narrow as immature female Allen's.

The most similar species to Rufous Hummingbird is Allen's Hummingbird (breeding mainly in California, but with migrants occurring more widely in the Southwest, and vagrants being found increasingly in the East). Relative to nominate Allen's Hummingbird, Rufous is slightly larger overall, but note that a slightly larger, longer-billed race of Allen's Hummingbird (*sedentarius*) is resident in a small area of southern California, and overlaps more in size with Rufous Hummingbird.

The best field identification characters for Rufous versus Allen's are the width and shape of certain rectrices. Overall, Rufous has broader rectrices than Allen's, taking into account age and sex: males have narrower rectrices than females, and adults have narrower rectrices than immatures (**Figures 2, 8**). This is often most noticeable on R5 and, with experience, can be useful (at least for males) in the field, *once the age/sex of a bird has been determined*. Also, the outer web of R2 on adult (and immature male) Rufous usually shows distinct emargination, lacking or poorly developed on Allen's and on most immature female Rufous (Pic. 24.3; **Figures 2, 8**); this tends to be difficult to see in the field. Remember that any evaluation of rectrix shape should take into account molt (are you really looking at R5, or R4?) and wear (heavily worn feather tips can affect the perceived width of a feather).

In summary, given typical views, the majority of female and immature Rufous and Allen's Hummingbirds are not safely identified to species in the field.

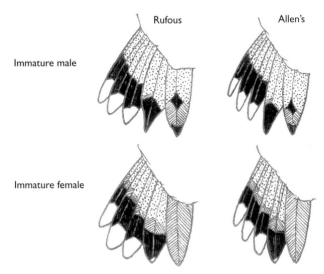

Figure 8. Tail shape and pattern differences in immature Rufous and Allen's hummingbirds. Hatching represents green, stippling rufous. Note narrower rectrices of Allen's and nipple-like tips of R2 on Rufous, both features being most distinct on immature males. Beware that tail patterns are highly variable, particularly the extent of rufous basally (e.g., see Figure 9), and appear not to be useful for specific identification.

Immature male   Adult female   Immature female

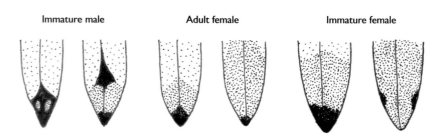

Figure 9. Shape and pattern differences in R1 of immature male, adult female, and immature male Rufous/Allen's hummingbirds. Sparse stippling represents rufous, dense stippling green. Note that immature male has narrowest R1, immature female widest. On females basal rufous typically abuts distal green, while on immature males rufous typically abuts black.

Adult males

The only problem here is between Allen's Hummingbird and a small percentage (up to 1–2%) of adult male Rufous that have all-green backs[12]; in this regard Rufous is the most variable of all adult male North American hummingbirds. Any adult or near-adult male with obvious rufous on the back should be a Rufous (if you look carefully you'll see that many adult male Rufous have from a few to many green feathers in their back). Even extensively green-backed male Rufous tend to have some rufous back feathers, but a few adult male Rufous appear to exactly match the pattern of adult male Allen's (Pics 23.3, 24.4). In areas where Allen's is common, mostly or fully green-backed male Rufous surely go undetected. Outside the range of Allen's, any green-backed adult male Rufous/Allen's should be scrutinized carefully. Numerically, male Allen's must greatly outnumber fully green-backed male Rufous, but Allen's should not be identified simply by probability, and the 'safest' course is to leave many birds unidentified to species. Also note dive-display differences (see under **Behavior**), useful in breeding season and perhaps during migration and winter.

With experience, and good views (e.g., birds fanning their tail in aggressive encounters), the width of the outer rectrices (especially R5) can be useful. While there is slight overlap in this feature, the narrowest, 'wire-like' R5 of Allen's is distinct from the widest R5 of Rufous (Pic. 24.3). A strongly emarginated notch on the outer web of R2 is diagnostic of Rufous; this is usually very difficult to discern in the field but can be captured by a photograph (e.g., Pic. 23.2).

Adult females

Adult female Allen's Hummingbird (mainly California) essentially identical in plumage to Rufous Hummingbird, and identification to species often not possible beyond default geographic range and probability. Note, however, that about 30% of adult female Allen's show distinct to extensive rufous edgings on their uppertail-coverts, versus narrow to absent edgings on adult female Rufous[7]. Thus, extensive rufous on the uppertail-coverts is strongly indicative of Allen's. Also, adult female Allen's of the race *sedentarius* have paler rufous sides with extensive green spotting, distinct from adult female Rufous. A knowledge of migration timings and migration routes is useful in this regard (see **Status and Distribution**). Observers very familiar with Allen's (nominate *sasin*) may be struck by the (albeit slightly) larger size of a Rufous Hummingbird when confronted with one, and *vice versa*.

Adult females are more worn in fall than immatures and have a mostly whitish chin and a central throat splodge of metallic flame color. They have slight to moderate rufous at the base of R1, and the rufous abuts a green subterminal band. Once age/sex is determined, identification can be attempted by studying width of R5 and shape of R2. Although there is slight overlap in both of these features, many birds can be identified in the hand and some in the field: Allen's has narrower rectrices and its closed tail may appear relatively narrow and pointed overall, compared to the relatively broader closed tail of Rufous. As on adult males, R2 of Rufous typically has the outer web distinctly emarginated (versus not or only slightly emarginated on Allen's). Allen's molts on average a month earlier than Rufous, although molt in *sedentarius* Allen's may be more variable.

Adult female Broad-tailed Hummingbird (mainly Great Basin and Rocky mountains) averages somewhat larger and heavier than Rufous, its tail is noticeably less graduated with a broader, blade-like R1 that is often < R2 (**Figures 2, 7**), and its primaries are slightly broader (with the P9/P10 projection beyond P8 relatively shorter). Its rectrices average wider with less rufous at the base (e.g., no rufous on R1 or inner web of R2). The face of Broad-tailed tends to be 'cold' with little or no rufous wash (often washed rufous on Rufous, so that the white post-ocular spot contrasts) and often shows a whitish eyering. Female Broad-tailed has a more diffuse and paler, more vinaceous-cinnamon wash to the underparts, compared with the brighter and more sharply demarcated cinnamon-rufous sides/flanks of female Rufous. The whitish forecollar and median underpart stripe are less contrasting, unlike the distinct white forecollar and strongly vested appearance typical of female Rufous. Female Broad-tailed's throat tends to be more evenly flecked with dusky, and any iridescent color is rose, versus an often larger central splodge of flame color on adult female Rufous. Upperparts of Broad-tailed average more bluish green, and molt averages about a month later than Rufous, which may be helpful for wintering birds. Call a higher and slightly more metallic *chip*.

Adult female Calliope Hummingbird (mainly W mountains) smaller with shorter and finer bill, broad rounded primaries, and noticeably short tail: at rest, wing tips usually project slightly beyond tail tip rather than falling short of tail tip, as on Rufous. Calliope tail has little rufous (often not noticeable) at the base, its throat is finely flecked with dusky, lacking a large central splodge of color, its lores are extensively white, and its sides and flanks are more diffusely washed vinaceous-cinnamon (much like Broad-tailed) rather than bright cinnamon-rufous with a vested appearance and white forecollar. Call a soft chip, and behavior relatively low-key, unlike the aggressiveness often shown by Rufous Hummingbirds at feeding aggregations.

Immature males

The same comments and criteria for separating adult females apply to **immature male Allen's and Rufous hummingbirds**, but also note dive-display differences (see under **Behavior**), useful from at least June into winter. Immature males have fresh plumage in fall, their extensively flecked throat and chin often have random spots of metallic flame color, and their sides/flanks average deeper rufous than females. Both species in this plumage have variable rufous on the uppertail-coverts, but limited rufous again appears more typical of Rufous than Allen's, which typically has extensive rufous in the uppertail-coverts. Often the mostly rufous uppertail-coverts merge with the rufous tail base, forming a wide band of rufous, unlike female Rufous and many female Allen's, and extensive rufous at the base of R1 abuts subterminal black and green (**Figures 8, 9**). Once age/sex is determined, identification can be attempted by studying width of R5 and shape of R2 (see above under adult female).

Immature male Broad-tailed and Calliope hummingbirds identified by much the same criteria that separate adult females from Rufous Hummingbird (see above), in particular note the less strongly graduated tail (with R1 often < R2), broader primaries, outer primary tip spacing, tail pattern, and paler, more diffusely cinnamon sides (lacking a contrasting white collar) of Broad-tailed, and small size, short tail, broad rounded primaries, and paler, more diffusely cinnamon sides (lacking a contrasting white collar) of Calliope.

Immature females

The same comments and criteria for separating adult females apply to **immature female Allen's and Rufous hummingbirds**. Immature females have fresh plumage in fall and their throats are more extensively flecked dusky than adults, rarely with spots of metallic flame color. The uppertail-coverts of immature female Rufous have narrow to indistinct rufous fringes (90% of birds) to fairly distinct rufous fringes (up to 10%), while most Allen's show distinct rufous on the uppertail-coverts[7], at times as extensive as on immature males; reduced rufous at the base of R1 is often not visible and abuts subterminal green (**Figures 8, 9**). Once age/sex is determined, identification can be attempted by studying width of R5 and shape of R2 (see above under adult female).

Immature female Broad-tailed and Calliope hummingbirds identified by much the same criteria that separate adult females from Rufous Hummingbird (see above), in particular note the less strongly graduated tail (with R1 often < R2), broader primaries, outer primary tip spacing, tail pattern, and paler, more diffusely cinnamon sides (lacking a contrasting white collar) of Broad-tailed, and small size, short tail, broad rounded primaries, and paler, more diffusely cinnamon sides (lacking a contrasting white collar) of Calliope.

Voice and Sounds

Calls very similar to those of Allen's Hummingbird and probably not safely distinguished; note that male calls tend to be higher than female calls. Common call a medium-hard to fairly hard ticking or clicking chip, *tik* or *chik*, given in flight and from a perch, at times repeated steadily by perched birds when may be given in slightly pulsating, irregular rhythm, including doubled and trebled notes, *chi chi chi-ti-ti chi-ti chi chi chi-ti...*, or *tik-tik tik tik-tik-tik...*, etc. Also simply doubled or trebled chip notes, *ch-tik* and *chi-ti-tik;* a nasal, slightly buzzy *jiuw* or *chíuw* in aggressive interactions; a slightly squeaky, buzzy *tsíiur* or *tsirr* in warning; and varied longer series in interactions, typically a warning note followed by a rapid-paced, slightly buzzy chatter or chipper, *tszir tzi-si si-si-chir,* or *zziir tí tíchip tí tíchip,* or *tsssir tsssir tsi tssir tsi*, and variations.

Male's wing-buzz often reveals his presence in an area, even though he may avoid visual detection, but wing-buzz reduced to absent when hovering and when P10 worn and molting (mainly in early winter). Wing-buzz loudest in shuttle displays. In dive display, male produces (with his tail?) a stuttering *ch-ch-ch-ch-chi* or *vr-du-duh du-duh*, as he pulls up in arc at bottom of dive (unlike drawn-out whine of Allen's), and also a stuttering *z-z-z-z-z-z-zzr* or *t-t-t-t-t-t-tr* in fluttering flight at end of J-dive.

Habitat

Breeds in open coniferous and mixed woodland, parks, gardens, forest edge, and nearby open and semi-open areas with shrubby vegetation and flower banks. Winters (in Mexico) mainly in open pine and pine-oak woods with flower banks. Migrants occur in a variety of open and semi-open habitats, including in lowlands.

Behavior

Feeds and perches mainly at low to mid levels, but territorial males in breeding season perch prominently high in or atop bush, tree, or on phone wire, etc. Feeds mainly with tail held closed, in or near body plane, and quivered or occasionally flashed. Tail flipped and fanned when hovering and maneuvering, e.g., to glean insects or on approach to feeders, and often fanned and flashed in territorial interactions. Notably aggressive, regularly chasing off larger species, e.g., Anna's and Broad-tailed hummingbirds.

In dive display, male flies from perch to starting point above subject, then ascends in variably steep climb to 10–25 m high, turns and power-dives down to pull up over subject in a slanted J-form trajectory typically followed by a short, horizontal fluttering flight; he then stops and turns to look back before ascending to repeat display one to several times; most dive-display sequences involve about five J-dives, unlike single and typically steeper J-dive typical of Allen's. Rufous J-dives are often repeated in more-or-less the same trajectory, back and forth over subject, or can involve ranging over a wider area when male may move in an arc around subject. From at least June into winter, immature males can give adult-like slanted J-dives or variations (but lacking in wing and tail noises). Adult male also has short-wavelength shuttles much like Allen's Hummingbird (which see). Closed-oval or ellipse dive-loops reported for Rufous Hummingbird by Robbins *et al.*[24] and Ortiz-Crespo[19], repeated by Johnsgard[10], not observed by Calder[3], nor seen by careful observers in Oregon[8,9,21,23] and British Columbia[2], and require substantiation, but note variation in power-dives exhibited by Broad-tailed Hummingbird.

Molt

Molts on winter grounds. Primary molt starts August to November, ends December (rarely November on adults, especially males) to March; averages later on immatures. Molt averages about a month later than in migratory Allen's Hummingbirds, and 1–2 months earlier than in Broad-tailed Hummingbird.

Description

Adult male: bright rufous overall, including back, with green crown and upperwing-coverts, white post-ocular spot (at times indistinct), iridescent flame gorget (upper chin rufous), broad white forecollar, and fluffy white vent band; underparts sometimes show whitish median stripe. Up to 1–2% of adult males have the back 95–100% green[12] (Pics 23.3, 24.4), and many birds have scattered green feathers in mostly rufous back. Extensively green-backed male Rufous tend to have some rufous back feathers, and in particular the lower rump is often mostly rufous. **Tail:** bright rufous, tipped dark green. Bill black, feet blackish.

Adult female: pale cinnamon supraloral stripe, white post-ocular spot, and diffuse pale buffy-cinnamon post-ocular line separate green crown from dark lores and dusky to rufous-washed auriculars that have variable bronzy-green spotting. Throat whitish to pale buff with lines of bronzy-green spots heaviest at lower sides and variable, iridescent flame splodge in center. Forecollar and median underparts whitish, with sides, flanks, and undertail-coverts cinnamon to cinnamon-rufous; at times with narrow cinnamon band extending mostly or completely across upper chest; up to 30% of birds show one to a few scattered green spots on sides and flanks; shorter undertail-coverts sometimes have small, bronzy-green centers. Upperparts golden green (bluer when worn) with indistinct (often virtually absent) rufous edgings to uppertail-coverts. **Tail (Figures 2, 9):** R1 bluish green to golden green with blackish tip and slight to moderate rufous at base (rarely none visible beyond tips of uppertail-coverts); R2–R5 rufous basally with black subterminal band (typically bordered basally by narrow band of green that can be hard to see in the field), and white tips to R3–R5.

Immature male: resembles adult female overall but plumage in fall fresher, upperparts with cinnamon to rufous tips and sides/flanks average brighter rufous, often with one or more green spots; rectrices narrower. Throat typically more heavily marked with lines of bronzy-green spots (that may fade by mid-winter) and usually with one or more scattered, iridescent flame feathers, at times with a central splodge of color suggesting adult female. Uppertail-coverts edged rufous, ranging from narrow, inconspicuous edgings (5–10% of birds) to extensive edgings that merge with extensively rufous-based tail to form a solid rufous 'rump patch.' **Tail (Figures 8–9):** on close views, note that rufous on tail base typically abuts subterminal black band (with no green in between), white tips to R3–R5 narrower and sometimes tinged buff.

Immature female: resembles adult female but plumage in fall fresher, upperparts with cinnamon to rufous tips; rectrices broader. Throat more uniformly marked with lines of bronzy-green spots, usually (but not always[13]) lacking iridescent flame feathers, sides and flanks lack green spots. Uppertail-coverts variable edged rufous, ranging from narrow, inconspicuous edgings (80–90% of birds) to extensive edgings (up to 10% of birds) that form a small rufous 'rump patch' on most heavily marked birds, but this is rarely contiguous with tail base. **Tail (Figures 8–9):** R1 typically has reduced rufous at base (often none visible beyond tips of uppertail-coverts), but some have more rufous than some adult females; white tips to R3–R5 sometimes tinged buff.

Hybrids

Apparently with Allen's Hummingbird[12,17]; studies of potential breeding overlap zone of these two species in NW California and SW Oregon are needed to address the nature of hybridization. Also with Calliope Hummingbird and possibly with Anna's Hummingbird[1]; reported with Broad-tailed Hummingbird[22] but apparently in error.

References

[1]Banks & Johnson 1961, [2]G. Brown pers. comm., [3]Calder 1993, [4]Conway & Drennan 1979, [5]Garrett & Dunn 1981, [6]Hill *et al.* 1998, [7]Howell 2001, [8]S. N. G. Howell pers. obs., [9]M. Hunter pers. comm., [10]Johnsgard 1997, [11]Kessel 1989, [12]McKenzie & Robbins 1999, [13]MVZ specimen no. 14250, [14]NAB 53:90 (1999), [15]NAB 53:276 (1999), [16]NAB 54:90 (2000), [17]Newfield 1983, [18]Ortiz-Crespo 1971, [19]Ortiz-Crespo 1980, [20]Phillips *et al.* 1964, [21]J. Plissner pers. comm., [22]Pyle 1997, [23]F. Ramsey pers. comm., [24]Robbins *et al.* 1966.

23.1 Adult male Rufous. Unmistakable. Many adults have some green mottling in their back (see Pics. 23.3, 23.4). Charles W. Melton. Gila Cliff Dwellings National Monument, New Mexico, 30 July 1999.

23.2 Adult male Rufous. In North America, a flame-colored gorget is found only on Rufous and Allen's hummingbirds. The relatively broad rectrices and distinctly notched tip of R2 are characteristic of adult male Rufous (cf. Pic.24.3). Jim & Deva Burns (Natural Impacts). Becker Lake, Arizona, August 1994.

23.3 Variation in amount of green on the back of specimens of adult male Rufous Hummingbirds. Kristof Zyskowski. Reproduced by permission of *Western Birds* 30:86–93 (cf. Pic. 24.4).

23.4 Adult female Rufous. Throat pattern indicates adult female, as does relatively worn plumage (in fall) with no rufous in uppertail-coverts; note also relatively 'cold' face with virtually no cinnamon wash, thus much like typical Broad-tailed. Identification to Rufous (versus Allen's) is based upon probability, but note lack of rufous in uppertail-coverts (Allen's often shows obvious rufous). In this view, best told from Broad-tailed by strongly graduated tail and relatively narrow and tapered primaries (e.g., P9–P10). Brian E. Small. Portal, Arizona, August 1993.

23.5 Adult female Rufous. Contrasting cinnamon-rufous on underparts and extensive rufous on tail base rule out Broad-tailed Hummingbird; also note cinnamon-washed face. Throat pattern, relatively worn plumage in fall, and notched tip to R2 indicate adult female Rufous. Charles W. Melton. Gila Cliff Dwellings National Monument, New Mexico, 4 August 1997.

23.6 Adult female Rufous. Tail pattern immediately indicates Rufous/Allen's, while geographic range and season strongly favor Rufous, supported by reduced rufous edgings to uppertail-coverts. Width of the retrices and only the hint of a notched tip to R2 appear equivocal, however, and identity should be confirmed by in-hand examination and measurements. Brian E. Small. Riverside Co., California, mid April 1986.

23.7 Immature male Rufous. Relatively narrow and tapered primaries, cinnamon-washed face, sharply contrasting cinnamon sides with white forecollar, and obvious rufous in strongly graduated tail eliminate Broad-tailed Hummingbird but identification to Rufous (versus Allen's) is based solely upon date and location. Fresh plumage in fall and extent of rufous in tail and dark on throat indicate immature male. Charles W. Melton. Boulder, Colorado, 10 August 1992.

23.8 Immature male Rufous. Extensive rufous in tail and uppertail-coverts, plus sharply contrasting rufous sides and white forecollar point to Rufous/Allen's. Fresh plumage in fall, heavily spotted throat, extent of rufous on inner rectrices, and notched tip to R2 indicate immature male Rufous. John H. Hoffman. Sonoita, Arizona, August 2000.

23.9 Immature male Rufous. By early winter many immatures attain extensively rufous backs, eliminating Allen's Hummingbird. Robert A. Behrstock. Houston, Texas, 14 February 1993.

23.10 Immature male Rufous. Rufous on flanks and in tail indicate *Selasphorus*, and fresh pumage in fall indicates an immature. Evenly spotted throat with two flame feathers and little rufous in uppertail-coverts and tail equivocal for sex determination. Relatively tapered and blackish tip to R1 and long projection of P9/P10 indicate Rufous/Allen's; identification as Rufous is based on date and location, supported perhaps by reduced rufous in uppertail-coverts. Larry Sansone. Miller Canyon, Arizona, 5 September 2000.

23.11 Immature male Rufous/Allen's. Fresh plumage in fall, throat pattern, and rump/tail pattern indicate immature male Rufous/Allen's. Within the geographic range of Allen's Hummingbird, this bird is not safely identifiable without in-hand examination although the date and location combined suggest Allen's is more likely. Note white dusting of pollen on crown. Charles W. Melton. Mount Pinos, California, 20 July 1994.

23.12 Immature male Rufous/Allen's. Fresh plumage in fall, throat pattern, and rump/tail pattern indicate immature male Rufous/Allen's, most likely Rufous based on geographic range. Charles W. Melton. Madera Canyon, Arizona, 18 August 2000.

23.13 Immature female Rufous/Allen's. The relatively extensive rufous edgings to uppertail-coverts, the strongly graduated tail, and boldly black-tipped R1 eliminate Broadtailed. Fresh plumage in fall and relatively little rufous in tail indicate immature female, and lack of iridescent flame throat feathers also supports immature female. Brian E. Small. Kern Co., California, September 1997.

24 Allen's Hummingbird

(Selasphorus sasin)

8–9 cm (3.2–3.5 in). Bill: nominate *sasin*
15–18.5 mm; *sedentarius* 17–21 mm
(female > male)
Pics x, 23.11–23.13, 24.1–24.10.

Identification summary

Breeds W N America. Small size. Tail
graduated. At rest, wing tips < tail tip.
Adult male rufous overall with green
crown and back, also note flame-colored
gorget and wing buzz. Female/immature
have variable throat markings (often
with some flame-orange feathers), white
forecollar, cinnamon-rufous sides/flanks,
and rufous in tail. Tail and throat patterns important for age/sex determination. Often not distinguishable in field
from Rufous Hummingbird.

A: nominate *sasin*, casual to rare in SE U.S. in
    winter
B: *sedentarius*

Taxonomy

Migratory mainland breeders comprise nominate subspecies *sasin*, while largely resident
birds of S California are subspecies *sedentarius*, which averages slightly larger than *sasin*
although this is unlikely to be noticeable in the field except perhaps for bill length. Adult
female *sedentarius* show distinct and fairly extensive green spotting on their sides and
flanks which average paler cinnamon and less sharply vested than nominate *sasin*, only
up to 30% of which show one to a few green spots on sides and flanks[8].

Status and Distribution

Nominate *sasin* a summer resident (mainly February to July) along W slope of coast
ranges from Ventura County, California, N to Coos County, coastal SW Oregon, with
occasional nestings and breeding season records slightly to S and N of these limits[4,5,14]. First males arrive in S breeding areas in January, in N areas through February,
and start to head S from early to mid June through July. Last fall migrants leave breeding areas mostly in August, with stragglers rarely into September.

Spring migrant (early January to early April) N from W Mexico through S
California, casually E through Arizona. Fall migration spreads farther E, with small
numbers rare but regular through Arizona (mainly July–August).

Casual N to Washington (May[10]) and NE to Massachusetts (August[22]). In fall and
winter (mainly August to February) casual to rare but increasing (or increasingly
detected?) E to SE U.S.[15,16]; casual N to Delaware[1]. Small numbers also winter locally in
coastal S California[4,21], possibly in central California[17].

Sedentarius breeds and mostly resident on California Channel Islands, whence spread in 1960s and 1970s to adjacent coast in vicinity of Palos Verdes Peninsula, Los Angeles County[23], with some post-breeding birds moving inland and upslope into nearby mountains[20]; casual S to San Diego[21]. In recent years, range of this subspecies has expanded inland through much of coastal slope of Los Angeles County and throughout Orange County[7], and resident populations of presumed *sedentarius* also occur now along the coast nearly to edge of breeding range of nominate *sasin* in Ventura County[3,14]; more work is needed on subspecies boundaries in this region. A specimen of this taxon reported from Louisiana[16] is remarkable and should be re-examined.

Range
Breeds extreme SW Oregon and W California, winters W Mexico. Local resident S California.

Field Identification

Structure
Small size. Bill medium length and straightish. Tail distinctly graduated with R4 clearly < R3; R1 of female/immature slightly tapered at tip; R2 typically lacks distinct emargination near tip (e.g., Pic. 24.3). At rest, wing tips < tail tip. Adult male P9 and P10 very narrow and sharply pointed. Female/immature P10 narrow and tapered (more so on immature male); P9/P10 project noticeably beyond P8.

Similar species
In North America, rufous in the tail and cinnamon-rufous sides/flanks essentially eliminate all but the other three species of green-and-rufous, small gorgeted hummingbirds: Rufous, Broad-tailed, and Calliope. (Bahama Woodstar, a casual vagrant to S Florida also has this plumage pattern, and some female/immature *Archilochus* have buffy-washed sides/flanks but all lack rufous in tail.)

Any identification in this group should start by determining the age and sex of a bird in question, because age/sex differences within a species can be greater than differences between the same age/sex of different species. Thus, immature female Allen's could have outer rectrices as wide as adult female Rufous, while immature male Rufous could have outer rectrices as narrow as immature female Allen's.

The most similar species to Allen's Hummingbird is Rufous Hummingbird (breeding farther N, with migrants occurring widely in the West, and vagrants being found increasingly in the East). Relative to Rufous Hummingbird, nominate Allen's is slightly smaller overall, while *sedentarius* overlaps more in size with Rufous.

The best field identification characters for Rufous versus Allen's are the width and shape of certain rectrices. Overall, Rufous has broader rectrices than Allen's, taking into account age and sex: males have narrower rectrices than females, and adults have narrower rectrices than immatures (**Figures 2, 8**). This is often most noticeable on R5 and, with experience, can be useful (at least for males) in the field, *once the age/sex of a bird has been determined*. Also, the outer web of R2 on adult (and immature male) Rufous usually shows distinct emargination, lacking or poorly developed on Allen's and on some immature female Rufous (Pic. 24.3; **Figures 2, 8**); this tends to be difficult to see in the field. Remember that any evaluation of rectrix shape should take into account molt (are you really looking at R5, or R4?) and wear (heavily worn feather tips can affect the perceived width of a feather).

In summary, given typical views, the majority of female and immature Rufous and Allen's Hummingbirds are not safely identified to species in the field.

Adult males

The only problem here is between Allen's Hummingbird and a small percentage (up to 1–2%) of adult male Rufous that have all-green backs[12]; in this regard Rufous is the most variable of all adult male North American hummingbirds. Any adult or near-adult male with obvious rufous on the back should be a Rufous (if you look carefully you'll see that many adult male Rufous have from a few to many green feathers in their back). Even extensively green-backed male Rufous tend to have some rufous back feathers but a few adult male Rufous appear to exactly match the pattern of adult male Allen's (Pics 23.3, 24.4). In areas where Allen's is common, mostly or fully green-backed male Rufous surely go undetected. Outside the range of Allen's, any green-backed adult male Rufous/Allen's should be scrutinized carefully. Numerically, male Allen's greatly outnumber fully green-backed male Rufous, but migrant Allen's should not be identified simply by probability, and the 'safest' course is to leave many birds unidentified to species. Also note dive-display differences (see under **Behavior**), useful in breeding season and perhaps during migration and winter.

With experience, and good views (e.g., birds fanning their tail in aggressive encounters), the width of the outer rectrices (especially R5) can be useful. While there is slight overlap in this feature, the narrowest, 'wire-like' R5 of Allen's is distinct from the widest R5 of Rufous (Pic. 24.3). A strongly emarginated notch on the outer web of R2 is diagnostic of Rufous; this is usually very difficult to discern in the field but can be captured by a photograph (e.g., Pic. 23.2).

Adult females

Adult female Rufous Hummingbird (W North America) essentially identical in plumage to Allen's Hummingbird, and identification to species often not possible beyond default geographic range and probability. Note, however, that about 30% of adult female Allen's show distinct to extensive rufous edgings on their uppertail-coverts, versus narrow to absent edgings on adult female Rufous[8]. Thus, extensive rufous on the uppertail-coverts is strongly indicative of Allen's. Also, adult female Allen's of the race *sedentarius* have paler rufous sides with extensive green spotting, distinct from adult female Rufous and nominate Allen's. A knowledge of migration timings and migration routes is useful in this regard (see **Status and Distribution**). Observers very familiar with Allen's (nominate *sasin*) may be struck by the (albeit slightly) larger size of a Rufous Hummingbird when confronted with one.

Adult females are more worn in fall than immatures and have a mostly whitish chin and central throat splodge of metallic flame color. They have slight to moderate rufous at the base of R1, and the rufous abuts a green subterminal band. Once age/sex is determined, identification can be attempted by studying width of R5 and shape of R2. Although there is slight overlap in both of these features, many birds can be identified in the hand and some in the field: Allen's has narrower rectrices and its closed tail may appear relatively narrow and pointed overall, compared to the relatively broader closed tail of Rufous. As on adult males, R2 of Rufous typically has the outer web distinctly emarginated (versus not or only slightly emarginated on Allen's). Nominate Allen's molts on average a month earlier than Rufous, although molt in *sedentarius* Allen's may be more variable.

Adult female Broad-tailed Hummingbird (mainly Great Basin and Rocky mountains) averages somewhat larger and heavier than Allen's, its tail is noticeably less graduated with a broader, blade-like R1 often < R2 (**Figures 2, 7**), and its primaries are slightly broader (with the P9/P10 projection beyond P8 relatively shorter). Its rectrices are wider with less rufous at the base (e.g., no rufous on R1 or inner web of R2). The face of Broad-tailed tends to be 'cold' with little or no rufous wash (often washed rufous on Allen's, so that the white post-ocular spot contrasts) and often shows a whitish eye-ring. Female Broad-tailed has a more diffuse and paler, more vinaceous-cinnamon wash to the underparts, compared with the brighter and more sharply demarcated cinnamon rufous sides/flanks of female Allen's. The whitish forecollar and median underpart stripe are less contrasting, unlike the distinct white forecollar and strongly vested appearance typical of female Allen's. Female Broad-tailed's throat tends to be more evenly flecked with dusky, and any iridescent color is rose, versus an often larger central splodge of flame color on adult female Allen's. Upperparts of Broad-tailed average more bluish-green, and molt averages 1–2 months later than Allen's, which may be helpful for wintering birds. Call a higher and slightly more metallic *chip*.

Adult female Calliope Hummingbird (mainly W mountains) smaller with shorter and finer bill, broad rounded primaries, and noticeably short tail: at rest, wing tips usually project slightly beyond tail tip rather than falling obviously shorter than tail tip, as on Allen's. Calliope tail has very limited rufous (often not noticeable) at the base, its throat is finely flecked with dusky, lacking a large central splodge of color, its lores are extensively white, and its sides and flanks are more diffusely washed vinaceous-cinnamon (much like Broad-tailed) rather than bright cinnamon-rufous with a vested appearance and white forecollar. Call a soft *chip*, and behavior relatively low-key.

Immature males
Same comments and criteria for separating adult females apply to **immature male Allen's and Rufous hummingbirds**, but also note dive-display differences (see under **Behavior**), useful from at least May into winter. Immature males have fresh plumage in fall, their extensively flecked throat and chin often have random spots of metallic flame color, and their sides/flanks average deeper rufous than females. Both species in this plumage have variable rufous on the uppertail-coverts, but limited rufous again appears more typical of Rufous than Allen's, which typically has extensive rufous in the uppertail-coverts. Often the mostly rufous uppertail-coverts merge with the rufous tail base, forming a wide band of rufous, unlike female Rufous and many female Allen's, and extensive rufous at the base of R1 abuts subterminal black and green (**Figures 8, 9**). Once age/sex is determined, identification can be attempted by studying width of R5 and shape of R2 (see above under adult female).

Immature male Broad-tailed and Calliope hummingbirds identified by much the same criteria that separate adult females from Allen's Hummingbird (see above). In particular, note the less strongly graduated tail (with R1 often < R2), broader primaries, outer primary tip spacing, tail pattern, broader outer rectrices, and paler, more diffusely cinnamon sides (lacking a contrasting white collar) of Broad-tailed, and small size, short tail, broad rounded primaries, and paler, more diffusely cinnamon sides (lacking a contrasting white collar) of Calliope.

Immature females

Same comments and criteria for separating adult females apply to **immature female Allen's and Rufous hummingbirds**. Immature females have fresh plumage in fall and their throats are more extensively flecked dusky than adult, rarely with spots of metallic flame color. The uppertail-coverts of immature female Rufous have narrow to indistinct rufous fringes (90% of birds) to fairly distinct rufous fringes (up to 10%), while most Allen's show distinct rufous on the uppertail-coverts[8], at times as extensive as on immature males; reduced rufous at the base of R1 is often not visible and abuts subterminal green (**Figures 8, 9**). Once age/sex is determined, identification can be attempted by studying width of R5 and shape of R2 (see above under adult female).

Immature female **Broad-tailed and Calliope hummingbirds** identified by much the same criteria that separate adult females from Allen's Hummingbird (see above), in particular note the less strongly graduated tail (with R1 often < R2), broader primaries, outer primary tip spacing, tail pattern, broader outer rectrices, and paler, more diffusely cinnamon sides (lacking a contrasting white collar) of Broad-tailed, and small size, short tail, broad rounded primaries, and paler, more diffusely cinnamon sides (lacking a contrasting white collar) of Calliope.

Voice and Sounds

Following refers to nominate *sasin* but *sedentarius* not known to be substantively different[13]. Calls very similar to those of Rufous Hummingbird and probably not safely distinguished; note that male calls tend to be higher than female calls. Common call a medium-hard to fairly hard ticking chip, *chik* or *chi*, from perch and in flight while feeding, at times repeated steadily by perched birds and including doubled and trebled notes, *chi chi chi chi chi chi-ti chi-ti chi chi…*, etc. Also simply doubled and trebled chips, *chi ti-ti* and *chi-tik*, etc; an abrupt, slightly buzzy to nasal *tseéu!* or *chíuw!* in aggressive interactions; a high, slightly wiry *tsirr* or *siirr* in warning; and varied chippering series in interactions and chases, typically introduced by warning call, *tssir tí-chi tí-chi*, or *tssir chípi tíchip*, or *tssiir tí chípi tíchip*, and variations.

Male's wing-buzz often reveals his presence in an area, even though he may avoid visual detection, but wing-buzz reduced to absent when hovering and when P10 worn and molting (mainly in early winter). Wing-buzz loudest in shuttle displays. In dive display, male also makes a high, drawn-out, shrieky whine as he pulls up in arc at bottom of dive, unlike stutter of Rufous; shrieky whine in *sasin* comprises 3–5 pulsating syllables run together and upslurred at end, *vrrizizheeeu* or *vrrizzhizhiu*[9], in *sedentarius* perhaps more often 4–5 syllables, *phphphphpheeew*[3,18]; more study needed. Immature *sasin* males can make a quieter whining *zzhieer* in pull-out of J-dives. In shuttle display and rocking series preceding J-dive, direction reversals of *sasin* accompanied by a stuttering *z-z-zzir* (produced by tail?) between bouts of wing buzzing; stutter can be given at end of last arc before climb for J-dive[9] and also at end-point of J-dive as bird stops.

Habitat

Nominate *sasin* breeds primarily in coastal 'fog belt' in open mixed and coniferous woodland, parks, gardens, forest edge, and nearby open and semi-open areas with chaparral, shrubby vegetation, and flower banks, often along alder-lined streams in coastal valleys. Winters (in Mexico) mainly in open pine and pine-oak woods with flower banks. Migrants occur in a variety of open and semi-open habitats. *Sedentarius* traditionally resident in sage scrub and associated riparian habitat on islands and

along the immediate mainland coast, but extensive non-native plantings (e.g., euca-
lyptus, cape honeysuckle, bottlebrush) have resulted in marked habitat and range
expansion in the past few decades[3].

Behavior

Feeds and perches mainly at low to mid levels, but territorial males in breeding season
perch prominently high in or atop bush, tree, or on phone wire, etc. Feeds mainly
with tail held closed, in or near body plane, and quivered or occasionally flashed. Tail
flipped and fanned when hovering and maneuvering, e.g., to glean insects or on
approach to feeders, and often fanned and flashed in territorial interactions. Notably
aggressive, regularly chasing off larger species, e.g., Anna's Hummingbird.

In dive display of nominate *sasin* (*sedentarius* considered virtually identical[18, 20]),
male flies from perch to starting point above subject and makes rhythmic, variably
deep swoops 4–12x (usually 4–8x) back and forth over subject in arcs of about 5–8 m
wavelength, gorget flared and aimed at subject, then climbs steeply from end point of
last arc up to 15–30 m and turns to power-dive back down and sweep up in shallow
arc over subject, stopping fairly abruptly, if briefly, at end point of its J-form trajectory before flying off to perch or, less often, retracing arc and climbing back to repeat J-
dive a second time. From at least May into first winter, immature males give swooping dive arcs similar to adult but often of shorter wavelength (e.g., 2–6 m) and lacking
in wing and tail noises; less often these are followed by adult-like J-dives. Adult male
also has intense, short-wavelength shuttles (0.5 m or less) rocking and twisting in
convoluted arcs in front of and over subject, holding tail cocked vertically over back,
and gorget flared; shuttles much like other *Selasphorus*. Exceptionally, adult male
Allen's (nominate *sasin*) can mimic Anna's dive-display trajectory, starting from hover
and climbing near-vertically to 30 m or more (but with bill pointed up, not towering
with bill angled down as in Anna's), then power-diving down to pull up in loop; these
displays given in tandem with displaying male Anna's[6].

Molt

Nominate *sasin* molts on winter grounds: primary molt starts August (and probably
July in some adult males) to October, ends November (on some adults, especially
males) to February; averages later on immatures. Molt averages about a month earlier
than Rufous Hummingbird. Main breeding season of *sedentarius* is December to May[3],
i.e., averaging about a month ahead of nominate *sasin*, so molt schedule can be
expected to vary accordingly; more study needed.

Description

Adult male: bright rufous overall with golden green to emerald-green (bluer when
worn) crown, back, upper rump, and upperwing-coverts, white post-ocular spot (at
times indistinct), iridescent flame gorget (upper chin rufous), broad white forecollar,
and fluffy white vent band. As far as known, Allen's do not show any obvious rufous
in their back[12]. **Tail**: bright rufous, tipped dark green. Bill black, feet blackish.

Adult female: pale cinnamon supraloral stripe, white post-ocular spot, and diffuse
pale buffy-cinnamon post-ocular line separate green crown from dark lores and dusky
to rufous-washed auriculars that have variable bronzy-green spotting. Throat whitish
to pale buff with lines of bronzy-green spots heaviest at lower sides and variable, iridescent flame splodge in center. Forecollar and median underparts whitish, with
sides, flanks, and undertail-coverts cinnamon to cinnamon-rufous (averaging paler

and less extensively cinnamon on *sedentarius*), at times with narrow cinnamon band extending mostly or completely across upper chest; up to 30% of nominate *sasin* show one to a few scattered green spots on sides and flanks, most if not all *sedentarius* show distinct and relatively extensive green spotting (see under Taxonomy); shorter undertail-coverts sometimes have small, bronzy-green centers. Upperparts golden green (bluer when worn), with variable (extensive on up to 30% of birds[8]) rufous edging to uppertail-coverts. **Tail (Figures 2, 9):** R1 bluish green to golden green with blackish tip and slight to moderate rufous at base (rarely none visible beyond tips of uppertail-coverts); R2–R5 rufous basally with black subterminal band (typically bordered basally by narrow belt of green that can be hard to see in field), and white tips to R3–R5.

Immature male: resembles adult female overall but plumage in fall fresher, upperparts with cinnamon to rufous tips and sides/flanks average brighter rufous, often with one or more green spots; rectrices narrower. Throat typically more heavily marked with lines of bronzy-green spots (that may fade by mid-winter) and usually with one or more scattered, iridescent flame feathers, at times with a central splodge of color suggesting adult female. Uppertail-coverts with variable, usually extensive, rufous edgings that merge with extensively rufous-based tail to form a solid rufous 'rump patch.' **Tail (Figures 8–9):** on close views, note that rufous on tail base typically abuts subterminal black band (with no green in between), white tips to R3–R5 narrower and sometimes tinged buff.

Immature female: resembles adult female but plumage in fall fresher, upperparts with cinnamon to rufous tips; rectrices broader. Throat more uniformly marked with lines of bronzy-green spots, usually lacking iridescent flame feathers; sides and flanks lack green spots (at least in nominate *sasin*; no *sedentarius* seen). Uppertail-coverts variably edged rufous, sometimes with extensive edgings that form a small rufous 'rump patch,' but this is rarely contiguous with tail base. **Tail (Figures 8–9):** R1 typically has reduced rufous at base (often none visible beyond tips of uppertail coverts), but some have more rufous than some adult females; white tips to R3–R5 sometimes tinged buff.

Hybrids

Apparently with Rufous Hummingbird[12,16]; studies of potential breeding overlap zone of these two species in NW California and SW Oregon are needed to address the nature of hybridization. Also with Anna's Hummingbird[2] and Black-chinned Hummingbird[11]. Report of hybrid with Broad-tailed Hummingbird[19] apparently in error.

References

[1]AFN 52:37 (1998), [2]Banks & Johnson 1961, [3]K. L. Garrett pers. comm., [4]Garrett & Dunn 1981, [5]Gilligan *et al.* 1994, [6]J. Green pers. comm., [7]Hamilton & Willick 1996, [8]Howell 2001, [9]S. N. G. Howell pers. obs., [10]Jewett *et al.* 1953, [11]Lynch & Ames 1970, [12]McKenzie & Robbins 1999, [13]Mitchell 2000, [14]D. E. Mitchell pers. comm., [15]NAB, [16]Newfield 1983, [17]Ortiz-Crespo 1971, [18]J. Plissner pers. comm, [19]Pyle 1997, [20]Stiles 1972, [21]Unitt 1984, [22]Viet & Peterson 1993, [23]Wells & Baptista 1979.

24.1 Adult male Allen's. Identification based upon range and season, and supported by apparent narrowness of rectrices (cf. Pic. 24.3). Brian E. Small. Newport Back Bay, California, January 1997.

24.2 Adult male Allen's. Identification based upon range and season, but note apparent narrowness of rectrices (cf. Pic. 24.3). Charles W. Melton. Prairie Creek Redwoods State Park, California, 16 May 1995.

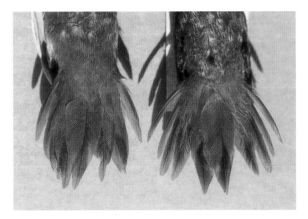

24.3 Tails of specimens of adult male Rufous (left) and adult male Allen's (right) hummingbirds. Note broader rectrices (often most noticeable on R4–R5) and strongly notched tip to R2 of Rufous. Kristof Zyskowski. Reproduced by permission of *Western Birds* 30:86–93.

24.4 Specimens of two adult male Allen's Hummingbirds (either side) and green-backed adult male Rufous Hummingbird (center). Kristof Zyskowski. Reproduced by permission of *Western Birds* 30:86–93.

24.5 Adult female Allen's (nominate *sasin* by range). Contrasting rufous sides, cinnamon-washed face, and relatively narrow and tapered primaries point to Rufous/Allen's. Throat pattern and context indicate adult female, and identification to Allen's is based on geographic location. Note uniform and relatively deep rufous sides cf. Pic. 24.6 of race *sedentarius*. Ian C. Tait. Near Bolinas, California, June 1971.

24.6 Adult female Allen's. Geographic range indicates this is the race *sedentarius*. The washed out flanks are mottled green, typical of *sedentarius* but atypical of nominate Allen's Hummingbird (cf. Pic. 24.5) and of Rufous Hummingbird, adult females of which typically have brighter rufous flanks with little to no green mottling. Larry Sansone. Malibu, California, 14 March 1992.

24.7 Adult female Allen's (nominate *sasin* by range). Contrasting rufous sides, cinnamon-washed face, and rufous-edged uppertail-coverts indicate Rufous/Allen's; throat pattern (heavily spotted on this individual, cf. Pic. 24.8) and season indicate adult female. Species identification based upon geographic location and probability, although Allen's (like this bird) often shows more rufous on uppertail-coverts than adult female Rufous (cf. Pics 23.4, 23.6). Mike Danzenbaker. Santa Cruz Co., California, 2 April 1988.

24.8 Adult female Allen's (nominate *sasin* by range). Contrasting rufous sides and cinnamon-washed face indicate Rufous/Allen's; throat pattern (typical on this individual, cf Pic. 24.7) and season indicate adult female. Species identification based upon geographic location and probability. Mike Danzenbaker. Santa Cruz Co., California, 2 April 1988.

24.9 Immature male Allen's (nominate *sasin* by range). Contrasting cinnamon-rufous sides, white forecollar, cinnamon-washed face, and extensively rufous uppertail-coverts point to Rufous/Allen's. Evenly spotted throat (with one or two iridescent flame feathers), plus fresh plumage overall, indicate immature male (extent of rufous on uppertail-coverts also more typical of immature male than female). Species identification based upon geographic location and date. John Sorenson. Big Sur, California, July 1992.

24.10 Immature female Allen's (nominate *sasin* by range). Contrasting cinnamon-rufous sides, white forecollar, cinnamon-washed face, and rufous-edged uppertail coverts point to Rufous/Allen's. Evenly spotted throat (with no iridescent flame feathers) and fresh plumage overall indicate immature female. Species identification based upon date and geographic location. Peter LaTourette. San Mateo Co., California, 12 June 1999.

Abbreviations and Terminology

Albino. Lacking in pigment and thus appearing white.

Arched. Refers to a bill that is 'decurved' through a shallow arch, versus simply down-curving throughout.

Attenuate. Tapered, in relation to primaries or rectrices whose tips narrow to a point; see truncate.

CBRC. California Bird Records Committee.

Cleft. Refers to tail shape where the outer feathers are slightly longer than the inners; see forked. A deeply cleft tail becomes forked.

Crissum. Undertail-coverts; mostly used when these feathers comprise a solid and often contrasting patch of color.

Double-rounded. Refers to tail shape where both the central and outermost rectrices are noticeably shorter than the others.

Falcate. Attenuated and slightly curved, or sickle-shaped.

Forecollar. A contrasting band (usually whitish in hummingbirds) across the front of the neck.

Forked. Refers to tail shape where the outer feathers are distinctly longer than the inners; see cleft. A shallowly forked tail becomes a cleft tail.

Gorget. A contrasting throat panel of brilliantly iridescent feathers.

Graduated. Refers to a tail where outer feathers are progressively shorter than inners (although R1 may be slightly shorter than R2), giving a wedge-like shape to the spread tail; see rounded.

Iridescent. Glittering or metallic-looking, e.g., refers to colors dependent on the interference of reflected light from a feather and which thus change in intensity depending on the angle of light.

Leucistic. Milky colored due to deficiency of pigmentation.

Monotypic. Literally, of one type. A monotypic species is one for which no subspecies are recognized, thus indicating that geographic variation is absent or weakly defined. A monotypic genus is one containing only a single species.

Notched. Refers to a tail where the inner feathers are slightly shorter; a deeply notched tail becomes cleft.

Post-ocular Spot. A spot (usually white) immediately behind, and usually slightly above, the eye.

Post-ocular Stripe. A pale (usually whitish) stripe starting immediately behind the eye and running along the upper edge of the auriculars.

P: primary. Primaries are the primary wing feathers (numbering 9–10 in most birds, 10 in hummingbirds) attached to the hand bone, or manus, and whose bases are protected by primary coverts.

R: rectrix. Rectrices (singular: Rectrix) are the main tail feathers (numbering 10–12 in most birds, 10 in hummers) that act as a rudder and whose bases are protected by tail-coverts.

Rounded. Refers to a tail whose outer feathers are slightly shorter than the inners, giving an evenly and relatively gently rounded shape to the spread tail; see graduated.

Rufous. Brownish red, or orangish in color.

Secondaries. The secondary wing feathers attached to the forearm bone (numbering 6–7 in hummingbirds) and whose bases are protected by secondary-coverts (often simply called wing-coverts).

Straightish. Refers to a bill that is more-or-less straight but at times can appear slightly decurved or arched; most North American species have straightish (versus dead straight) bills.

Superspecies. A taxonomic term relating to two or more closely related species that replace one another over a geographic range, and whose ranges do not, or barely, overlap.

Tail closed. The tail is largely held closed, rather than partially or fully spread.

Tail fanned. The tail is spread open, like a fan.

Tail flashed. The tail is periodically spread from the more typical closed position, potentially flashing any white tail corners.

Tail partly spread. The tail is held about 'half open,' not closed or widely spread, or fanned.

Tail quivered. The tail is mostly closed but the outer feathers may spread and close slightly; more expressive quivering grades into flashing.

Tail rigid. The tail is held largely in the same vertical plane, without strong wagging.

Tail wagged. The tail is moved up and down noticeably, with a steady motion, typically partly spread or fanned. Longer tails often have a pumping action when wagged.

TBRC. Texas Bird Records Committee.

Tertials. Third-degree (or tertiary) flight feathers, usually used in reference to the inner secondaries and numbering three in hummingbirds (and most passerines).

Tomium (plural: Tomia). Cutting edge(s) of the maxilla and mandible.

Truncate. Blunt and relatively broad tipped, usually used in relation to rectrices; see attenuate.

Uropygial gland. A gland on the rump (= uropygium), i.e., at the base of the tail feathers.

Vinaceous. Pale pinkish in color.

Literature Cited

Aldrich, E. C. 1956. Pterylography and molt of the Allen Hummingbird. *Condor* 58:121–133.

American Ornithologists' Union. 1931. Checklist of North American Birds, 4th edition. American Ornithologists' Union, Lancaster, Pennsylvania.

American Ornithologists' Union. 1957. Checklist of North American Birds, 5th edition. American Ornithologists' Union, Washington, D.C.

American Ornithologists' Union. 1998. Checklist of North American Birds, 7th edition. American Ornithologists' Union, Washington, D.C.

Anderson, J. O., and G. Monson. 1981. Berylline Hummingbirds nest in Arizona. *Continental Birdlife* 2:56–61.

Andrews, R., and R. Righter. 1992. *Colorado Birds*. Denver Mus. Nat. Hist.

Bain, M., and D. Shanahan. 1999. Cross Canada round-up. *Birders Journal* 8:276–279.

Baldridge, F. A., L. F. Kiff, S. K. Baldridge, and R. B. Hansen. 1983. Hybridization of a Blue-throated Hummingbird in California. *Western Birds* 14:17–30.

Baltosser, W. H. 1987. Age, species, and sex determination of four North American hummingbirds. *North American Bird Bander* 12:151–166.

Baltosser, W. H. 1989. Costa's Hummingbird: its distribution and status. *Western Birds* 20:41–62.

Baltosser, W. H. 1995. Annual molt in Ruby-throated and Black-chinned hummingbirds. *Condor* 97:484–491.

Baltosser, W. H., and S. M. Russell. 2000. Black-chinned Hummingbird. No. 495 in Poole, A., and F. Gill (eds.). *The Birds of North America, Inc.* Philadelphia, Pennsylvania.

Baltosser, W. H., and P. E. Scott. 1996. Costa's Hummingbird. No. 251 in Poole, A., and F. Gill (eds.). *The Birds of North America*. The Academy of Natural Sciences, Philadelphia, PA, and the American Ornithologists' Union, Washington, D.C.

Banks, R. C., and N. K. Johnson. 1961. A review of North American hybrid hummingbirds. *Condor* 63:3–28.

Berlioz, J. 1932. Notes critiques sur quelques Trochilidés du British Museum. *Oiseau* 2:530–534.

Binford, L. 1997. First state record: Broad-billed Hummingbird. *Michigan Birds* 4:47–49.

Browning, M. R. 1978. An evaluation of the new species and subspecies proposed in Oberholsers' *Bird Life of Texas*. *Proc. Biol. Soc. Wash.* 91:85–122.

Buden, D. W. 1987. *The Birds of the Southern Bahamas. An Annotated Checklist*. British Ornithol. Union Checklist No. 8.

Calder, W. A. 1993. Rufous Hummingbird. No. 53 in Poole, A., and F. Gill (eds.) *The Birds of North America*. The Academy of Natural Sciences, Philadelphia, PA, and the American Ornithologists' Union, Washington, D.C.

Calder, W. A., and L. L. Calder. 1992. Broad-tailed Hummingbird. No. 16 in Poole, A., and F. Gill (eds.) *The Birds of North America*. The Academy of Natural Sciences, Philadelphia, PA, and the American Ornithologists' Union, Washington, D.C.

Calder, W. A., and L. L. Calder. 1994. Calliope Hummingbird. No. 135 in Poole, A., and F. Gill, (eds.) *The Birds of North America*. The Academy of Natural Sciences, Philadelphia, PA, and the American Ornithologists' Union, Washington, D.C.

Campbell, R. W., N. K. Dawe, I. McT.-Cowan, J. M. Cooper, G. W. Kaiser, and M. C. E. McNall. 1990. *The Birds of British Columbia*, vol. 2. Royal British Columbia Museum, Victoria.

Contreras, A. 1999. New historic records of Anna's Hummingbird from Oregon. *Western Birds* 30:214.

Conway, A. E., and S. R. Drennan. 1979. Rufous Hummingbirds in eastern North America. *American Birds* 33:130–132.

Crossley, R. 1997. Black-chinned Hummingbird (*Archilochus alexandri*) first New Jersey record. *Records of New Jersey Birds* 23:53–54.

Cruickshank, H. G. 1964. A Cuban Emerald Hummingbird. *Florida Naturalist* 37:23, 32.

DeBenedictis, P. A. 1991. ABA Checklist Report, 1990. *Birding* 23:190–196.

DeBenedictis, P. A. 1992. ABA Checklist Report, 1991. *Birding* 24:281–286.

DeBenedictis, P. A. 1994. ABA Checklist Report, 1993. *Birding* 26:320–326.

Erlich, P. R., D. S. Dobkin, and D. Wheye. 1988. *The Birder's Handbook*. Simon and Schuster. New York.

Ficken, M. S., K. M. Ruschi, S. J. Taylor, and D. M. Powers. 2000. Blue-throated Hummingbird song: a pinnacle of nonoscine vocalizations. *Auk* 117:120–128.

Friedmann, H., L. Griscom, and R. T. Moore. 1950. Distributional Checklist of the Birds of Mexico, Part 1. *Pacific Coast Avifauna 29*. Cooper Ornithol. Club.

Gaines, D. 1992. *Birds of Yosemite and the east slope*. Artemesia Press, Lee Vining, California.

Garrett, K., and Dunn, J. 1981. *Birds of Southern California. Status and Distribution*. Los Angeles Audubon Society, Los Angeles, California.

Gilligan, J., D. Rogers, M. Smith, and A. Contreras (eds.). 1994. *Birds of Oregon. Status and Distribution*. Cinclus Publications, McMinnville, Oregon.

Graves, G. R., and N. L. Newfield. 1996. Diagnoses of hybrid hummingbirds (Aves: Trochilidae). 1. Characterization of *Calypte anna* x *Stellula calliope* and the possible effect of egg volume on hybridization potential. *Proc. Biol. Soc. Wash.* 109:755–763.

Graves, G. R., and S. L. Olson. 1987. *Chlorostilbon bracei* Lawrence, an extinct species of hummingbird from New Providence Island, Bahamas. *Auk* 104:296–302.

Greenwalt, C. H. 1960. *Hummingbirds*. Doubleday and Co., Garden City, New York.

Grinnell, J., and A. H. Miller. 1944. *The distribution of the birds of California*. Pacific Coast Avifauna No. 27. Cooper Ornithol. Club.

Griscom, L. 1934. The ornithology of Guerrero, Mexico. *Bull. Mus. Comp. Zool.* 75:367–422.

Hainebach, K. 1992. First records of Xantus' Hummingbird in California. *Western Birds* 23:133–136.

Hamilton, R. A., and D. R. Willick. 1996. *The Birds of Orange County, California: Status and Distribution*. Sea and Sage Audubon Society, Irvine, California.

Heidcamp, A. 1997. *Selasphorus* Hummingbirds. *Birding* 29:18–29.

Heindel, M. and S. N. G. Howell. 2000. A hybrid hummingbird in southeast Arizona. *Western Birds* 31:265–266.

Hill, G. E., R. R. Sargent, and M. B. Sargent. 1998. Recent change in winter distribution of Rufous Hummingbirds. *Auk* 115:240–245.

Howell, C. A., and S. N. G. Howell. 2000. Xantus' Hummingbird. No. 554 in Poole, A., and F. Gill (eds.). *The Birds of North America*, Inc. Philadelphia, Pennsylvania.

Howell, S. N. G. 2001. Field identification of female Allen's and Rufous hummingbirds. *Western Birds* 32: 97–98.

Howell, S. N. G., and S. Webb. 1995. A Guide to the Birds of Mexico and Northern Central America. Oxford University Press, Oxford, U.K.

Hubbard, J. P. 1970. *Checklist of the Birds of New Mexico*. New Mexico Ornithol. Soc. Publ. No. 3.

Jewett, S. G., W. P. Taylor, W. T. Shaw, and J. W. Aldrich. 1953. *Birds of Washington State*. Univ. Washington Press.

Johnsgard, P. A. 1997. *The Hummingbirds of North America*, 2nd edition. Smithsonian Institution Press, Washington, D.C.

Jones, L. 1983. California's first "Ruby-throated Hummingbird." *Birding* 15:231–235.

Kaufman, K. 1990. *A Field Guide to Advanced Birding*. Houghton Mifflin Co., Boston, Massachusetts.

Kessel, B. 1989. Birds of the Seward Peninsula, Alaska. Univ. Alaska Press, Fairbanks.

Lasley, G. W., C. Sexton, W. Sekula, and M. Lockwood. 1996. Texas Region. *Field Notes* 50:968–972.

Lehman, P. E. 1997. First record of Calliope Hummingbird in New Jersey. *Records of New Jersey Birds* 23:54–57.

Lynch, P., and P. L. Ames. 1970. A new hybrid hummingbird, *Archilochus alexandri* x *Selasphorus sasin*. *Condor* 72:209–212.

Marven, D. 1999. Rare birds in Canada in 1998: British Columbia. *Birders Journal* 8:247.

Mayr, E., and L. L. Short. 1970. *Species Taxa of North American Birds*. Publ. Nuttall Ornithol. Club, No. 9.

McKenzie, P. M., and M. B. Robbins. 1999. Identification of adult male Rufous and Allen's hummingbirds, with specific comments on dorsal coloration. *Western Birds* 30:86–93.

McLaren, I. 1999. Photographic identification of *Archilochus* hummingbirds in Nova Scotia. *Birders Journal* 8:151–153.

Mitchell, D. E. 2000. Allen's Hummingbird. No. 501 in Poole, A., and F. Gill (eds.). *The Birds of North America*, Inc. Philadelphia, Pennsylvania.

Monroe, B. L. Jr. 1968. *A distributional survey of the birds of Honduras*. Ornithological Monographs No. 7. American Ornithologists' Union.

Moore, R. T. 1937. Four new birds from northwestern Mexico. *Proc. Biol. Soc. Wash.* 50:96–101.

Navarro-S., A. G., and A. T. Peterson. 1999. Comments on the taxonomy of the genus *Cynanthus* (Swainson), with a restricted type locality for *C. doubledayi*. *Bull. Brit. Ornithol. Club*. 119:109–112.

Newfield, N. L. 1983. Records of Allen's Hummingbird in Louisiana and possible Rufous x Allen's hummingbird hybrids. *Condor* 85:253–254.

Oberholser, H. C. 1974. *The Bird Life of Texas*. Univ. Texas Press, Austin.

Olson, S. L. 1993. Contributions to avian biogeography from the archipelago and lowlands of Bocas del Toro, Panama. *Auk* 110:100–108.

Ortiz-Crespo, F. I. 1971. Winter occurrences of *Selasphorus* hummingbirds in the San Francisco Bay region. *Bird Banding* 42:290–292.

Ortiz-Crespo, F. I. 1980. Agonistic and foraging behavior of hummingbirds co-occurring in central coastal California. Unpubl. PhD thesis. Univ. California, Berkeley.

Owre, O. T. 1976. Bahama Woodstar in Florida: first specimen for continental North America. *Auk* 93:837–838.

Phillips, A. R. 1975. The migrations of Allen's and other hummingbirds. *Condor* 77:196–205.

Phillips, A. R. 1982. Hummingbirds. Pp. 11–14 in C. Chase (ed.). Third Denver Museum of Natural History and Colorado Field Ornithologists' taxonomy clinic. *Colorado Field Ornithologists' Journal* 16:5–15.

Phillips, A., J. Marshall, and G. Monson. 1964. *The Birds of Arizona*. Univ. Arizona Press, Tucson.

Pyle, P. 1997. *Identification Guide to North American Birds, Part 1*. Slate Creek Press, Bolinas, California.

Pyle, P., S. N. G. Howell, and G. Yanega. 1997. Molt, retained flight feathers, and age in North American hummingbirds. Pp. 155–166 in Dickerman, R. W. (compiler). *The Era of Allan R. Phillips: A Festschrift*. Horizon Publications, Albuquerque, New Mexico.

Pytte, C. and M. S. Ficken. 1994. Aerial display sounds of the Black-chinned Hummingbird. *Condor* 96:1088–1091.

Raffaele, H., J. Wiley, O. Garrido, A. Keith, and J. Raffaele. 1998. *Birds of the West Indies*. Princeton Univ. Press.

Ridgway, R. 1898. Description of a new species of hummingbird from Arizona. *Auk* 15:325–326.

Ridgway, R. 1911. The Birds of North and Middle America. *Bulletin of the United States National Museum, No. 50, Part 5*. Washington, D.C.

Robbins, C. S., B. Brun, and H. S. Zimm. 1966. *A Guide to Field Identification for Birds of North America*. Golden Press, New York.

Robinson, T. R., R. R. Sargent, and M. B. Sargent. 1996. Ruby-throated Hummingbird. No. 204 in Poole, A., and F. Gill, (eds.) *The Birds of North America*. The Academy of Natural Sciences, Philadelphia, PA, and the American Ornithologists' Union, Washington, D.C.

Rosenberg, G. H., and Witzeman, J. L. 1998. Arizona Bird Committee Report, 1974–1996: Part 1 (Nonpasserines). *Western Birds* 29:199–224.

Russell, S. M. 1996. Anna's Hummingbird. No. 226 in Poole, A., and F. Gill, (eds.) *The Birds of North America*. The Academy of Natural Sciences, Philadelphia, PA, and the American Ornithologists' Union, Washington, D.C.

Schuchmann, K. L. 1999. Family Trochilidae (Hummingbirds). *In* del Hoyo, J., A. Elliott, and J. Sargatal (eds.). *Handbook of the Birds of the World*, vol. 5. Lynx Editions, Barcelona, Spain.

Short, L. L., and A. R. Phillips. 1966. More hybrid hummingbirds from the United States. *Auk* 83:253–265.

Shuford, W. D. 1993. *The Marin County Breeding Bird Atlas*. Bushtit Books, Bolinas, California.

Sibley, C. G., and B. L. Monroe, Jr. 1990. *Distribution and Taxonomy of Birds of the World*. Yale Univ. Press, New Haven, Connecticut.

Sibley, D. A. 2000. *The Sibley Guide to Birds*. Knopf, New York.

Stejskal, D., and Rosenberg, G. H. 1992. Southwest Region, Arizona. *American Birds* 46:1161.

Stevenson, H. M., and B. H. Anderson. 1994. *The Birdlife of Florida*. University Press of Florida, Gainesville, Florida.

Stiles, F. G. 1971. On the field identification of California hummingbirds. *Western Birds* 2:41–54.

Stiles, F. G. 1972. Age and sex determination in Rufous and Allen's hummingbirds. *Condor* 74:25–32.

Stiles, F. G. 1973. Food supply and the annual cycle of the Anna Hummingbird. *Univ. Calif. Publ. Zool.* 97:1–109.

Stiles, F. G., and A. F. Skutch. 1989. *A Guide to the Birds of Costa Rica*. Cornell Univ. Press.

Swarth, H. S. 1904. Birds of the Huachuca Mountains, Arizona. *Pacific Coast Avifauna* 4. Cooper Ornithol. Soc.

Texas Ornithological Society. 1995. *Checklist of the Birds of Texas, 3rd edition*. Capital Printing Inc., Austin, TX.

Thompson, M. C., and C. Ely. 1989. Birds in Kansas. Vol. 1. *University of Kansas Museum Natural History, Public Education Series No. 11*. Lawrence, Kansas.

Toochin, R. 1998. A Xantus' Hummingbird in British Colombia: a first Canadian record. *Birders Journal* 6:293–297.

Unitt, P. 1984. The Birds of San Diego County. *San Diego Society of Natural History Memoir No. 13*.

Van Rossem, A. J. 1939. A race of the Rivoli Hummingbird from Arizona and northwestern Mexico. *Proc. Biol. Soc. Wash.* 52:7–8.

Veit, R. R., and W. R. Peterson. 1993. *Birds of Massachussetts*. Mass. Audubon Soc.

Wagner, H. O. 1945. Notes on the life history of the Mexican Violet-ear. *Wilson Bull.* 57:165–187.

Wagner, H. O. 1946. Observaciones sobre la vida de *Calothorax lucifer*. *Anales del Instituto de Biología* 17:283–299.

Weller, A.-A. 1998. On types of trochilids in the Natural History Museum, Tring. I. *Amazilia sumichrasti* Salvin, in relation to morphology and biogeography within the *A. beryllina* complex. *Bull. Brit. Ornithol. Club* 118:249–256.

Wells, S. A. and L. F. Baptista. 1979. Breeding of Allen's Hummingbird (*Selasphorus sasin sedentarius*) on the southern California mainland. *Western Birds* 10:83–85.

Wells, S., R. A. Bradley, and L. F. Baptista. 1978. Hybridization in *Calypte* hummingbirds. *Auk* 95:537–549.

Wetmore, A. 1968. The birds of the Republic of Panama, part 2. *Smithsonian Misc. Collection, vol. 150.*

Williams, S. O., III. 1994. Southwest Region, New Mexico. *American Birds* 48:138, 160.

Williamson, F. S. L. 1956. The molt and testis cycle of the Anna Hummingbird. *Condor* 58:324–366.

Wilson, R. G., and H. Ceballos. 1993. *The Birds of Mexico City, 2nd edition.* BBC Printing and Graphics, Burlington, Ontario, Canada.

Witzeman, J. 1979. Plain-capped Starthroats in the United States. *Continental Birdlife* 1:1–3.

Yanega, G. M., P. Pyle, and G. Geupel. 1997. The timing and reliability of bill corrugations for ageing hummingbirds. *Western Birds* 28:13–18.

Zimmerman, D. A. 1973. Range expansion of Anna's Hummingbird. *American Birds* 27:827–835.

Zyskowski, K., A. T. Peterson, and D. A. Kluza. 1998. Courtship behaviour, vocalizations, and species limits in *Atthis* hummingbirds. *Bull. Brit. Ornithol. Club* 118:82–90.

Index

References to pages with photos and figures in *italic*, main species accounts in **bold**

Notes

Notes

Notes